T0355221

Union Booms and Busts

Union Booms and Busts

The Ongoing Fight Over the U.S. Labor Movement

JUDITH STEPAN-NORRIS

Professor Emerita
Department of Sociology
University of California, Irvine

JASMINE KERRISSEY

Associate Professor
Department of Sociology and Labor Center Director
University of Massachusetts, Amherst

OXFORD
UNIVERSITY PRESS

OXFORD
UNIVERSITY PRESS

Oxford University Press is a department of the University of Oxford. It furthers
the University's objective of excellence in research, scholarship, and education
by publishing worldwide. Oxford is a registered trade mark of Oxford University
Press in the UK and certain other countries.

Published in the United States of America by Oxford University Press
198 Madison Avenue, New York, NY 10016, United States of America.

Library of Congress Cataloging-in-Publication Data
Names: Stepan-Norris, Judith, 1957– author. | Kerrissey, Jasmine, 1977– author.
Title: Union booms and busts : the ongoing fight over the U.S. labor movement /
Judith Stepan-Norris and Jasmine Kerrissey.
Description: New York, NY : Oxford University Press, [2023] |
Includes bibliographical references and index.
Identifiers: LCCN 2022054565 (print) | LCCN 2022054566 (ebook) |
ISBN 9780197539859 (hardback) | ISBN 9780197539873 (epub)
Subjects: LCSH: Labor movement—United States. | Labor unions—United States.
Classification: LCC HD8066 .S737 2023 (print) | LCC HD8066 (ebook) |
DDC 331.0973—dc23/eng/20230207
LC record available at https://lccn.loc.gov/2022054565
LC ebook record available at https://lccn.loc.gov/2022054566

DOI: 10.1093/oso/9780197539859.001.0001

Printed by Integrated Books International, United States of America

For Rick and Kurt

Contents

List of Illustrations

Figures

Tables

Preface and Acknowledgments

The history of the U.S. labor movement presents several puzzles for interested participants, labor scholars, and the public. Why were workers relatively successful in forming unions in some industries and some time periods, but not in others? How much do the economic, political, and legal contexts of the time matter for union density? How have race and gender dynamics impacted unionization prospects? What have unions and employers done to enhance their power vis-à-vis their opponents and to change the terrain on which their subsequent struggles occur?

Scholars have addressed these and many more questions, usually within relatively short timeframes and focusing on certain industries, labor federations, or individual unions. Some have a more long-term historical focus, while others tend to be more data driven. Our study builds upon this body of earlier analyses. But this book is different—very different. Our distinctive contribution lies in an analysis based on our unique and extensive longitudinal data set covering 115 years of U.S. labor union and employer activity in eleven industries. Using this broad and long-term approach, we seek to explain what accounts for the cyclical fluctuations of union successes and failures as represented by union density.

Originally, we sought to collect and analyze data by union. Indeed, some of our data is coded by national/international union. But many of the factors we consider are not systematically available at the individual union level. So, instead, we opted to identify broad industry-level patterns of union strength within three major time periods using comparative and historical analysis. We supplement these analyses with illustrations of events within individual unions and industries that typify these patterns. Since our focus is broad, we necessarily omit many interesting and even important events and developments.

Answers to the historical questions of this book, we believe, remain key for understanding potential paths forward for today's labor movement. This analysis seeks to pinpoint the conditions under which unions were more likely to successfully organize and maintain workers as union members and when they were more likely to fail. Juxtaposing patterns that emerged during certain times and in particular industries with actions (or inactions) on the part of unions and employers has the potential to provide compelling lessons for moving forward.

Our research for this project began with visits to several archives, including the U.S. National Archives (College Park, DC), George Meany Archives (Silver Springs, MD, most of the data we found here pertain only to the AFL or AFL-CIO), Department of Labor (Wirtz) Library (Washington, DC), American Catholic History Center and University Archives (Washington, DC), NYU Tamiment Library (New York, NY), Cornell Catherwood Library/ Kheel Center (Ithaca, NY), and Wisconsin Historical Society (Madison, WI). We are grateful to these archives and libraries for allowing us to use their collections. We also use data that have been available online. Some data that we assessed online are no longer available at those sites.

The data that we have accumulated from all of these organizations and sources are extensive. There are many types of analysis that would benefit by their use. Therefore, we make this data trove available to everyone at no cost. The data are accessible through the authors' faculty profiles at the University of California, Irvine and the University of Massachusetts, Amherst. We hope that others will take advantage of this data to further our collective understanding of the U.S. labor movement.

Our project began in collaboration with Caleb Southworth. He spent many hours visiting archives, researching, and establishing and working on the complex data set we assembled. He has remained connected with the project by providing valuable feedback. We greatly appreciate his contributions and emphasize that we are solely responsible for the arguments and data that are represented in this book.

Early funding for this project was generously provided by the National Science Foundation (grant to Caleb Southworth and Stepan-Norris, and dissertation grant to Kerrissey), the University of California, Irvine Academic Senate and administration, and UCI's Center for the Study of Democracy.

We relied on scholars for crucial feedback. Early on, we assembled an advisory board to inform our data collection decisions. We are appreciative of this board, which consisted of the following individuals: Art Shostack (Drexel University), Randy Hodson (Ohio State University), Kim Voss (University of California, Berkeley), Dan Cornfield (Vanderbilt), Leo Troy (Economics), Neil Shefflin (Economics, Rutgers), Barry Hirsch (Policy Studies, Georgia State), Maurice Zeitlin (UCLA), Andrew Martin (Ohio State University), Howard Kimeldorf (University of Michigan), Kate Bronfenbrenner

(Cornell ILR), Dan Clawson (University of Massachusetts, Amherst), and Margaret Levy (University of Washington). We are also grateful for the well-argued and insightful comments and suggestions we received on various chapters (or the entire manuscript) from the following scholars: Dan Clawson, Mary Ann Clawson, Marc Dixon, G. William Domhoff, Michael Goldfield, Howard Kimeldorf, Tyson Patros, Caleb Southworth, and anonymous Oxford reviewers. The members of the UMass Five College Social Movement Group gave us early stage, helpful feedback. We also thank the faculty, staff, and graduate students of the UMass Labor Center, whose many conversations helped to sharpen our thinking.

Several then UCI graduate students (all now PhDs) helped us with research, data collection, coding, and analysis. We are grateful to Ben Lind, Daniel Schneider, Tyson Patros, Christopher Zoeller, and Langou Lian. We also owe thanks to current UCI graduate students Spencer Potiker, Sabrina Nasir, and Darnell Calderon for helpful research, coding, and analyses, as well as UMass graduate student Nathan Meyers. Early on, UCI undergraduate students Christina Nizar and Daniel Rojas helped with coding and later, Kai Soto-Dessen helped with coding large strike information. Then high school student Jadyn Tiong was also very helpful in the large strikes coding project.

We are both indebted to our families and friends who have provided support and encouragement during this long-term project. Stepan-Norris is especially grateful to her husband, Rick, who read many drafts and provided valuable feedback and for the regular interesting and stimulating dinner conversations with her grown children and their partners. Kerrissey is thankful for the support of her (growing) family during the many stages of this book, especially the care from her partner-in-all Kurt, the laughter from Ansel and Brio, and the encouragement from her parents, Paul and Carol. And we acknowledge the working people who struggled and sacrificed throughout the last 115 years by organizing unions to better workers' lives, reduce inequalities, and to increase overall democracy.

Union Booms and Busts represents our long-term academic partnership; it is a fully joint work.

Abbreviations and Acronyms

ACORN	Association of Community Organizations for Reform Now
AFL	American Federation of Labor
AFL-CIO	American Federation of Labor-Congress of Industrial Organizations
AFT	American Federation of Teachers
ANA	American Nurses Association
BEA	U.S. Bureau of Economic Analyses
BLS	U.S. Bureau of Labor Statistics
CBTU	Coalition of Black Trade Unionists
CEO	Chief Executive Officer
CES	U.S. Current Employment Statistics
CETA	Comprehensive Employment and Training Act
CIO	Congress of Industrial Organizations
CLUW	Coalition of Labor Union Women
CPI	Consumer Price Index
CPS	U.S. Census Current Population Survey
CtW	Change to Win
CUAIR	Construction Users Anti-Inflation Roundtable
DOL	Department of Labor
EEOC	Equal Employment Opportunity Commission
EFCA	Employee Free Choice Act
FIRE	Finance, Insurance, and Real Estate industry
FLU	AFL Federal Labor Union
FMCS	U.S. Federal Mediation and Conciliation Service
HERE	Hotel Employees and Restaurant Employees Union
ITU	International Typographical Union
IWW	Industrial Workers of the World
NAFTA	North American Free Trade Agreement
NAM	National Association of Manufacturers
NCF	National Civic Federation
NEA	National Educational Association
NLRA	National Labor Relations Act
NLRB	National Labor Relations Board
NRA	U.S. National Recovery Administration
OSHA	U.S. Occupational Safety and Health Administration

PATCO	Professional Air Traffic Controllers Organization
RWDSU	Retail, Wholesale and Department Store Union
SEIU	Service Employees International Union
TCU	Transportation, Communications, and Utilities industry
Trade	Retail and Wholesale Trade industry
TUEL	Trade Union Education League
TUUL	Trade Union Unity League
UAW	United Automobile Workers Union
UFCW	United Food and Commercial Workers Union
ULP	Unfair Labor Practice
ULU	United Labor Unions
UMW	United Mine Workers Union
UNITE-HERE	United Needletrades, Industrial, and Textile Employees—Hotel Employees and Restaurant Employees Union
USCIR	U.S. Commission on Industrial Relations
WLB	War Labor Board
WTO	World Trade Organization
WTUL	Women's Trade Union League

1

Introduction

Forming and defending unions in the United States has always been a herculean task. Employers have a long history of fighting vigorously to bust strikes and prevent workers from organizing—and, ultimately to dis-organize unions. The government, including politicians, local officials, and the courts, has provided unions only sporadic support—and sometimes it directly opposed them. This challenging terrain for unions characterizes labor relations in the 2000s, just as it did in the early 1900s.

And yet, throughout the last century, large numbers of workers successfully formed unions, with national trends in union strength developing a wave-like pattern. In the early 1900s, about one in ten workers were unionized; by mid-century, that number had risen to one in three. But by 2015, union density resembled the circumstances from a century earlier, with approximately one in ten workers unionized.

Scholars, union activists, and anti-union agents alike hope to better understand what makes unions strong and what drives these patterns of union booms and busts (Ashenfelter and Pencavel 1969; Clawson 2003; Goldfield 1987; Southworth and Stepan-Norris 2009; Western 1999). Researchers have analyzed a range of issues, including laws, economic factors, industry structures, and the actions taken by employers and unions. Getting it right matters: the fate of unions constitutes the single most important force for elevating or sidelining workers' collective voice, growing or checking income inequality, deteriorating or improving working conditions, and perhaps augmenting democracy itself (Fletcher and La Luz 2020; Lafer 2017; MacLean 2017).

This book tackles these long-standing debates from a unique angle. We ask: Why have some industries become highly unionized in certain historical contexts while others have not? Most scholarship focuses on *aggregate* national union density. We show that an *industry-level* approach over a long period of time reveals important patterns. For example, an entertainer—say, a musician—was very likely to be unionized in the early 1900s, while a factory worker was not. However, by mid-century, factory workers were among the

Union Booms and Busts. Judith Stepan-Norris and Jasmine Kerrissey, Oxford University Press.
© Oxford University Press 2023. DOI: 10.1093/oso/9780197539859.003.0001

most unionized. Only a few decades later, success in manufacturing unions was surpassed by public sector workers, who had previously been largely unorganized. What drives these industry-level differences in unionization over time, and what can we learn from them?

These debates have never been more important: by the twenty-first century, union density had slid to an almost unimaginable low. The economic and social consequences of mass de-unionization are staggering, including increasing poverty, health disparities, and racial and gender inequities. The largest contemporary employers, Walmart and Amazon, are largely union-free in the United States. While their workers face considerable challenges, the owners of these mega-corporations are among the richest in the world. Even union strongholds—from manufacturing to the public sector—face serious obstacles. The intense union organizing efforts of the 1990s and 2000s did little to move the needle on union strength. Among labor circles, many are asking: What is to be done? Historical analysis can help give us insight about the contemporary issues that workers and unions face in America today.

Our expansive and detailed data set covering labor issues from 1900 to 2015 includes estimates of yearly memberships by union and industry level, and data on union density, strikes, elections for union representation, filings of unfair labor practices (ULPs), and workers' occupations, gender, and race. These data afford analytical traction to address ongoing debates about union power and resulting union fates in the cycles of booms and busts.

Key Questions for Unions and Employers

Several key debates among the major players have resurfaced repeatedly over the 115 years we study. For unions, the key question has been how to build power, especially when the conditions appear to be unfavorable. Part of this debate has focused on the proper strategy for organizing. Who should be included, and who should be excluded? One strategy has been to build power based on exclusive skills, with the idea that workers' power is maximized when they are able to reduce employers' capacity to find replacements for striking workers. This was the general approach of American Federation of Labor (AFL) craft unions in the early 1900s, which consisted of mostly skilled workers (and mostly white men), and aimed to control the pool of available skilled labor. Inclusionary power, in contrast, builds power by broad organization. We could think of race and gender here as well as skilled and unskilled, supervisors and supervised, allies and community members. Through expansive solidarity—extending the terrain of struggle beyond individual workplaces or specific groups of workers—unions have aimed to shift power relations through inclusion. The goal here is to use solidarity to get all workers onboard with unions' main objectives, so that none are willing to serve as replacements during strikes. Historically, the inclusionary vision has garnered workers' support, from the massive Industrial Workers of the World (IWW) strikes in the early 1900s, to the formation of the more inclusionary Congress of Industrial Organizations (CIO) unions in the 1930s. However, this orientation has also received intense pushback, from the state (especially against radicals), employers, more conservative unions, and some workers intent on upholding race and gender hierarchies.

Strikes and union militancy are another major touch point in labor history. What strategies and how much militancy should the collective use (e.g., single workplace strikes vs. general strikes; boycotts vs. using the union label; NLRB elections vs. other actions to win power)? Under which conditions do strikes compel employers to concede or state governments to create more favorable laws? If workers are not well-positioned to win strikes, what other actions might work? How could unions maneuver themselves into being better positioned to win strikes?

Unions have also debated how to improve laws and conditions that are hostile, with an eye toward weakening strong employers and strengthening workers' rights. What is the balance among political efforts, community alliances, and direct action? Other debates have centered on questions of how unions should operate. Should they primarily "service" members or should they have more of a participatory social movement orientation? How should resources be deployed?

Employers have also debated how to organize themselves, and what sort of strategies to use to dis-organize unions, to gain state and public support, and to minimize the impact of strikes. A main question has been how best to influence laws and the geographic scope of laws. At various points over the twentieth century, employers also had to consider just how much worker militancy they were willing to endure. During the massive strikes and government actions of the 1940s, many employers were forced to bargain. Decades later, more favorable options were readily available to them. Many employers chose to relocate to union-free areas, hire contingent workers who would be less likely to unionize, use anti-union consultants to beat election attempts, or break laws to minimize unionization.

As we show, the contexts that unions and employers faced differed by industry. Throughout the book, we examine industry-level union dynamics to identify the factors that contribute to building or breaking unions. In doing so, we shed new light on these long-standing debates about what empowers or weakens both unions and employers.

The Theoretical Argument in Brief

Structural explanations dominate existing union density scholarship, emphasizing the importance of favorable structures for unionization, such as laws, institutional arrangements, tight labor markets, and the location of workers within the economic system (e.g., Ashenfelter and Pencavel 1969; Kimeldorf 2013; Wallace, Griffin, and Rubin 1989; Wright 2000). Research that compares country-level unionization rates shows that institutions and political alignments strongly shape union trajectories (Eidlin 2018; Western 1999). These studies suggest that how the state manages labor relations and the institutional climate is key to understanding union density.

What employers do, and what the state allows them to do, also shapes the prospects for unionization. Extensive research identifies the "employer offensive" as key to undermining union strength (Domhoff 2015; Goldfield 1989b; Lafer 2017; Windham 2017). Many employers, with their vast resources, have the advantage of being able to withstand long strikes, engage in lengthy and costly court cases, hire expensive union-avoidance consultants, make large political donations to employer-friendly candidates, and engage in long-term planning. Their offensive plays out in multiple arenas, including workplaces, courts, and the halls of Congress.

Workers, for their part, have aimed to organize themselves and their communities, weaken employers, and gain greater protection from the state. Scholarship considering unions' and workers' options focuses on the actions that unions themselves have taken to overcome unfavorable political climates and hostile employers. Much of this scholarship elucidates how unions have captured workers' hearts and minds and developed social movement orientations (Clawson 2003; Ganz 2000; Stepan-Norris and Zeitlin 2003; Voss and Sherman 2000).

We draw on both structural and agentic perspectives to build a dynamic understanding of industry-level unionization in America. Structures matter, but real people—along with their collectives—must act to realize structural potential and to change unfavorable structures over the long term. Employers' and workers' organizations, sometimes with internal competition and differing strategies, have struggled to further their class interests. We consider the major organizations on each side but mostly tend to how these actors have aimed to shift the terrain of struggle to their advantage by influencing political and legal climates and by building (or undermining) the abilities of workers to effectively strike and organize.

Several related mechanisms have shaped industry-level union density since 1900. First, the *state and macro context* set the stage for labor relations, including laws, institutions, and major events such as wars. Both employers and unions have tried to influence this stage over the 115 years that we study. Second, *replacement costs* of workers influence unionization patterns. Workers are better positioned to form and maintain unions when they are difficult to replace. If employers can easily replace strikers or union leaders with "docile" workers, unions flounder. Third, *organizing strategies of unions and employers*—or how they make or break solidarity—also shape unionization. We pay particular attention to how unions aim to build strikes and solidarity—and how employers try to break them. Finally, although less of a mechanism and more of a correlate, *race and gender dynamics* permeate U.S. labor relations. Women and workers of color have been disproportionately employed in industries with lower unionization levels, due to employers' hiring patterns, opportunities for skill acquisition, and laws, and they have faced unique challenges to organizing.

These factors evolved over the century, as both employers and unions experimented with new strategies to build power. We distinguish between three broad periods of labor relations, each the subject of a chapter: unregulated (1900–1934), regulated (1935–1979), and dis-regulated (1980–2015). For each period, we examine how these major mechanisms relate to union density. We then summarize the main actions and strategies that employers and unions used to fortify their positions during these periods.

What the state did (or didn't) do is crucial to understanding unionization— and both unions and employers have sought to influence the basic terrain of struggle. Sometimes conditions provide openings for unions to secure state support. These occur most often when replacement costs are high, disruptive capacity is high (through strikes or other actions), and workers provide strong support for progressive politicians who are willing to push for workers' rights. Likewise, maintaining state support is dependent on union power and workers' disruptive capacities: as union power declines, pro-labor legislation erodes. Still, even in unfavorable political climates, some workers have had success unionizing. We mainly see this success when workers' replacement costs are high, strikes are high, workers have a union (rather than a professional association) orientation, and where employers are relatively less aggressive against union efforts (such as in the public sector during our later periods). We find that race, gender, and skill divisions (or solidarities) intertwine with union prospects in each period.

A Bird's-Eye View of Union Power

We take a bird's-eye view of union power, stepping back to see broad trends in industry-level unionization over time. We capture union power by measuring *union density*, which is the ratio of unionized workers to all workers. Higher union density not only means that more workers are unionized but also helps unions to be more powerful. With less non-union competition, unions have a more credible "threat" effect vis-à-vis non-union employers (Western and Rosenfeld 2011), which helps them to secure better working conditions and attract new members. Higher overall union density also means that unions have a larger base with which to influence the political arena (Kerrissey and Schofer 2013). Union density doesn't capture all of the complex ways that organized workers may be powerful. It does not account for workers involved in worker centers or political organizations. It also doesn't account for instances of low density but the presence of a highly mobilized membership (or vice versa, high density, but a membership that is not mobilized). However, union density does provide a useful measure that can be compared across time and industry, and we think it is the best measure available.

Figure 1.1 presents the aggregate union density over the last century through 2015. Aggregate unionization was relatively low but rising in the early 1900s, peaked mid-century, and steadily declined for the next fifty-plus years.[1]

---

[1] The 1950s peak is similar to union density estimates by the Congressional Research Service (2004), which estimates the peak in 1954 to be 28.3 percent of total employment (and 34.8 percent of all wage and salary employment). To remain consistent over the 115 that we study, we use census employment estimates (the employment base includes agricultural workers and independent contractors). See "Methods" section for details.

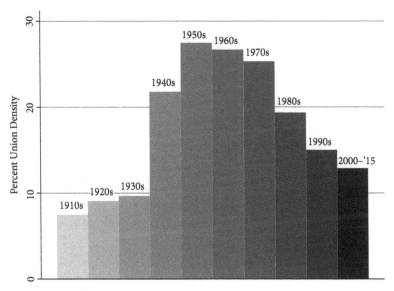

Figure 1.1 Aggregate union density, average by decade.

But industry-level analyses reveal a far more interesting story, due to substantial variation by industry (see Figure 1.2). We analyze eleven major industries since 1900 (see "The Census and Industry Categories" section of this chapter for details): agriculture, forestry, and fisheries; mining; construction; manufacturing; transportation, communication, and utilities (TCU); wholesale and retail trade; finance, insurance, and real estate (FIRE); personal services; entertainment; health services; and public administration and education.

A handful of industries maintained moderate to high levels of unionization for most of the twentieth and early twenty-first centuries: construction, mining, TCU and entertainment. Two industries moved from relatively low unionization to much higher: manufacturing and public administration/education. Personal services and health services established some union presence over the century. A handful of industries had minimal unionization throughout the period, including retail and wholesale trade; FIRE; and agriculture, fisheries, and forestry.

All industries grew in unionization during the regulated period (1935–1979) and several secured major gains. In fact, all of the industries that had higher density in the early 1900s (construction, mining, TCU, and entertainment) as well as manufacturing gained over 50 percent density during the

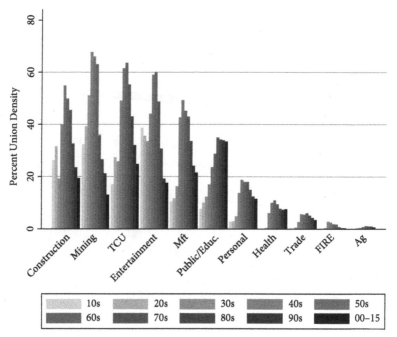

Figure 1.2 Union density by industry, average by decade.
TCU, transportation, communication and utilities; Entertainment, includes arts and recreation,
Mft, durable and nondurable manufacturing; Public/Educ, public administration and education;
Personal, personal services, including lodging; Health, hospitals and all other health facilities; Trade,
wholesale and retail trade; FIRE, finance, insurance, and real estate; Ag, agriculture, fisheries, and
forestry.

regulated period. Unionization then generally eroded, especially after the
1970s. However, the extent of the erosion also varied. Mining experienced
a huge decline—from over 60 percent density mid-century to 13 percent in
the twenty-first century. Personal services, health, and trade were not initially highly unionized but also did not experience as severe a decline. Public
administration/education, on the other hand, did not experience a similar
drop, and was unique in its success in maintaining relatively high unionization levels into the twenty-first century.

A key question is what we should consider to be high, medium, or low
union density. We base our answer on the specific U.S. context we study. We
deem high density to be industries where over 20 percent of workers were
unionized. This threshold would be considered far too low for many other
industrialized countries, and it is even low for the height of our second period. However, within the U.S. context over 115 years, there aren't many time

periods or industries that sustain over 20 percent density, making it a reasonable cutoff. A more apt description would be "high density for the U.S. 20th and early 21st context." We deem medium industry density to be 5–20 percent density and low industry density to be under 5 percent. We use these high, medium, and low categories as a useful way of categorizing union strength.

Because union density is the ratio of union members to employment, and employment grew and shifted over the century, density does not map directly onto the number of union members by industry. Industries with high density did not necessarily have the most union members. For example, construction, mining, TCU, and entertainment were high density for most of the twentieth century. However, their absolute membership numbers pale in comparison to manufacturing and, in later decades, to public administration/education, as Figure 1.3 shows. By contrast, health services and trade both had less impressive union density in the late twentieth century—but still had more absolute members than the historically highly organized industries such as mining and entertainment.

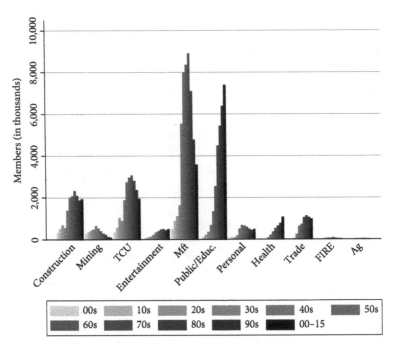

Figure 1.3 Number of union members by industry, average by decade.

Overall employment, as well as industry employment, changed dramatically over the century. Figure 1.4 shows employment by industry, based on census estimates beginning in 1910. Even in the early 1900s, manufacturing employed a substantial proportion of the labor force, and by mid-century it had become the dominant employer. While manufacturing had only 10 percent organized in 1910, it grew to nearly 50 percent union density by the 1950s. Had that unionization surge not occurred, the aggregate union density trajectory would have been much smaller—and the actual working conditions of manufacturing workers would have been much different. In other words, a good part of the surge in aggregate density that we see in Figure 1.1 is due to the organization of manufacturing.

As the economy changed, the labor movement faced new challenges. By the twenty-first century, retail and wholesale trade had come to dominate employment, surpassing the employment numbers in the union strongholds of manufacturing and public administration. Low union density in this large industry pulled overall density downward. Going forward, it is difficult to imagine a contemporary increase in aggregate union density without organizing the trade sector. An opposite dynamic occurred in agriculture: it had large

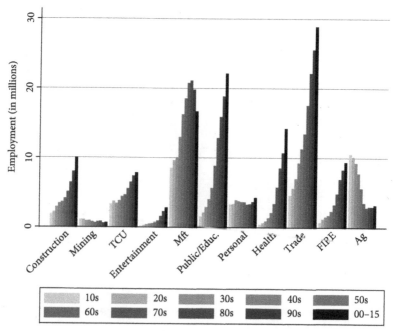

Figure 1.4 Employment by industry, average by decade.

employment and very low union density in the early period, contributing to overall low density. In later periods, its union density remained very low, but agricultural employment declined drastically. So by the dis-regulated period, its consequence for overall union density had declined.

The majority of Americans (and workers) report that they approve of labor unions, and that has been true for almost every year since the Gallup Poll began polling in 1936 (Gallup Poll 2022). But, as we discuss in Chapter 4, organizing new union workplaces has become increasingly difficult in recent decades, and unions made few new inroads, especially in the growing trade sector. Unions working there need new strategies and reinvigorated support to counter the structural and employer-based obstacles they face. As we discuss in Chapter 3, two industries that were union-resistant early on— manufacturing and public administration—grew to have large employment by mid-century and, with great effort, unions won widespread unionization there. It can happen in trade, too.

Orienting Mechanisms: Understanding Union Booms and Busts by Industry Over Time

To understand union booms and busts by industry, we focus on the evolution of key mechanisms: the role of the state and macro context, replacement costs, and union and employer organizing strategies. Throughout, we consider the role of race and gender dynamics. As actors act on and change these factors, they create altered conditions for each subsequent period.

The State and Macro Context

State actions and macro-contexts set the stage for labor relations. In particular, laws and institutions that effectively protect the ability of workers to organize and maintain unions are important to understanding union density.

Cross-national comparative studies stress the importance of state institutions for explaining union density. The scholarship is clear: countries with more robust labor institutions and supportive political configurations have had higher density—or at least less decline in the contemporary era— than countries with less supportive institutional arrangements. Scholars point to the strength of factors such as leftist political parties, centralized collective bargaining, and union-administered unemployment insurance to account for differences in union strength (Carré and Tilly 2017; Ebbinghaus and Visser 1999; Eidlin 2018; Wallerstein and Western 2000; Western 1999).

Our analyses build on this literature in two ways. First, we document how employers and unions have attempted to influence state actions and the macro-context in the United States since 1900. Second, we show how state actions and macro-contexts have varied by industry, which in turn has impacted where and how unions grow.

Employers and unions are well aware that labor laws, political alignments, and economic policy shape the playing field, and both have worked hard to impact them. As aptly put by U.S. labor historian Erik Loomis (2018, 7): "There is simply no evidence from American history that unions can succeed if the government and employers combine to crush them. All the other factors are secondary." Throughout our three periods, employers fought relentlessly to win the support of the state—or at least lax enforcement of labor laws (De Leon 2015; Domhoff 2015; Griffin, Wallace, and Rubin 1986; Lafer 2017). For their parts, unions and workers have also aimed to influence laws and policies through lobbying and rallying around labor-friendly politicians. Importantly, workers' strike waves have been critical to winning big institutional change. Most major advances to U.S. labor law have come on the heels of widespread strikes and disruption (Goldfield 1989a, 1989b).

For most of its history, the United States has had relatively decentralized bargaining and weak labor institutions, especially compared to many European countries. However, within the United States, the role of the state has varied over time, and some industries have received greater state support than others. In the early 1900s the state did very little to bolster the existence of unions. The institutional environment changed dramatically in the 1930s with the passage of the National Labor Relations Act (NLRA). Importantly, the NLRA regulated union activity for most private sector industries. It also created the National Labor Relations Board (NLRB) to govern union elections and ULP cases. Notably, the NLRA and subsequent laws did not cover some types of workers, including those disproportionately comprised of women and workers of color, such as the public sector, agricultural workers, and domestic workers (Perea 2011). Later, after significant strikes, many states adopted laws to allow for public sector collective bargaining (Dixon 2020; Goldfield 1987; Valletta and Freeman 1988). By the turn of the twenty-first century, many of the laws established during the New Deal and later in individual states were either weakened or less protective in practice due to changes in the organization of work, court decisions that narrowed workers' rights, and the passage of newer restrictive laws. Courts have played an especially central role in shaping U.S. labor relations policy. While New Deal legislation in the 1930s established workers' rights to organize and strike, in decision after decision, the courts have slowly chipped away those rights (McCammon 1993). The cumulative effect has eroded workers' right to organize and placed extreme limitations on their right to strike. A host of new regulations also emerged that further eroded union strength, such as the deregulation of transportation industries in the 1980s, which made union organizing in trucking and air more difficult.

Although political power is important in understanding state actions, throughout our 115-year coverage, the United States maintained a two-party system, and neither of the parties proports to directly or even predominantly represent workers and unions. Rather, U.S. unions have been junior partners in the Democratic Party coalition, and no matter their contributions to political campaigns, normally receive only partial attention in return. Still, the more favorable court and government appointments as well as legislation enacted by Democratic politicians have been more beneficial to unions than those enacted by Republicans.

The state's decisions to enter wars, implement trade deals, and deploy the National Guard, as well as its reaction to major economic swings also have important consequences for labor relations. New wartime demand for munitions and war supplies drives the development of political representation schemes (National War Labor Boards) to negotiate the new economic dynamics, including labor shortages, augmented production schedules, wage and price freezes, and so forth. The War Labor Board during World War II restricted workers' right to strike (though workers did not always comply) in exchange for other union fortifications. And much of the New Deal legislation, following the upheavals spurred by the Great Depression, aimed to protect union organizing and to institutionalize collective bargaining. Conversely, trade deals, such as the North American Free Trade Agreement (NAFTA), created new possibilities for capital flight and global competition over wages.

Economic factors also set the stage for unionization prospects. Unions operate within specific economic contexts, which lay the foundation for their organization. Economists have stressed the importance of economic factors, from inflation and unemployment to business cycles (Ashenfelter and Pencavel 1969) in determining unions' fate. The economic context is intertwined with our concept of replacement costs and state actions, because business cycles and government policies tighten or loosen the demand for labor, thereby situating more or less power with employers or unions. Usually unemployment, by increasing the available supply of labor, lowers workers' bargaining power. Yet during the Great Depression, the most extreme economic downturn of the twentieth century, accumulated grievances among workers and the unemployed helped to fuel the rise of the CIO. Inflation decreases the value of wages, thereby increasing workers' sense that their wages are insufficient.

It is also important to note that in addition to regulating labor relations, the government also employs federal, state, and local workers. The public sector differs from the private sector in significant ways, and this difference has shaped union trends. Unionism came first in the private sector due to harsh laws and policies in force in the public sector during the unregulated period. For example, the executive order known as the gag rule (1902–1912) forbade federal workers from seeking to "influence legislation in their own behalf 'individually or through associations, save through the heads of their departments.'" And after World War I many local governments passed laws prohibiting public servants (police, firefighters, teachers) from organizing and striking (Spero 1972, 3–4). This strong aversion to public unionism extended through the 1950s, when new legislation began to provide collective bargaining rights to some public workers (with restrictions on the right to strike and some collective bargaining issues) (Budd 2008). However, the strong aversion to public sector unionization faded somewhat with the spread of collective bargaining laws and the growth of public sector unionism. Public sector employment grew substantially over the century, and by the late twentieth century, public sector employers took less aggressive anti-union positions than private sector employers. Public sector unions were much more likely to win union elections (Bronfenbrenner and Juravich 1994), and these workers were more successful in forming and defending their unions compared to many private sector workers at the turn of the twenty-first century. The unique characteristics of the public sector create important differences in the ways public sector unions organize and use strikes. Public sector unions tend to focus on their political positions and coalition building rather than their market positions. And unlike in the private sector, much public sector work is regulated at the state level, with varying strike restrictions by state, occupation, and time period. One of the eleven industries that we analyze (public administration/education) is almost entirely public and another (health services) has a substantial public component.

In sum, the state plays a major role in union formation—and precisely because of that, employers and unions have tried to influence laws, institutions, and politics. We see that industries have had different experiences with state regulation, which partially explains variations in union density. Next, we turn to another important factor in shaping union density: replacement costs.

Replacement Costs

We define replacement costs as the ease with which employers replace workers when they act collectively, especially when they strike. Strikes are the most powerful form of direct action because they have the potential to create crises for employers—and occasionally for politicians. However, when employers more easily replace strikers with non-striking workers (also called "scabs") and continue business as usual, they are better able to diffuse strikes' power. At their core, replacement costs are about power relations. Workers were able to form and maintain unions because they had power to do so— they raised employers' costs until they relented. Although strikes have historically been the main arena for replacements, some employers have also sought to replace workers who *may* become engaged in collective action, including by firing leaders of organizing drives or moving entire plants to non-union locations.

Both employers and unions have actively aimed to shape replacement costs to their favor. While some replacement cost factors reflect structural features, they also reflect the strategies and actions of workers and employers. On the structural side, labor laws (and their enforcement) impact whether workers can be replaced when they strike or engage in collective actions. In addition, some workers have greater disruptive capacities because of their strategic locations, especially those able to produce "bottlenecks" in interdependent economic systems. Workers in logistics and some manufacturing industries possess this sort of positional power to disrupt production (Perrone 1983; Wallace, Griffin, and Rubin 1989). Similarly, the concept of "structural power" shows how some workers are better positioned in the economic system to disrupt production (Silver 2003; Wright 2000). Still, we see instances where workers were successful in organizing "non-strategic" industries, such as entertainment. While strategic and locational advantages are helpful for unionization, we focus on how both structures and actions impact replacement costs, which we think is key to understanding union density.

We build on the work of Howard Kimeldorf (2013), who shows that high replacement costs were critical to explaining where unions were able to gain footholds in the early 1900s. Kimeldorf argues that some workers had greater disruptive capacity because they had a higher cost of being replaced during strikes. These workers were able to generate strikes that were costly for employers—and therefore more likely to be successful. In turn, they were able to form durable unions. Three conditions were associated with high replacement costs in the early 1900s: scarcity of skilled labor, time-sensitive tasks that made replacement workers impractical, and geographically isolated worksites that raised the cost of importing strike breakers (Kimeldorf 2013). We extend this work by expanding the concept of skill (to include professional and technical workers), by showing how strikes mattered, and by analyzing how these features interacted with race, gender, and professional organizations.

We demonstrate how replacement costs evolved over time, and we consider how new factors influenced replacement costs over time. New laws, organizing tactics, and work arrangements all shaped relative replacement costs as the century progressed, giving unions the advantage at mid-century. By the close of the dis-regulated period, employers regained the upper hand in terms of replacement costs, and in turn, unions struggled to maintain themselves.

Scarcity of Skilled Labor

One component of high replacement costs is a scarcity of "skilled" labor. Highly skilled workers have higher replacement costs because their skills are scarce, and therefore fewer workers are available to serve as strike breakers. The concept of "skill" is itself shaped by gender and race, with occupations dominated by women and workers of color considered less skilled and compensated at a lower rate (Branch 2011; Steinberg 1990). Most scholarship of the early 1900s identifies craft work as high skill. We broaden this conceptualization, adding that technical and professional workers were also high skill, holding unique skills that required training and/or education, and could not easily be replaced with untrained workers. These workers, in theory, could have more readily formed unions, as they had the potential to leverage their replacement costs. However, most of these technical and professional workers did not form unions until much later in the twentieth century.

We use broad occupational categories to identify workers who may be hard to replace due to rare skills, credentials, or other forms of closure: craft workers and technicians and professionals. Here we use "high skill" to identify work that is hard to replace due to either the technical skills that workers master after long-term training (apprenticeship) processes (such as carpenters and plumbers) and/or licensing/credentialing requirements that specify the procedures required before individuals are allowed to perform certain work (such as teachers and nurses). Both types create closure—the ability to restrict labor supply, thus heightening workers' power and their leverage to make demands (Weeden 2002).

Table 1.1 presents census data on the percent of the workforce characterized in craft or professional/technical occupations by industry, which change over time. The construction industry had far more craft workers than any other industry in all periods. Professional and technical workers were always the most prevalent in health services, public administration/education, and entertainment. As we show, occupational features contributed to, but did not define, replacement costs.

Table 1.1 Percent of Employment by Occupation: 1910, 1960, and 2015

	Craft			Professional or Technical		
	1910	1960	2015	1910	1960	2015
Construction	69	54	41	1	5	3
Mining	9	22	16	1	8	18
TCU	19	22	14	1	4	11
Entertainment	6	8	5	50	24	28
Manufacturing	24	20	15	1	8	18
Public Administration	1	5	2	56	41	55
Personal Services	2	3	2	1	3	7
Health Services	1	3	1	75	45	50
Trade	7	7	3	2	2	5
FIRE	1	2	2	1	3	14
Agriculture	0	1	5	0	1	7

TCU, Transportation, Communication, and Utilities; Public Administration, Public Administration, and Education; Trade, Wholesale, and Retail Trade; FIRE, Finance, Insurance, and Real Estate; Agriculture, Agriculture, Forestry, and Fishing.

Both unions and employers have aimed to influence the scarcity of craft labor. Especially in the early 1900s, unions developed extensive apprenticeship programs that aimed to control the number of skilled crafts people (and hence the ability to replace union labor in the common event of a strike). Employers, on the other hand, have sought to deskill work processes, rendering tasks more easily interchangeable among workers (Braverman 1974). They have also adopted scientific management, automation, and computerization as strategies to avoid dependence on skilled labor (Kristal 2013). Changes in the construction industry illustrate these shifts: in 1910, 69 percent of construction workers were craft workers; by 2015, that number had dropped to 41 percent.

We also conceptualize professional and technical workers as skilled (unlike Kimeldorf 2013), as these workers had the potential for closure and higher union density. In the early 1900s, both public administration/education and health services had at least 50 percent professional and technical workers. However, these industries remained largely union-free during the early century, only moving towards unionization later in the century. By contrast, the entertainment industry had high proportions of professional/technical workers and was relatively successful in unionizing in the early 1900s. These industry-level differences suggest that high skill is one component of union strength and replacement costs, but not sufficient to explain variation.

The benefits of high skills are mediated by other factors, including race, gender, professional orientation, and willingness to strike. Scarcity of skilled labor can also arise from professional closure though credentialing and licensing. Professional status is somewhat elusive. While certain professions have captured the spoils of professional status (doctors and lawyers), others have not quite made it (nurses and teachers). As they pursued professional status, both education and health workers largely ignored the possibility for unionization, and thus, both industries had low union density during the early twentieth century. Encouraged by professional associations and cultural gender norms, these workers pursued professional avenues in their workplaces. But they never fully accomplished their desired professional status, along with its financial and other rewards. Not until later in the century did these workers turn from their professional orientation and forge a union identity, at which point their licenses and credentials became a way to increase their replacement costs during strikes.

Finally, major events can influence the labor supply. Wars, in particular, instigated a scarcity of skilled labor as enlisted soldiers left the workforce, and the demand for war production ramped up. World War II temporarily shifted the balance of power in favor of manufacturing workers, including women and workers of color who were able to enter coveted manufacturing jobs as northern men left for the war (Milkman 1987; Ruiz 1987).

Timing

Whether an industry is time sensitive serves as another factor in high replacement costs. If striking workers cannot quickly be replaced, strikes in these time-sensitive industries can more readily disrupt production or service. When transportation workers strike in a city dependent on public transportation, widespread disruption in all travelers' workday routines occur, placing pressure on employers to settle the strikes quickly and thereby affording unions more power. Employers have used various strategies to reduce their time sensitivity, including automation and stockpiling. Workers, on the other hand, often used timing to strategize when to strike.

Spatial Factors: Isolation and Capital Flight

Socially isolated workers are difficult to replace for several reasons. First, geographical distance may complicate the delivery of replacement workers. Second, workers in isolated communities tend to develop cohesive communities that are able to sustain collective action (Kerr and Siegel 1954). So isolation contributes to high replacement costs, especially in mining in the early period (Kimeldorf 2013). However, as transportation technologies developed, workplace isolation became rare in the United States.

As the century progressed, new spatial factors became increasingly relevant to union organization. The most important of these was capital flight, which ramped up over the century. Facing the threat of strikes in union-dense cities, employers who were mobile, especially in manufacturing, often relocated to non-union areas, what Silver (2003) calls a "spatial fix." As Bronfenbrenner (2000) demonstrated, employers regularly used the threat of plant closure when workers made demands. Plant closures and capital flight are the ultimate replacement mechanisms—(potentially) striking workers are replaced by non-union workers in a different production location. But some industries are much more place-bound, including health services and public administration/education. Workers in these industries enjoy the spatial advantage of not being as easily replaced during strikes or relocated if there is a hint of union activity.

Organizing to Limit Replacements

By the 1930s, workers and unions had secured additional ways of increasing replacement costs. The newly formed CIO championed industrial organizing, or wall-to-wall organizing rather than the dominant AFL approach of organizing by craft. At the same time, the new labor legislation of the NLRA protected "concerted activity," giving strikers a legitimacy that they did not previously enjoy. Workers also took up a new tactic, the sit-down strike, which required replacement workers to physically remove striking workers from the workplace in order to resume production. These innovations helped unskilled workers discourage would-be replacements. But soon thereafter, sit-down strikes were outlawed, and the 1938 Mackay decision declared permanent replacement workers legal. Picket lines were another tool used to block (or at least made it very uncomfortable for) replacements to enter the workplace and pleas for solidarity with potential replacements sought to keep the use of replacements at bay, especially when the replacement workers had limited rights and replacement jobs were considered temporary (it is more difficult to justify the negative aspects of crossing a picket line for a temporary job). Replacements were also harder to obtain when the community supported striking workers.

Contingent Work, Subcontracting, and Other Profit Sources

The growing use of contingent workers also eroded workers' high replacement costs. Contingent workers are temporary workers, part-time workers, or independent contractors who are not in permanent full-time positions (Kalleberg 2009; Katz and Krueger 2019). Such work arrangements create a pool of labor that is insecure, theoretically mobile, and even potentially available as direct replacements during strikes. Some of these workers, such as independent contractors, are not covered by the NLRA, which complicates their ability to unionize (Boris and Klein 2015; Viscelli 2016).

Likewise, subcontracting allowed employers to more readily replace demanding workers. With competition among subcontractors, employers could select an arrangement to their liking and dismiss any subcontractor if a dispute arose.

Firms' structures also evolved over time, generating profits from a range of new sources (such as in conglomerate organization and financial activities) and responding to new economic pressures (such as financialization). Strikes are less impactful when employers are not dependent solely on labor to generate profits. The need to replace workers is less acute, as profits continue to roll in. Increased financialization in the late twentieth century contributed to this dynamic (Lin and Tomaskovic-Devey 2013), with some firms able to increasingly rely on financial income rather than on income from productions and sales. Importantly, financial income has also created a new hierarchy of pressures on firms. The rise of conglomerates that span multiple industries or geographic locations also changes the landscape for both firms and workers/unions.

Weakening of Legal Strike Protections and Norms

Finally, how the law is interpreted and acted upon shapes replacement costs. Since 1938, it has been legal to replace workers who are on strike for economic reasons. However, employers rarely acted upon this right until President Reagan permanently replaced striking air traffic controllers in the 1981 PATCO strike. Once Reagan signaled the cultural shift in the use of replacement workers, the floodgates opened up for employer action (LeRoy 1995b; McCartin 2006). Collective bargaining contracts that increasingly included "no strike" clauses and mandatory arbitration also weakened workers' strike protections.

Recap of Replacement Costs

In sum, our use of the replacement costs concept traces how workers' and employers' use of skill, timing, spatial, and other factors changed over the century. Race, gender, and professional orientation as well as deskilling and automation all shaped the enactment of replacement costs based on skill. Replacement costs based on spatial factors changed over the century: isolation became irrelevant while capital flight became a powerful employer spatial strategy. The timing mechanism, which is determined by the nature and delivery of the work, remained relatively constant. New factors impacting replacement costs arose over time. Inclusive solidarity and sit-down strikes, as embodied in the CIO, enabled unskilled workers to raise replacement costs and to organize during the 1930s and 1940s. By the dis-regulated period the use of contingent work and employers' use of alternative profit sources both reduced replacement costs. And importantly, state actions, especially the dwindling of strike protections and norms against replacing striking workers, reduced replacement costs. In general, in the U.S. context, replacement costs mattered most when workers acted upon them by striking. Strikes put the concept of replacement costs to the test.

Union and Employer Strategies: Making and Breaking Unions

During most of the 115 years we study, unions built power through solidarity, strikes, and other strategic actions, such as holding NLRB elections. And conversely, employers and employer organizations acted to break strikes and solidarity, and to dis-organize unions. Some of these efforts map directly onto influencing replacement costs or state context, but they also extend to an additional set of strategies and tactics used to organize or dis-organize unions. The efforts on both sides have shaped the booms and busts of union density over the century.

Employer Offensive: The Disorganization of Worker Solidarity and Strikes

A key theme in American labor history is the intense, sustained employer offensive against unions, a response many scholars point to as a main reason that unions are weak in the United States (Clawson and Clawson 1999; Friedman 1988; Goldfield 2007). Employers have tried to shift the law in their favor, and they have seen remarkable success. Perhaps their most significant accomplishment in this quarter was in their role in creating and supporting the Taft-Hartley Act of 1947, which rolled back many of the key worker protections established during the New Deal. In addition to political involvement, employers have tried many tactics to dis-organize unions. Arguably most consequentially, throughout the century they formed powerful employer associations. These associations were key to organizing employer offensives. In the early 1900s, they often hired spies and anti-union detectives to monitor and break union actions. They also attempted to undermine solidarity through hiring practices and strike breaking that pitted workers against each other due to race, ethnicity, and gender divisions (see Chapter 2). By the mid- to late twentieth century, they had created the demand for a large and innovative "union avoidance" industry, which ran the gambit from anti-union lawyers to strike consultant firms (Logan 2006).

As part of our context that frames each period, we trace the main currents of employers' actions to undermine unions, strikes, and solidarity. One data series that underscores this offensive is the record of ULP charges filed by unions with the NLRB. Union-filed ULPs, reported yearly by the NLRB, are

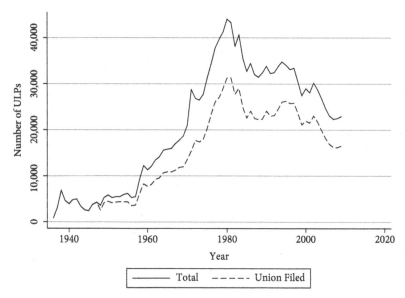

Figure 1.5 Unfair labor practice cases, total and union-filed by year.

one indicator of the willingness of employers to break labor laws, and they have been used as a measure of employer aggression (Goldfield 1987; Stepan-Norris and Southworth 2010).

Figure 1.5 shows the aggregate number of total ULPs and those filed by unions. Total ULPs and union-filed union ULPs increased steeply from the 1960s to the 1980s. This was true in the aggregate and for individual industries. This sharp increase in ULP filings reflects the employer offensive against unions, as employers sought to undo the gains that unions had made in the previous decades. The number of ULPs filed declined (for most, but not all industries) as strikes, NLRB activity, and union density declined in the 1980s and on.

Strikes

Strikes aim to create a crisis that forces employers to negotiate and/or for the state to take action. They are often the most powerful tool in workers' arsenal because they can stop production and impact employers' bottom line or branding and, in turn, compel employers to recognize unions, improve wages and working conditions, attend to workers' grievances, and to allow unions to recruit new members. Workers used a range of tactics besides strikes to pressure employers into recognizing unions or winning contracts, including boycotts, sabotage, comprehensive campaigns, and symbolic protest. However, strikes have been the dominant form of disruption in U.S. labor relations. Strikes are inherently risky for workers, and the history of U.S. strikes has been fraught with bloodshed (Taft and Ross 1969). As Morris and Clawson (2005, 696) argue about the labor movement and the civil rights movement, "Victory takes huge sacrifices."

Strikes and union strength are related. Both union density and strikes declined over the last fifty years. By the turn of the twenty-first century, unions struggled to win their strike demands (Rosenfeld 2014). Strikes, especially successful ones, often help to grow unions. Studies examining country-level patterns and disaggregated union-level data have found that strikes are associated with union growth (Cohn 1993; Cregan 2013; Hodder et al. 2017). Successful strikes can lead to growth for multiple reasons—they change the way that workers view power and their chances of success, they bring material gains that attract new members, and sometimes they may lead to changing laws or the degree of employer opposition to unions. Joe Burns (2012) and others argue that strikes must be revitalized as a central tactic used by the labor movement.

Did workers win strikes? We don't have much systematic data. The limited data generally suggest that when workers did strike, they often won. During the unregulated period, U.S. Bureau of Labor Statistics (BLS) data (1916 to 1936) show the union win rate hovering around 50 percent (with lower rates in the 1920s, and higher rates in the late teens and early 1930s). From the 1950s to the 1970s, the BLS collected results on only large strikes, those with over ten thousand workers. Workers won roughly 75 percent of these very large strikes. But beginning in the dis-regulated period, large strikes became less frequent as well as less successful, with about a 50 percent win rate (according to our coding of large strike outcomes; the BLS ceased reporting strike outcomes in the 1980s).

While winning strikes leads to membership growth, losing strikes can result in breaking unions, losing jobs, accepting concessions, or spreading the belief that unions cannot bring about change—all of which present challenges to robust unions. Losing strikes, especially multiple high-profile strikes (such as in the 1980s), can have a chilling effect for the larger labor movement and impact the likelihood of future strikes. When workers see other workers losing, they may be less likely to take the risk that strikes entail.

Workers may be more likely to strike when the context seems favorable or they have recently seen other workers win, because this helps them see that they can win also. As we show in Chapter 2, the number of strikes was associated with winning strikes: when workers were winning strikes, other workers struck more often. Workers are also more likely to strike when they are union members; though in some periods, substantial numbers of strikes sought union recognition and defense. Therefore, strikes relate to the perceived ability to win, union presence, and solidarity (Dixon et al. 2004; Dixon and Martin 2012; Rubin 1986). In the United States, all strikes—not just large strikes—became less frequent by the end of the twentieth century. We see the declining strike rate in recent decades as reflecting workers' and leaders' perception that they would have difficulty winning strikes.

We show that strikes have been linked to union density throughout most of the period we study. As we show in the following chapters, high replacement costs alone were not sufficient to generate high union density. For most of the twentieth century, workers had to strike in order to win and maintain union power. Surges in unionization often followed strike waves, as in both manufacturing and public sector unionization. Some strike waves have "encouraged" new legislation that is favorable to unions (Goldfield 1989a, 1989b). In other words, strike activity is sometimes due to the institutionalized presence of unions and their ability to win, but it also can create institutionalized union presence through successful strikes.

Figure 1.6 shows the number of workers involved in strikes each year. Three observations stand out. First, we see several sharp spikes, or strike waves. Both 1919 and 1946 had over 4 million workers involved in strikes, and 1952, 1970, and 1971 were not far behind with well over 3 million workers on strike. Second, the regulated period was characterized by workers on the move. Most years during this period saw over a million workers on strike. Third, the number of workers involved in strikes plummeted in the 1980s.

Strike rates illustrate how prevalent strikes were across the decades. Figure 1.7 shows the national strike rate by decade, or the total number of workers involved divided by employment.[2] The 1920s, the first decade with consistent aggregate strike data, had under 2 percent of workers involved in strikes.

---

[2] We use total employment from the census, which provides a relatively consistent measure over the 115 we study. These rates are similar (with small discrepancies) to the BLS statistics on the percent of workers involved in strikes, available from 1927 to 1979 (U.S. BLS Analysis of Work Stoppages, 1979, Table 1).

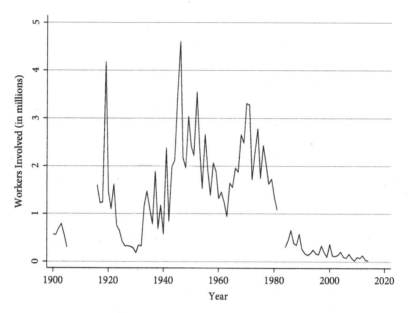

Figure 1.6 Number of workers involved in strikes, by year.

Note: U.S. BLS data available most years, 1900–1981 (no data available 1906–1915). No data available 1982–1983. Federal Mediation and Conciliation Service (FMCS) data 1984–2014.

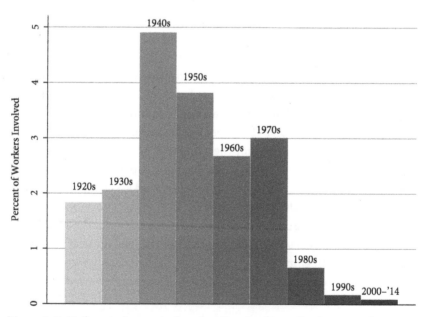

Figure 1.7 Strike rate (percent of workers involved in strikes), average by decade.

Note: U.S. BLS data 1920–1981. Federal Mediation and Conciliation Service (FMCS) data 1984–2014.

That percentage increased in the 1930s to over 2 percent, and then jumped even higher to a peak of almost 5 percent in the 1940s, when workers were on the move. Rates fell to under 4 percent in the 1950s, and the 1960s and 1970s hovered between 2.5 and 3 percent on strike. Thus, in each decade between the 1930s and the 1970s, between 2 and 4.8 percent of workers were involved in strikes. By contrast, the rate fell to well under 1 percent by the 1980s and later.

While the aggregate picture tells part of the story, industry-level analyses locate where workers were striking over the century. And, as we maintain, replacement costs alone were not sufficient to build union density, especially without state laws and agencies that provided some support to union efforts; it took strikes, too. The combination of high replacement costs and strikes was a successful recipe, which we determined to be the pathway to high union density in the early 1900s.

Figure 1.8 presents strikes rates by industry starting in the 1930s. During the mid-century, strike rates were over 5 percent for several decades in construction, mining, TCU, and manufacturing, which represented the bulk of organized workers during that period. Manufacturing workers, who struggled to win strikes in the early 1900s, gained leverage through industrial organizing, the formation of the NLRB, and expanded wartime employment. Mining had relatively small employment and was very strike prone, often with multiple strikes in a year involving the same workers. Although on a much smaller scale compared to earlier decades, public sector workers generated a strike wave in the late 1960s and 1970s, preceding the turn toward widespread public sector unionization.[3]

Union Elections and the National Labor Relations Board

The formation of the NLRB in 1935 created an alternative route to form unions for most private sector workers—one that did not rely as much on

---

[3] The public category includes workers employed with the Works Projects Administration (WPA), which employed job seekers for public works projects from 1935 to 1943. WPA workers were somewhat strike prone and large numbers struck (123,000 workers were out for at least one day) in 1939 to protest budget cuts to the WPA, which is reflected in the 1930s strike rate of public administration/education workers. Strike statistics for public workers were not consistently available from the BLS until 1933.

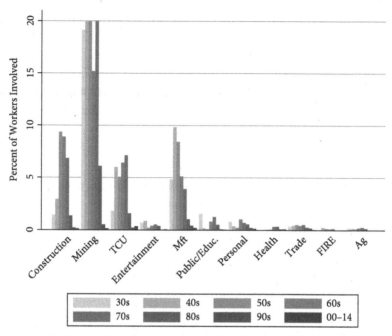

Figure 1.8 Strike rate by industry (percent of workers involved in strikes), average by decade.

Note: BLS strike data by industry starts in 1927. Strike rates were above 20 percent for mining in the 1940s, 1950s, and 1970s.

high replacement costs or striking for recognition. The NLRB provided for union elections, fortified by legal rights to organize, to file ULPs, and to strike. The sheer number of workers that organized through the NLRB during the regulated period in the United States was staggering. As Figure 1.9 shows, over a million workers per year were eligible to vote in NLRB elections in the mid-1940s.[4] Until 1980, that number hovered around half a million and then halved again in later decades.

Although NLRB elections were used by workers across most of the private sector, they were by far most important to manufacturing. Manufacturing workers accounted for the bulk of workers involved in elections and even

---

[4] Eligible workers are those who qualify to vote for or against union representation in their workplace. Election numbers dipped in 1948 due to the reorganization of the NLRB and new requirements for unions (Thirteenth Annual Report of the National Labor Relations Board, 1948: 3). The numbers reflect cases closed. Beginning in 1964, they report all elections held, including decertification elections (which is how the NLRB annual reports organized industry-level data). Decertifications, however, comprise a small percent of total elections.

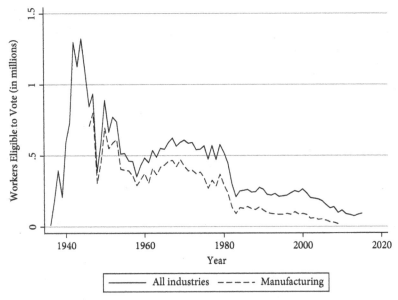

Figure 1.9 Workers eligible to vote in NLRB elections, by year.
Note: See Footnote 4 regarding 1948.

when standardizing by employment size, manufacturing workers stand out as the primary group to benefit from NLRB elections. In the mid-1940s, over 4 percent of all manufacturing workers were eligible to vote in NLRB elections. Though that number halved in the 1950s and 1960s to 2 percent, manufacturing workers also continued to have the highest election rate of any industry. The creation of the NLRB election process aided in introducing hundreds of thousands of mostly manufacturing workers into the union fold.

As we discuss in Chapter 3, manufacturing was the core industry targeted by the CIO, which used both strikes and elections to solidify their union efforts. In addition, manufacturing workers were concentrated in large workplaces. For example, in 1954, only 25.6 percent of manufacturing workers were in workplaces with under one hundred employees, while 83 percent of retail workers were in similarly small units (Sutch and Carter 2006, Tables Ba4707, Ba4704). Although these large workplaces were difficult to win, when they were won they provided a foothold for industry-level bargaining. The early success of the sit-down strikes in manufacturing created momentum throughout many manufacturing workplaces. On the other hand, small workplaces required exponential effort, given that individual

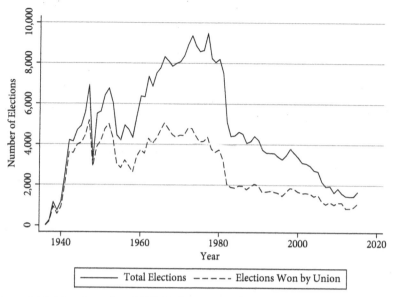

Figure 1.10 Number of total NLRB elections and union-won elections, by year.

elections (or strikes) would need to be held at every workplace. Eventually, aided by trade deals and capital mobility, many manufacturing employers were able to flee to new locations, making the threat of capital flight a serious problem for winning NLRB elections in the dis-regulated era.

In the first two decades of the NLRB's existence, unions won far more often than not, as shown in Figure 1.10. However, by the 1960s the gap between elections and those won by unions widened considerably. The number of elections dropped dramatically in the 1980s. Unions began to win a higher percentage in the 2000s, but the absolute number won pales in comparison to the 1940s. In other words, by the turn of the twenty-first century, unions no longer brought in substantial numbers of workers through NLRB elections. However, we see industry-level differences in NLRB elections, a trend we un-pack in later chapters.

Expansive Solidarity

Worker solidarity also drives unionization. A large body of labor scholarship maintains that solidarity is crucial to union strength. A vein of this schol-arship argues that solidarity among coworkers alone is often not enough to build widespread union power, especially in unfavorable institutional settings. Clawson (2003) argues that under neoliberal capitalism, workers must build their strength through new relationships between unions and other sectors of the working class. These relationships "fuse" union and community work in creative ways that may be able to tilt power away from employers.

The views, support, and potential solidarities with affinity groups can make big differences in outcomes. During the unregulated period, this was especially true for the use of the union label and boycotts (which required consumers to direct their purchasing choices toward aiding union struggles), as well as strikes. During all three periods, strikes oftentimes benefited from non-labor organizations' support, including financial and person power help as well as general community solidarity with strikes and organizing drives (Fantasia 1988). Prominent examples of non-union allies' support of the labor movement include the Highlander School, which played an important role in educating CIO union and other leaders; the role of radical political leaders in the tumultuous 1930s and beyond (Goldfield 1989b; Stepan-Norris and Zeitlin 2003); and the role of leader cross-over between labor and other like-minded organizations (Ganz 2000). Dixon and Martin (2012) though, found that participation by coalition partners was "fairly rare" in strike events during the 1990s–2000s.

When workers lack in other key arenas—say, state support or high replacement costs—one available strategy is to expand the terrain of solidarity. This concept differs from what Silver (2003) and Wright (2000) call "associational power," which is workers' power built through labor unions and political parties. We saw expansion of solidarity in the upsurge in manufacturing. Instead of relying on solidarity among mainly highly skilled craft workers, the new industrial approach embraced by the CIO built solidarity among the skilled, semi-skilled, and unskilled, men and women, and among all races. Later, in the 1960s and 1970s, the upsurge in public sector unionization drew upon deep connections between unions, civil rights groups, and feminist organizations (Isaac and Christiansen 2002; Johnston 1994). Farm workers drew on ties to clergy and student groups, and later the Justice for Janitors campaigns embraced a social movement orientation (Chun 2011; Shaw 2008). More recently, worker centers, which are community- rather than workplace-based, also expand the bounds of workers' solidarity (Fine 2006).

Expansive solidarity broadens the terrain of struggle beyond the dominant organizing paradigm. It has the capacity to expand who is included in struggles for class, race, and gender equity, and it can build power beyond the workplace. This orientation has been especially important in recent decades, as state support has evaporated and employer offensives have accelerated.

Workers and Their Union Leadership: Shaping Strategies Around Strikes and Solidarity

Over time and across industries, specific unions, factions, caucuses, and leaders have differed considerably in defining what outcomes are possible and how to arrive at those outcomes. Leadership impacts strategy, strikes, and solidarity. Union leadership and democracy (incorporating workers' voices into union policy) in these ways play important roles in union growth (Ganz 2000; Stepan-Norris and Zeitlin 2003; Voss and Sherman 2000). However, systematically capturing leadership dynamics across industry is difficult (in large part due to internal industry variations). Instead, we follow the major twists and turns of the main labor federations and their decisions/actions on behalf of their members as part of our context characterizing each period.

Beginning in the Progressive Era (1896–1916), the main labor federation was the AFL. Early on, it had a progressive agenda of broad social reform aimed at challenging dominant organizations and values. In the early 1900s, it turned in a more narrow and conservative direction in order to counter aggressive use of injunctions against strikes and boycotts. Going forward, especially in comparison to the policies of its rivals (the IWW, Trade Union Unity League [TUUL], and CIO), the AFL was more conservative.

The CIO leadership break from the AFL, along with worker upheaval and enhanced union power based on New Deal initiatives, had tremendous consequences for union density in the regulated period. The CIO, with more leftist leadership, was more egalitarian and progressive. In 1955, the two federations merged to create the AFL-CIO. The challenge by the twenty-first-century rival federation, Change to Win to the AFL-CIO, was less consequential than the CIO's challenge in the 1930s.

During periods when social movement unionism took hold, union democracy and worker involvement peaked. But in other times, many unions embraced what is called "business unionism," especially during the mid-twentieth century and later. With business unionism, union staff took responsibility for collective bargaining, enforcement of the contract, and other union operations, with little worker input. This approach meant that rank-and-file workers had less involvement and experience in running their own unions. By the 1990s, many were calling for a pivot from business unionism to social movement unionism—though this shift often proved difficult to achieve and maintain (Clawson 2003; Voss and Sherman 2000).

Race and Gender

Labor scholars have traced the many ways that race and gender have shaped union dynamics (e.g., Boris and Klein 2015; Fletcher and Gapasin 2008; Hill 1985; Honey 1993; Jung 2006; Kelley 1990; Milkman 2016; Ruiz 1987; Windham 2017). However, most analyses of union density over time ignore race and gender. We seek to redress this dearth in the scholarship. To this end, we attend to how employment by race and gender map onto union density patterns. Race and gender unionization patterns were clearly tilted toward white men in the early 1900s: the industries with high union density were all dominated by a white, male workforce. This relationship weakened and even reversed direction as the century progressed.

Employment in the United States has been organized around a split labor market, with the best jobs dominated by white workers, and the secondary labor market—characterized by insecure and low-pay work—dominated by workers of color and women, especially Black women (Bonacich 1976; Branch 2011).

In the early 1900s, employer hiring practices and societal race and gender norms contributed to the occupational segregation of women and workers of color. In addition, many unions prohibited membership and access to apprenticeship programs for women and workers of color. This discrimination kept workers of color and women out of the highly skilled jobs and higher paying industries (Milkman 2016). Combined, employer and union practices relegated women and workers of color to industries that were unlikely to have high replacement costs. As the century progressed, Black workers, immigrants, and women were more likely to be employed as contingent workers. These workers had low replacement costs, but some began to innovate with new forms of organizing, including using worker centers (Chun 2011; Hatton 2014; Milkman and Ott 2014; Polivka 1996).

Table 1.2 Percent of Employment by Race and Gender: 1910, 1960, and 2015

	White			Male		
	1910	1960	2015	1910	1960	2015
Construction	93	91	81	99	96	90
Mining	94	97	87	99	95	85
TCU	90	92	71	95	83	75
Entertainment	92	91	75	79	69	57
Manufacturing	95	93	77	83	75	71
Public Administration	95	90	76	54	54	38
Personal Services	70	64	66	25	28	28
Health Services	95	87	71	63	30	23
Trade	96	93	74	80	62	52
FIRE	96	96	78	87	54	45
Agriculture	78	86	82	87	90	77

TCU, Transportation, Communication, and Utilities; Public Administration, Public Administration, and Education; Trade, Wholesale, and Retail Trade; FIRE, Finance, Insurance, and Real Estate; Agriculture, Agriculture, Forestry, and Fishing.

Table 1.2 presents census data on the race and gender composition by industry. In the earlier decades of the 1900s, personal services and agriculture employed far more workers of color. Women were far more likely to work in personal services, health services, and public administration/education. As the century progressed, the race and gender composition shifted in most industries, with increases of women and workers of color in almost all industries.

In addition to occupational segregation, employers stoked race, gender, and citizenship tensions to diminish the prospects for unionization. Employers aimed to undermine strikes and solidarity by hiring strike breakers based on race and ethnic divisions (Griffin et al. 1986). Perpetrated by the state, employers, and white vigilantes, racial violence was commonplace in the South when Black workers tried to organize under Jim Crow (Honey 1993). Some white workers struck in order to keep workers of color out of their union ranks.

Workers in women-dominated industries experienced other challenges. Most early AFL unions refused to organize women or placed them in secondary organizations called Federal Labor Unions. Women also faced paternalistic laws and employers. For example, in the early century, some employer practices' restricted women's actions, including restrictions on performing certain "heavy" (and higher-paying) jobs, and on their ability to work while pregnant or as mothers of small children.

Laws also reinforced race and gender subordination. The foundational Fair Labor Standards Act and the National Labor Relations Act both excluded industries dominated by women and workers of color, while being more protective of the jobs dominated by white workers or men (Perea 2011).

Union federations have differed in their enthusiasm for organizing women and workers of color, and these differences were particularly pronounced in the early 1900s. Some embraced their white male membership, while mainly excluding women and workers of color either explicitly or implicitly. Others, especially the IWW and TUUL, worked to forge solidarity among workers, sometimes with success (Cole 2010; Rabinowitz 2017). Some international unions found themselves in industries with rapidly changing demographics, especially during World War II (Milkman 2016). The rise of CIO industrial organizing strategies in the 1930s ushered in significant numbers of workers of color and women, who had long been at the bottom of the occupational hierarchy, into the union fold. Unfortunately, the postwar CIO campaign to organize the South in "Operation Dixie" underestimated the role that race would play, both among workers and employers, and ultimately failed (Honey 1992).

As the century progressed, space for women and workers of color began to open up, though significant challenges remained (Fletcher and Gapasin 2008; Milkman 2016; Windham 2017). By the late 1960s, public sector organizing expanded unionization for both women and Black workers. In the 1970s and later, unionized women workers in the public sector, along with women's rights activists, led the charge to implement "comparable worth" programs to win equal pay for occupations that had been devalued by gender discrimination, and these efforts and others resulted in greater pay equity for union women and workers of color in the public sector (Acker 1989; Johnston 1994; Kerrissey and Meyers 2022). Meanwhile, caucus groups within unions began to agitate for greater gender and racial justice within labor organizations. By the twenty-first century, women constituted almost half of all union workers, immigrants were deemed to be "organizable," and Black workers were far more likely to be union members than white workers, controlling for labor force size (Milkman 2006; Rosenfeld and Kleykamp 2012).

Methodology and Data

We apply comparative and historical methods within three main historical periods. At the beginning of each chapter, we introduce the legal, political, and economic factors that provide the broad context for that period. While contexts change, sometimes gradually, over the century, we maintain that these broad divisions characterize the three main contexts that unions faced over this long time period. We also emphasize that the main actors of concern—workers and unions versus employers and their organizations—worked within each period to change those conditions to their own advantage. Actions on the part of both sides, along with state and other actors, account for the altered contexts we see in subsequent years.

Comparison seeks to identify similarity and difference among cases and to assess how various factors help to explain patterns in the outcome variable. Considerable variation exists in union density across industries, and in the timing of the booms and busts by industry. Aggregate analyses are insufficient because in any given year increases in one industry may obscure or entirely erase declines in another. Industry analyses allow us to capture much of those differences. For instance, prominent patterns across industries were dramatic during the dis-regulated period, when both employment and union density in many of the private sector industries began to fall, while employment in public administration/education and health grew and their union density remained steady. Extending this logic, it is possible to scrutinize even more precisely to consider a smaller unit of analysis: the union. Within the same industry, some unions grew while others merged or disappeared. Analyzing data at the lowest level of aggregation is the best solution. But data on all relevant factors is not always available to do so. Our solution is to analyze at the industry level.

Comparison is a powerful tool for examining combinations of factors related to an outcome. We have a small number of cases (eleven industries) over a long time period (115 years), which we divide into three basic periods. This configuration allows us to analyze how labor regimes impact overall trends of union density and specific industries differently.

Our primary methodological strategy is John S. Mill's method of agreement. This method categorizes cases with regard to a common outcome (in our case, union density) and then attempts to identify common factors associated with that outcome. This process finds factors that are consistently present (or absent) in cases with one outcome and not present (or absent) in cases with the opposite outcome. We organize industries by three basic levels of union density: high, medium, and low. We ask how our factors of interest—state actions, replacement costs, union and employer strategies, and race and gender—explain high, medium, and low levels of union density in each period. We also selectively use the method of difference, whereby we assess cases (industries) that have some or many of the factors we deem to be important for building high union density, but don't achieve high density.

Comparative and historical research allows for some generalization and theory building, but hypothesis testing is limited. We aim for our analysis to provide a compelling comparative and historical account of union density over time, to provide new evidence, to afford some important lessons, and to raise new questions about future trajectories.

The data for this book come from government documents, union reports, and secondary sources. Our data set provides an uninterrupted century of labor data by industry. The data and methodology are described in Appendix B and are publicly accessible through a data repository. See authors' faculty profiles at the University of California, Irvine and the University of Massachusetts, Amherst for links to data repository.

We went to great lengths to make our extensive data as accurate as possible, but several caveats should be noted. As is true of any research that spans over one hundred years, our data have some limitations. Data sources and definitions change over the period, and some data are only available for certain years. We use a combination of sources: government records, organizational records, data assembled by other scholars, and secondary sources. Each source used unique procedures to collect and record its data, and those differences may matter for the consistency of data across time and industry.

In addition, we base union membership numbers on union reports, which may be rough estimates. Also, in later decades, unions were more likely to span multiple industries; we use sparse reports of the percentage of members in each industry to allocate unions' members to our industry categories. For these reasons, our estimates of membership, density, strikes, and accompanying data are inevitably approximate. We present averages over decade periods to indicate broad trends, rather than yearly changes.

As many scholars have shown, geography is important for union density throughout our long period (Dixon 2020; Troy 1956). At the extremes, the industrial Northeast has traditionally been the most heavily unionized and the South the least organized. We acknowledge this important pattern, but abstract from it in this work for one main reason: the lion's share of our data is not available by location.

All of these caveats matter. But, because we aim to provide a sweeping investigation into U.S. union density over a long time period, they are less likely to interfere with our overall analysis and conclusions. Our industry-level analysis allows us to consider whether and how the variations we identify help explain the differences we observe, using the lowest level of aggregation possible. One may disagree with some of our data or periodization decisions, but we are confident that the overall patterns that we present are accurately portrayed over time and industry.

The Census and Industry Categories

The decennial census offers the longest and most consistent source of employment data. It includes information on gender, race, occupation, and industry, and began to track industry in 1910. We follow the work of Sobek (2001), who constructed a method to create consistent census employment data over time by industry. Our industrial categories, which shift boundaries over time, are constructions of official recordkeepers and represent approximations of work done, products made, and services delivered in similar settings and/or for similar purposes. Hence, they are estimations.

We analyze eleven major industries. A primary consideration in constructing these categories is how they relate to other data sources. Some data, including for strikes and NLRB elections, differed in the level of specificity in industry categories. We aimed to construct meaningful categories that were also broad enough to be comparable across data sources. We do not include business services or "other services" in the analyses because these category definitions were particularly likely to vary across data sets. They also have low unionization rates throughout the time period studied. For more information, see the methodological appendix and the online data repository. Thus, we examine:

1. Agriculture, forestry, and fisheries. We refer to this as "agriculture," as that is the dominant industry in this group.
2. Mining
3. Construction
4. Manufacturing. We combine durable and nondurable manufacturing.
5. Transportation, communication, and utilities, which we abbreviate as "TCU."

6. Trade. We combine wholesale and retail trade.
7. FIRE. This is finance, insurance, and real estate.
8. Personal service. This includes accommodations, laundry, beauty salons, and other categories.
9. Entertainment. This includes entertainment, arts, sports, and recreation.
10. Health services. This includes hospitals, other health facilities, and social assistance.
11. Public administration and education. This includes federal, state, and local levels as well as educational services. Most workers in this category are public sector. However, other industries may also include some public sector workers (e.g., public hospitals).

Some of our industries are amalgamations of several unique operations (e.g., transportation, communications, utilities) that may have different relationships to our variables of interest (e.g., timing, skill). This may be true even within seemingly singular industries, such as mining: some mines are more isolated than others, and different types of mining (e.g., anthracite coal, bituminous coal, hard rock) may create different social relations among workers and employers. Again, our aim is to provide a general sweep of union density over a long period of time; these internal industry differences must be acknowledged, but we accept them as the best categorizations available for our analysis.

Union Density, Membership, and Characteristics

We compile yearly union membership numbers and organizational characteristics for every major union in the United States, 1900–2015. We exclude small unions that do not have contracts in multiple states, and we exclude members who are not working in the United States. We rely primarily on union reports on their memberships to government agencies and later, other organizations, which are available for most unions for most of our time period. When these reports are unavailable, we use internal union reports on per capita dues or secondary sources.

Unions, especially in the last fifty years, often represent workers in multiple industries. Because we are interested in industry-level trends, we use AFL-CIO reports, BLS reports, and subsequent Directories (various years) to assign union memberships to industries, along with prior scholarship, including Hannan (1988), Fink (1977), and union websites that report industry breakdowns of their members.

This approach differs from union membership estimates derived from the Current Population Survey (CPS), a survey frequently used by contemporary U.S. labor scholars to obtain union membership numbers. The CPS asks questions about the primary jobs of wage and salary workers, including union membership and coverage. However, CPS industry-level data are only available beginning in 1983. Compared to union reports, CPS union estimates tend to result in slightly lower membership numbers by industry. While it is possible to disagree on which approach best captures actual membership, both the CPS and our approach of union reports show similar membership trends within industries. Because we are interested in a long time period, we opt to use union membership reports, similar to other scholars examining union trends prior to the 1980s.

Union density is the total U.S. union members divided by employment at the industry level. The most consistent employment data comes from the census, which began collecting industry-level employment in 1910. To calculate density, we use data on union membership and employment by industry, averaged over each decade. This approach allow us to produce rough estimates of union density over a long period of time. Union density often varies somewhat by different sources, depending on the method of capturing union membership (the numerator) and employment source (the denominator).

Our measure of union density summarizes three relative categories that fit the U.S. context: high density (over 20 percent unionized), medium density (5–20 percent), and minimal density (under 5 percent). As mentioned above, although the "high" category of over 20 percent is quite low for other countries (and even for our middle period), it is appropriate for the United States, which has had on average under 20 percent density during both before the 1930s and after the 1980s.

Strikes, Union Elections, and Other Data

We use multiple government and union sources to track work stoppages by industry. Work stoppages include both strikes and lockouts; however, the vast majority are strikes, rather than lockouts, and lockouts often occur within the context of a labor dispute. We follow the earlier BLS practice of simply referring to these types of labor disputes as "strikes." The data sources have some measurement differences over the century, which we detail in Appendix B. We use U.S. BLS reports covering all strikes for most of the unregulated and regulated periods, 1900–1981. Because these reports were missing in some of the unregulated years, we also use AFL convention proceedings that documented strikes to fill in missing years. The BLS stopped collecting data on all strikes during the dis-regulated period (it continued to track only large strikes). In its place, we use data on all strikes collected by the Federal Mediation and Conciliation Service (FMCS) starting in 1984. We track numbers of workers involved, number of strikes, and when possible, strike issue and outcome.

The NLRB published annual reports from 1936 to 2010. These reports include information on ULPs, NLRB decertification elections, and NLRB elections, including the number of elections, the number of workers covered, and election outcome. The NLRB changed its annual reporting methods for the tail end of our study (2011–2015), so we opt to not report on it for those years.

We also use data from the BLS and other sources to capture employment trends that are relevant to replacement costs, including contingent work and displacement from mass layoffs.

We include other data when they are available and relevant, including information on union apprenticeship programs and gender and race requirements for union membership.

Time Periods: Unregulated, Regulated, and Dis-regulated Periods

Union Booms and Busts is organized into three time periods, each with a fairly distinct labor regime, that we call unregulated, regulated, and dis-regulated periods. Scholars disagree on exact periodization dates. Many developments unfolded over the century; therefore, it is difficult to select exact beginning and ending dates for periods and subperiods. For example, the National Labor Relations Act passed in 1935 but took several years to implement. And the trends that we identify in the 1980s (the dis-regulated period) had roots in the regulated period. Moreover, we end our analyses in 2015, though we do not claim the dis-regulated period to be over. There are no "correct" cutoff points for our periods. We analyze broad trends over a long timeframe, select the most consequential turning points, and set our periods accordingly. In general, we are less concerned with pinpointing dates than with addressing general dynamics.

Chapter 2 considers the "unregulated period," which covers 1900 to 1934. In this period, labor relations were mostly unregulated, and courts tended to interpret laws in employers' favor. This span was the "wild West" of union organizing—with few laws, disruptive capacity (strikes and to a lesser extent, boycotts) and employers' countermeasures reigned supreme. A combination of three characteristics co-occurred in highly unionized industries: high replacement costs (work that was high skill and where workers accomplished job closure through apprenticeship programs, time sensitivity, or isolation), high strike frequency and success, and employment mainly of high-status workers—white men. Industries that did not have all of these characteristics had lower levels of unionization.

Chapter 3 examines the "regulated period," from 1935 to 1979. The regulated period saw a dramatic rise followed by a fall in union density in many—though not all—industries. Unlike the unregulated era, this period had greater state support of unionization. After mass strikes and protests, the passage of the NLRA and the onset of World War II helped to institutionalize unions, with some notable differences by industry. Favorable laws and access to NLRB election procedures helped some industries to unionize. Concurrently, the rise of industrial organizing and the adoption of the sit-down strike tactic presented new opportunities for disruptive action, especially for un- and semi-skilled workers in mass production industries who benefited from an expanded notion of solidarity. Although some scholars characterize this era as one of a "social compact," the strike data tell a different story. Unionization did not come easily; workers sacrificed much to make it happen, mainly by striking.

High-density industries during the regulated period continued to have the same three co-occurring characteristics: high replacement costs, substantial strike rates, and employment of mostly white male workers (though this pattern began to slowly fade, especially after the rise of public sector unionism and the retrenchment of Jim Crow). The two industries that experienced major booms in union density, manufacturing and public administration/ education, both had co-occurring worker disruption, organizing drives, and new beneficial legislation.

Chapter 4 focuses on the "dis-regulated period," covering 1980 to 2015. In this era, many of the regulations established mid-century were curtailed through employer and state actions. Unions faced an increasingly hostile climate, including legal setbacks, the use of permanent replacements during strikes, bold employer anti-union campaigns, capital flight, and increasing employment of contingent workers. Despite presidential administrations that were roughly half Democratic during this period, political leaders were either unable or unwilling to weaken employers' or to fortify workers' rights in meaningful ways. These conditions helped erode employment in union strongholds and rendered traditional union organizing approaches less successful. They also led to wage stagnation, greater income inequality, and related crises for many twenty-first-century workers.

Most industries with high replacement costs were able to maintain, or at least curb, the decline in union density. But the labor climate had deteriorated for most workers, making winning new unions and defending contracts difficult. Union strikes collapsed in all industries as the dis-regulated period proceeded. Strikes were far less frequent in this period compared to the regulated period. Unions' NLRB election efforts also collapsed. We see both of these collapses—strikes and NLRB elections—as partly a reaction to the unfavorable terrain, where the ability to win was heavily tilted toward employers. In light of the hostile climate, unions were most successful in industries that had footholds in the public sector—where a combination of spatially fixed work, favorable legislation, and less severe employer opposition fortified unions. Faced with these challenges, a renewed logic of expansive solidarity arose in this period, which focused on community-based organizing, worker centers, and coalitions, though it is too early to tell whether this will translate into higher union density. The demographics of all industries shifted away from white male dominance. In contrast to the early 1900s, in the 2000s, women and workers of color had become key members of the union movement.

Finally, we conclude the book with insights on what matters for union density. Given that employers will continue to act to disorganize unions, what lessons does history offer to unions?

2

Union Density in the Unregulated Period (1900–1934)

In the early 1900s, workers faced serious challenges: low wages, long hours, hazardous conditions, and few protective laws. Forming unions was a major avenue to improve their lives. But only some workers were successful: the formation and maintenance of unions was highly uneven across industries. While some industries had minimal unionization, in a handful of industries, including construction, mining, entertainment, and transportation, communications, and utilities (TCU), unions managed to attain over 20 percent density. Some of these industries had subindustries (or occupations) with union density as high as 80 percent. Given the harsh conditions, what accounts for this organizing success?

To illustrate these divergent outcomes, we begin with three accounts of union organizing in this early period: a successful route to unionization by book and newspaper printers, moderate success by manufacturing workers, and minimal success by agricultural workers.

Early Success in Organizing Printers

The case of book and newspaper printers illustrates an early and successful route to unionization. With very few government protections for unions, the workers with the most success in forming unions relied on building their replacement costs and striking. They succeeded despite employers' fierce opposition. We begin the story before 1900 because their early organizing success helps to explain their later success.

In the 1830s, New York printers faced declining wages, competition from runaway apprentices and new immigrant labor, and unsanitary and dangerous conditions (poor air circulation and light). In June 1831, disgruntled printers met to establish equitable prices and wages. A few weeks later, they

Union Booms and Busts. Judith Stepan-Norris and Jasmine Kerrissey, Oxford University Press.
© Oxford University Press 2023. DOI: 10.1093/oso/9780197539859.003.0002

formed the Typographical Association of New York, which circulated the new scale of prices to employing printers. Initiates to the union pledged to abide by the scale, and the union pledged to provide members with strike, unemployment, health, and death benefits. The hours were long, with newspaper printers often working up to seventeen hours per day, and rapidly changing technology rendered some printers' five-to-seven-year training obsolete (Stevens 1913, 107–111).

Most employers accepted the price scale and awarded the increased wages, but some "altogether refused." Non-cooperating employers developed a strategy armed with multiple tactics to avoid union labor and higher wages. Their first task was to secure control over the supply of printers. Printers normally controlled apprenticeship training, which worked to ensure a limited supply of eligible workers (Motley 1907). But boys indentured as apprentices in printing shops often got restless and eloped from their masters before completing their training. Non-cooperating employers jumped on the chance to reduce their wage bills, hiring these runaway apprentices as "halfway" journeymen, paying them wages just a bit higher than those paid to apprentices. This scheme increased the supply of printers and depressed all printers' wages. Printers' unions reacted swiftly by forming committees to find ways to control the number of apprentices and the employment of halfway journeymen. They disseminated "rat" circulars (unfair lists) to identify journeymen and master printers who violated union rules. Furthermore, they tried requiring printers leaving the city to carry traveling cards in order to receive employment elsewhere.

Another tactic non-cooperating employers used was to recruit skilled printers from Great Britain by advertising that U.S. wages were high and positions plentiful. Printers successfully responded with their own circular and emissary to Great Britain to warn printers there that the recruitment was a "well-laid plan" of a few master printers to create a "glut in the labor market that would result in a reduction of wage and possible dissolution of the union" (Stevens 1913, 69, 143, 73, 107, 147). For their part, printers built formidable unions that fought to improve working conditions and secure their power: many were able to win higher wages, shortened hours, improved working conditions, standardized payment methods, the banning of piecework, and closed/union shops (Lipset, Trow, and Coleman 1956, 21). What explains their success?

Printers adroitly used their striking power to disrupt the timing of publications like newspapers. But success was neither guaranteed nor immediate. Printers had to strike often and win, and this required a strong sense of solidarity. Printers' solidarity was rooted in their literacy, elite skills, and propensity to socialize among themselves outside of the workplace due to their night-shift work (they were off work when others were working). And according to Lipset, Trow, and Coleman (1956, 31): "Not the least part of their power comes from the fact that many of their employers produce a highly perishable commodity for a local market. Newspaper publishers have always been extremely vulnerable to strikes, and since they operate within a local market, they are able to pass on the increased costs to the readers or advertisers."

While other workers continued to work long hours, printers' unions secured the nine-hour day before 1900 and, by relying upon their militancy, were one of the first to adopt a resolution (in 1906) for an eight-hour day. They engaged in a significant and costly struggle to this end (in doing so, they suffered the loss of some locals). They used locals that had won the eight-hour day as their starting point. Once enough locals were onboard, the union required all local unions to strike if employers refused to grant an eight-hour day schedule (and they suspended locals that did not agree to strike, which meant that members lost their traveling cards). The United Typothetae (employers in the book and job branch) "refused to concede a second reduction without a struggle" (Ulman 1955, 496), so strikes became commonplace. The international union leveraged printers' solidarity by taxing members of locals that already won the eight-hour day to financially support its striking locals: "No organization involved in difficulty with employers carried its members on strike and benefit rolls as long as the International Typographical Union in the eight-hour difficulty" (Ulman 1955, 499). At significant cost, the printers won the important and long-standing gain of an eight-hour day.

Another battle occurred when employers introduced new technology that reduced skilled employment. In the 1890s, employers instituted linotype machines and proposed that a lower-skilled and lower-paid workforce operate them (Lipset, Trow, and Coleman 1956). The International Typographical Union (ITU) "responded by incorporating linotype training into its apprenticeship program and requiring that all workers (including those on linotype machines) complete apprenticeship training in all skills. The ITU called several strikes over this issue, and finally, employers accepted the union's rule. Workers were more productive with the new machine, which allowed the union to argue for shorter hours and the elimination of piece-rate work" (Lipset, Trow, and Coleman 1956, 21). Later in the twentieth century, employers introduced the teletype machine, which ushered in another battle, ultimately reducing printers' timing advantage. Printing employers also organized to protect their interests. A significant proportion of newspaper and book publishers joined employer associations to counter union power. These associations also covered lithography, electrotype, and photo-engraving occupations. Some were belligerent toward unions, working aggressively to break them.

In sum, printers organized early on and used their skill- and timing-based power along with their solidarity and militancy to successfully push for improving workers' hours, pay, and working conditions. Employers also organized and sought to employ non-union workers and to reduce the need for skilled workers by introducing novel technology. In the early years, printers gained the upper hand. In 1910, printers had 34 percent union density and by 1920, 50 percent (Wolman 1924, 141, 151).

Moderate Success in Organizing Manufacturing Workers

The manufacturing and public administration/education industries lagged behind, with more moderate levels of density in the 6–11 percent range, not because workers in these industries did not attempt to unionize, but because they were less successful at securing union members. We select one manufacturing subindustry, mill workers, to provide a case in point.

Mill workers in the early 1900s faced sweatshop conditions. The work was grueling: long hours, an ever-quickening production pace, unsafe conditions, and barely subsistence-level pay. Women and children did most of the work, and dozens of nationalities were represented on the factory floor. By any account, these workers needed a union. But the dominant federation of the time, the American Federation of Labor (AFL), was uninterested in organizing them. Mill work was viewed as unskilled, and the AFL's main strategy was to build power through skilled work. Mill workers, however, saw things differently, and the workers of Lawrence, Massachusetts, illustrate the promises and challenges that the era's mill workers faced, as depicted by Loomis (2018). As early as the 1880s, women workers struck the mills in Lawrence. Their male coworkers did not support them, and they lost. By the early 1900s, a small portion of the English-speaking workers who occupied more skilled jobs were unionized in the United Textile Workers, an AFL-affiliated union. But the masses of immigrant workers toiling for pittances did not receive the support of the AFL.

In 1912, a new Massachusetts law limited women's work hours to fifty-four hours a week—two hours less than before. In practice, this restriction resulted in a pay cut. When workers saw their reduced pay, they immediately walked out, effectively shutting down the city of Lawrence in the "Bread and Roses" strike. The Industrial Workers of the World (IWW), a radical alternative to the AFL, sent skilled organizers, who often spoke multiple languages and had prior strike experience, to support the strikers. Unlike the AFL, the IWW embraced semi-skilled and unskilled workers, women, and ethnic and racial minorities. They believed in "one big union" and in the power of strikes and direct action.

Mill owners, elites, and police aimed to close down the strike immediately. In the first days of the strike, mill agents stoked division by fabricating a lie meant to divide workers—that the bosses had agreed to the workers' demands. When the workers did not budge, the police, in subfreezing temperatures, sprayed fire hoses at the strikers from the mill roofs, and jailed strikers who threw the ice back at them. Harvard students, representing the elite of the time, volunteered to strike break. The Harvard president allowed participating students to reschedule their final exams in order to take part. Within two weeks, police had killed a striker and framed strike leaders, imprisoning them for eight months without trial.

When the women strikers sent their children away from Lawrence to the safe haven of neighboring states, where families volunteered to care for them, the national media increased its coverage of the strike. Hundreds of strikers' children were put on trains and met by strike sympathizers, and in late February, another train was set to leave with 150 children. The police intervened, beating women and children to prevent the departure. Outrage spread about the brute force. Concerned about the publicity, the company quickly settled. The strikers had won, including wage increases of 5–20 percent as well as overtime pay. Strikers negotiated their return to work, and eventually the release of the framed strike leaders who had been jailed. These events were very timely for the strikers as hunger and discouragement were already driving workers back to their jobs.

Although the victory was resounding, in just two years, the union was in ruins. At the height of the strike, ten thousand Lawrence mill workers were card-carrying IWW members; by 1914, only four hundred remained (Loomis 2018). A central impetus for the union collapse was the IWW's refusal to establish long-range organization in workplaces after strikes. They saw collective bargaining contracts as a step toward capitulating to capitalism and refused to sign agreements. Without contracts, wins quickly eroded. After strikes, IWW leaders typically moved on to the next battle, without leaving organizational infrastructures. This pattern is demonstrated by Matilda Rabinowitz, an immigrant mill worker turned IWW organizer, who recounted organizing workers at the Bread and Roses strike (Rabinowitz 2017). Afterward, she moved to support a similar strike in New York—filled with police violence, imprisonment, ploys by the company, and thousands of striking immigrant women using highly creative tactics. That strike was lost, and Rabinowitz proceeded to the next struggle.

The story of Lawrence mill workers underscores the medium-level unionization among manufacturing workers. These workers were often militant unionists facing strong anti-union employers. They struck, but they did not always win. The bulk of workers were low-skill, women workers, who did not fit into the AFL's main focus on skilled worker organizing.

Limited Success in Organizing Agricultural Workers

Workers in the remaining industries accomplished minimal levels of unionization, 2 percent or less—agriculture; trade; finance, insurance, and real estate (FIRE); health services; and personal services. We profile an attempted organizing activity in agriculture to illustrate some of the challenges that some of these workers faced, drawing on Megan Ming Francis's (2014) work and others.

In 1919, a group of Black sharecroppers met in a church in Elaine, Arkansas. Landowners were continuously demanding higher and higher profits from them, leaving little for survival. They wanted fairer compensation, and they were meeting to make a plan, along with a prominent white lawyer who supported them. Some had joined a union, the Progressive Farmers and Household Union of America. Rumors were already circulating among the local white communities that it was an "insurrection" against the white population.

The sharecroppers knew it was risky: racial violence permeated the area. Only two generations earlier, their grandparents had been enslaved. The convict leasing system had recently been in full swing, rounding up "convicts"—primarily Black workers with minor infractions—and forcing them to work on chain gangs and for private companies. Aware of the violence, some of the sharecroppers brought their rifles to the meeting. That evening, local white men, some of whom were associated with law enforcement, showed up outside of the church and fired shots into it. The sharecroppers returned fire. A white man was killed.

The state response was swift and clear: the punishment for Black workers associated with this sort of labor organizing would be deadly. The governor sent in five hundred troops. The local newspaper reported the troops were to "round up" the "heavily armed negroes" and had orders to "shoot to kill any negro who refused to surrender immediately." The troops exceeded their charge. Working with local vigilantes, they killed at least two hundred Black men, women, and children—perhaps many more. During the massacre, five whites were killed. The local authorities blamed the union for instigating a "deliberately planned insurrection" against whites (Francis 2014).

The Elaine Massacre was not an isolated event. Agriculture in the United States was built on racialized labor exploitation—through enslavement, sharecropping, and unprotected immigrant workers. The entire system depended on this cheap labor. As in the case of the Elaine Massacre, white locals and state forces combined to violently repress union activity. And history had shown that elites had reason to worry: Black people had and perhaps could again use their strike power to deeply change society. W. E. B. Du Bois (1935) argued that the Civil War was in part a mass general strike led by enslaved Black people, who collectively ceased to work. This strike was a key factor in ending slavery.

But such collective resistance was extremely difficult to maintain. Sharecroppers faced geographic challenges to collective organization (dispersed workplaces), in addition to violent repression (Kelley 1990). Sharecroppers were at the edge of plantations, often separated by several miles from the next tenant. Much of the sharecroppers' resistance was more individual or isolated in nature—sabotage, theft, and the like. More collective organization came during the Great Depression. Facing almost unsurvivable conditions, sharecroppers began to work with and through one of the few organizations interested in organizing them, the Communist Party. They formed new unions and issued demands, such as being paid cash instead of in kind. Similar to the response to the Elaine Massacre, oppression was swift. Groups of white vigilantes terrorized union activists while local authorities sometimes refused to protect activists and other times offered direct aid to vigilantes. In 1931, Tallapoosa, Alabama, for example, deputized vigilantes raided a union meeting, brutally beat men and women there; attacked the union leader's house, murdered him and beat his wife, leaving her with a fractured skull; and later murdered another leader.

It is not that workers in other industries did not face violent repression for labor action—they often did. But deeply racialized violence against sharecroppers perpetrated by state forces as well as local vigilantes rose to a level unrivaled in other types of work. At the same time, traditional labor organizations, like the AFL, offered little support to these workers, instead focusing on shoring up the conditions of skilled workers. It comes as little surprise, then, that agricultural unions did not flourish during this era, despite the efforts of these workers.

Union Density in the Unregulated Period

In this chapter, we examine the conditions that employers and workers faced in the early 1900s, and the strategies that they used to prevent or organize unions. Union efforts and outcomes differed dramatically by industry. Of our three examples, the successful printers' strategies and conditions allowed for strong unions; mill workers' strikes had more mixed outcomes, and they had more difficulty building and maintaining unions; agricultural workers' organizing efforts were met with harsh repression, and they faced considerable challenges due to racialized violence and work structures, leading to little success in unionization.

Figure 2.1 shows union density for each industry, averaged by decade for the 1910s, 1920s, and 1930s. Four industries have the highest union density compared to the others: construction, mining, TCU, and entertainment. More moderate unionization levels appear in manufacturing and public administration and education, and lower levels characterize the remaining industries. Density for each industry also varies by decade, with some becoming more organized over time and others becoming less organized.

We return to our four broad factors that serve to explain differences in union densities: the state and macro context; replacement costs; union and employer strategies; and race and gender dynamics. These factors change even within our first time period, in part as a result of employers' and unions' reactions to changes in their environments and development of new strategies and tactics to enhance their positions.

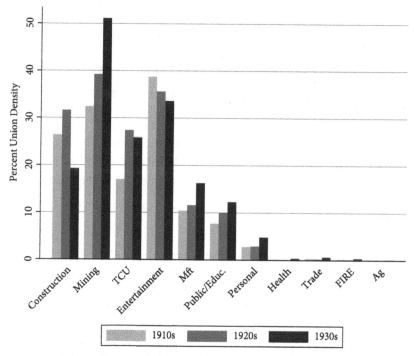

Figure 2.1 Unregulated period: Union density by industry, average by decade.
TCU, transportation, communication and utilities; Mft, manufacturing; Public/Educ, public
administration and education; Health, health services; Personal, personal services; Trade, wholesale
and retail trade; FIRE, finance, insurance, and real estate; Ag, agriculture, fisheries, and forestry.

Lacking favorable laws or state institutions to rein in employers, unionization developed mostly in industries where workers had high replacement
costs and also acted on that capacity via disruption. While boycotts and the
union label were fairly common union tactics, the dominant form of disruptive action in this period was strikes—or the collective withholding of labor
to force employers to recognize unions and improve wages and conditions.

Workers with high replacement costs were better positioned to form
unions and accomplish high union density during American labor's formative years (1897–1910), including workers with high and scarce *skills* (making
workers indispensable to production and replacement workers hard to secure during strikes), *time-sensitive* work (making work stoppages particularly potent), and *geographic isolation* from cities or towns (making it difficult
to find and transport replacement workers to a strike) (Kimeldorf 2013).

Replacement costs relate to workers' position within the economic
structure, but this highly structured orientation only tells part of the story.

Employers worked to reduce—and unions worked to increase—workers' replacement costs. In *The Principles of Scientific Management* (1911), Frederick Taylor advocated breaking workers' skills down into their constituent parts whenever possible and solidifying knowledge and power among management to prevent workers from "soldiering" or setting their own pace of work. In some industries, employers heeded Taylor's call to deskill work (Form 1987), thereby reducing workers' leverage in strikes. Workers and unions resisted. Simultaneously, unions attempted to accomplish labor market closure, limiting the supply of skilled workers by controlling access to apprenticeship programs (Motley 1907).

Importantly, several industries with skilled workers did *not* widely unionize—such as workers in the health services and education workers. Given their workplace power, why didn't they organize? In industries where workers had high replacement costs, we observe two major routes to worker representation. One route focused on maintaining workers' advantage (through apprenticeship programs and capitalizing on timing and/or geographically isolated workplaces) and utilizing work-based power to successfully strike for better wages and working conditions. These acts resulted in union formation and suggest that there is "power in the union." They also required that workers had a sense of union identity and solidarity. Alternatively, highly skilled workers whose work was associated with a "higher calling" and/or "service to the public" were more likely to affiliate with professional associations than unions. In some of these industries, gendered concepts of care and work mapped onto the possibilities of unionization.

In industries where workers had high replacement costs, it was only when those workers identified with unions and leveraged their power through disruption that they accomplished and sustained higher union density. Absent supportive state institutions and embedded in an unfriendly political climate, workers' main route to union formation during this period was by winning strikes. All industries in which workers realized high or moderate unionization levels also had substantial and successful strike activity during this period.

Race and gender composition of workers was important to understanding unionization. In this early period, unions were strongest in industries that disproportionately employed white male workers. Multiple factors contributed to this outcome, including hiring practices, exclusionary practices of some AFL unions, the legal and cultural barriers to collective action that women and workers of color faced, the male breadwinner mentality, and the preference for professional associations (that were in direct competition to unions) in "women's" occupations (i.e., teaching and health).

The State and Macro Context

U.S. Labor Legislation and the Courts' Interpretations

Although the U.S. economy underwent industrialization and urbanization beginning in the nineteenth century, the nation did not develop a "consistent and unified national labor policy" until the 1930s (Zieger 1969, 1). The labor policy that did exist generally favored employers. For the most part, unions were not illegal, but legislation did not protect them from employers' attacks. At the federal level, several acts were particularly important to controlling workplaces, workers' rights, and labor unions. During the start of our period, the Sherman Antitrust Act of 1890, which was intended to ban monopolistic business practices, was also applied to trade unions.

Throughout the first quarter of the century, the courts increasingly issued rulings that severely limited workers' allowable collective action in strikes and boycotts. Employers took advantage of friendly legal interpretations by routinely filing injunctions to quash strikes and injunctions became a "well established . . . weapon in the fight against unionization" (Taft 1976, 33). In the early 1900s, 3 percent of strikes encountered injunctions; by the 1920s, 25 percent of all strikes and 46 percent of sympathy strikes faced injunctions. Injunctions were especially prevalent in railroad, industrial, and organizing strikes (Forbath 1989, 1151–1152, 1252). And employers regularly used private guards as strike police, and worker arrests were common (Forbath 1989, 1188, 1190). Although the Clayton Act of 1914 excluded unions from the Sherman Antitrust Act, courts later voided many of its provisions. Not until the Norris-LaGuardia Act (1932) was the use of labor injunctions severely restricted (Smith 1951). A precursor to the Wagner Act, the Norris-LaGuardia Act delimited the use of injunctions against workers during peaceful labor disputes and outlawed the "yellow-dog" contract (where employers required workers to commit to not joining a union as a condition of employment).

Additional court cases and legal provisions also affected the balance of power during this period. A Supreme Court decision in 1908 led to the atrophy of unions' use of the boycott, and another ended the AFL's use of its "unfair" companies list (Bernstein 1972, 194; Dubofsky 1994, 46–47). At the very end of this period, the National Industrial Recovery Act (NIRA) of 1933, specifically Section 7(a), guaranteed collective bargaining rights to unions and authorized the president to regulate industry. Although this legislation set the stage for broad unionization, it lacked enforcement mechanisms. It was also missing business support, caused considerable consternation, and was declared unconstitutional in 1935.

While the union climate was hostile in all industries, public workers faced an additional set of limitations. A "gag rule" (repealed in 1912 by the Lloyd-La Follette Act) prohibited federal workers from lobbying the government. After the 1919 Boston police strike, Congress passed a law prohibiting the unionization of police and firefighters in the District of Columbia. Similar struggles followed in many municipalities (Spero 1972, 283–294). In response, the AFL encouraged public sector unions to include "no-strike" clauses in their collective bargaining agreements.

Even beyond wartime conditions, railways, airlines, and shipping fulfilled crucial industry transportation needs for much of this century, and therefore work stoppages in these domains received special attention. First, Congress enacted the Railroad Labor Board in 1920 to settle wage labor disputes. Then, the 1926 Railway Labor Act and its amendments gave railway and airline workers the right to organize and established mediation machinery to settle conflicts. With this act, railways, the major form of transportation during this period, became the first industry to receive greater government protection for union activities; it gave other private sector industries protections a decade later.

States also passed pointed anti-union legislation during this period. Between 1917 and 1920, twenty states (mainly in the West, including Alaska and Hawaii) passed criminal syndicalism laws that criminalized the advocacy of syndicalism (the support of radical political or economic change). These laws were used against the revolutionary IWW and, to a lesser extent, the left-wing Trade Union Unity League (TUUL); AFL unions didn't contest them (Bernstein 1972, 222).

Toward the end of the unregulated period, the Davis-Bacon Act (1931) required federal contractors to pay the prevailing wage to all workers on federal construction projects. This provided a boost to building trades unions, since it limited the ability of (non-union) contractors to undermine unions.

During this early period, few workplace-focused health and safety standards existed, and injured workers had little recourse for compensation. In 1910, New York was the first state to enact comprehensive worker compensation laws; in 1948, Mississippi was the last. Children continued to be active in the American workforce throughout the period (they constituted about 6 percent of the labor force in 1900). The National Child Labor Committee promoted state reforms, but enforcement was uneven and eventually it pushed for national legislation. Two national acts were passed and then declared unconstitutional by the Supreme Court. Laws prohibiting child labor were not permanently put into place until 1938 with the passage of the Fair Labor Standards Act (Boone 2015).

Employers Leverage State Power through Injunctions

Employers requested—and courts routinely issued—injunctions to restrain workers from engaging in strikes, pickets, and boycotts. Since the 1880s, "the injunction ha[d] been the most important legal instrument in employers' hands against the acts of organized labor" (Mason 1930, 466; see also Aaron 1962). Witte (1932, 84) counts 1,845 injunctions issued by federal and state courts against unions before May 1931, and the actual number of injunctions is likely to be five times higher (because most were issued by lower courts). While the Sherman Anti-Trust Act was initially intended to control business trusts and monopolies, employers extensively used injunctions to limit union activities beginning in 1893.

Unions were not able to reverse employers' use of injunctions or the courts' willingness to go along. But in rare cases, they filed injunctions against employers. Witte (1930) documents seventy-three cases in which unions did so (compared to around two thousand filed by employers). Given that the AFL opposed the use of injunctions, most were filed by unions that were not affiliates, and in the end, they were not very successful.

Political Context

During the unregulated period, the Republican Party occupied the White House for all but one presidency (Woodrow Wilson, 1913–1921) prior to Franklin D. Roosevelt's first administration, beginning in 1933. Due to labor's relative weakness, national leaders felt little pressure to address workers' concerns in earnest. The national political orientation toward labor during this early period was mixed, with some support for "anti-labor extremism" and the open shop campaign[1] that developed in the 1920s (Ziegler 1969, 12). Unions were mostly unsuccessful in winning favorable legislation, though there were a few important labor successes on the political front. One was the AFL's ability to incorporate its personnel and preferences into President Wilson's policymaking on labor concerns (McCartin 1997, 15–16); another was rescinding the gag rule on federal employees in 1912.

U.S. presidents more frequently deployed the National Guard on employers' behalf to end labor disputes during this period, compared to later in the century. During the 1920s and 1930s, for example, approximately 6,200 troops per year were called, and those numbers were higher during World War I due to the urgency of wartime production (Adams 1995). Likewise, governors more commonly dispatched state militias to end labor disputes during this period. As discussed above, elected judges also demonstrated their biases in favor of employers by commonly granting injunctions to them under the Sherman Antitrust Act, despite the fact that this was not the act's original intention.

Although there was considerable geographic variation, many local political actors also showed employer bias, especially during labor disputes. Labor radicalism was a major concern for many mayors and local police across the United States, in part due to the advertised and demonstrated militancy of the IWW and other groups. For example, police departments in Portland and Seattle "played major roles in planning, organizing, and carrying out efforts to suppress radicalism during this time" (Hoffman and Webb 1986, 341; see also Donner 1990; La Follette 1941). During this early period, violence during strikes was extreme. Between 1901 and 1939, there were 685 deaths, and the vast majority were strikers (Lipold and Isaac 2009).[2]

Among Western democracies, the U.S. labor movement is unique in that it has never formally affiliated with a national political party. In the early 1900s, labor concerns were not central to either major party, and unions usually sided with progressive Democrats or progressive Republicans, such as Robert

---

[1] "Open shop" refers to an establishment that does not recognize or deal with labor unions. The Open Shop Campaign of the 1920s attempted to weaken unions by spreading the prevalence of open shop establishments.

[2] For the period 1870 to 1947, strikers account for an estimated 64 percent of the deaths, strike breakers 12 percent, bystanders 10 percent, company agents 6 percent, state agents 6 percent, and company executives/government officials 2 percent (Lipold and Isaac 2009).

La Follette and Theodore Roosevelt. But a substantial minority of union members—mostly members of industrial affiliates of the AFL—clamored for political action via the Socialist Party. Former labor leader Eugene Debs, who was head of the party, won 6 percent of the national presidential vote in 1912. In that same year, over two thousand socialists held political office at various levels, often through support from various labor activists (Murolo and Chitty 2018).

So, after a fairly progressive political start, and considerable socialist influence during the nineteenth century, the policy of pure and simple unionism (providing worker benefits, strike funds, and often centralization of control over strikes) took hold among most AFL unions (Laslett 1984) and the AFL took a conservative political turn. It eschewed direct political involvement in favor of its "voluntarist" political policy of "rewarding friends and punishing enemies" at the ballot box.

The AFL's main rival, the IWW, also shunned traditional political participation, but did so from the left, in favor of anarcho-syndicalist (mass strike) activities. And the Trade Union Educational League (TUEL), which "bored-from-within" the AFL during the early-to-mid-1920s, then the TUUL, which briefly rivaled the AFL in the late 1920s and early 1930s, were organized through and supported by the Communist Party.

While overall, organized labor lacked significant national political influence during this early period, the AFL worked with the lone Democratic administration, President Wilson, to give substantial input into the development of the Department of Labor and the U.S. Commission on Industrial Relations (USCIR) (McCartin 1997, 15–16). During Wilson's presidency, wartime conditions (beginning in 1915 with foreign purchasing and ramping up with full wartime production with the U.S. entry into the war in 1917) led to extraordinary new demand. The conditions spurred the initiation of government labor boards in transportation, clothing, shipbuilding, and leather, as well as in other industries, thereby securing AFL union representatives a voice (Wolman 1924, 36). The IWW was entirely excluded from these bodies (and probably would not have participated even if invited); but more importantly, IWW opposition to World War I served as an impetus for more severe repression against its leaders who spoke out against the war, leading to the beginning of the end of the IWW as a viable labor organization.

The need for quick and peaceful settlement of disputes prompted the organization of the first tripartite National War Labor Board (WLB), with participation by government representatives, and employers' and workers' organizations (the AFL, but not the IWW). This first WLB "implied renunciation of strikes by the Federation [AFL]; it also implied acceptance of collective bargaining by the employers. Employers agreed not to discriminate against employees due to union membership; unions were not to coerce employers or employees in their organizing activities" (Ulman 1961, 391). The AFL's power was thereby briefly institutionalized (but only during wartime). The favorable conditions contributed to a steady and substantial increase in union membership through 1920—most dramatically, of course, in the industries most affected by the war: textiles, metal, transportation, clothing, leather, and building groups. Certain unions and their leaders, such as in the garment trades, gained leverage due to their indispensability. Relatedly, the return to peacetime conditions led to severe union declines in these same industries (Wolman 1924, 38).

Thus, the U.S. entry into World War I and the importance of maximizing production hastened thinking about the "labor problem." Production needs drove temporary solutions to labor disputes through the tripartite WLB and the president's Mediation Committee as well as actions favorable to labor regarding the railroads (Zieger 1969, 7).

This "acceptance" was not extended to the more radical unions. During World War I and into the postwar period, the federal government raided IWW offices that supported anti-war rhetoric. And in response to a series of bombings in 1919–1920 came the first "Red Scare" along with the Palmer Raids,[3] which targeted suspected anarchist and Communist activists among ethnic and immigrant communities with the aim to deport them. The government's repression was not reserved only for IWW radicals: it also used the wartime Lever Act to intervene in a 1919 coal strike (Zieger and Gall 2002, 41).

The Economy

The twentieth century began with a newly consolidated national economy, spurred on by developments in technology and managerial control. In response, unions called for a model of national organization beyond the local,

---

[3] Attorney General Mitchell Palmer led U.S. Department of Justice raids in 1919 and 1920 that sought to arrest and, where possible, deport various leftists.

with strikes and boycotts as its centerpiece. Successful strikes "impelled the federal government to intervene in labor-capital relations and to grope somewhat blindly toward a national labor policy" (Dubofsky 1994, 3–4). This growing unrest, national coordination, and the beginnings of a labor policy accompanied growing unions.

Scholars have varying views on how business cycles and major economic events such as depressions and wars affect union density (Bernstein 1954). In these pages, we consider two main indicators of the business cycle: employment and the consumer price index (CPI). Employment by industry is a component of our measure of union density and is presented in our analyses within each period. Because the CPI affects workers in all industries in similar ways, we treat it in the context section of each chapter.

According to Wolman (1924), many unions were still fledgling organizations at the turn of the century and sensitive to business cycles. He finds losses in union membership in this period to be associated with economic recessions and depressions. Both business decline and membership losses occurred in 1904–1906, 1908–1909, 1913–1915, and 1920–1923. Conversely, membership generally increased during times of business revival (Wolman 1924, 33). The effects of economic booms and busts were not experienced uniformly or synchronically across all industries; in mining and quarrying and textiles, fluctuations were typically more volatile. Unions experiencing the least variance with economic changes during this period include dominant and well-established unions in building, transportation, and printing as well as smaller unions in entertainment and public service (mainly postal workers) (Wolman 1924, 34–35).

Economists emphasize the roles of both unemployment and CPI in workers' proclivity to unionize. The prices workers faced for daily necessities directly affected how effectively their wages met their needs. The U.S. Bureau of Labor Statistics (BLS) measured and reported the cost of living beginning in 1913, with an early focus on food prices, and later diversified to include clothing, rent, fuel, and furnishings (Reed 2014). Inflation was sharp with the onset of World War I (19 percent increase in the CPI per year between July 1916 and November 1918), and with the postwar expansion (17 percent increase between November 1918 and June 1920), followed by a drop during the postwar period recession (almost a 10 percent annual drop between June 1920 and September 1922). Then, throughout most of the 1920s, prices remained fairly stable. The U.S. BLS reports a 3.5 percent annual increase in the CPI during the 1913–1929 period. With the onset of the Great

Depression, between December 1929 and June 1933, the CPI dropped 8 percent per year.

Employment numbers varied greatly by industry (see Figure 2.2). Agriculture, fisheries, and forestry employed nearly ten million workers, and we count these workers as part of the employment base when we calculate union density. Manufacturing had upwards of eight million workers, followed by trade. Construction, personal services, public administration and education, and TCU had closer to three million workers each; mining, FIRE, and health had even fewer workers. The smallest industry we analyze is entertainment, which averaged only a quarter million workers in this early time period. Toward the end of this period, the stock market crash of 1929 devastated many investors, caused drops in consumer spending and investment, and then reductions in industrial output and employment. The Great Depression had a drastic effect on workers through catastrophic increases in unemployment.

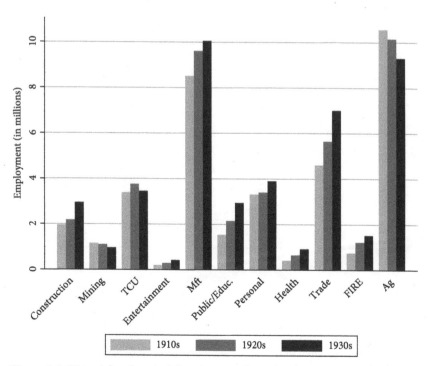

Figure 2.2 Unregulated period: Employment by industry, average by decade.

Replacement Costs

Replacement costs influenced unions' and employers' differing leverage during strikes. During the unregulated period, workers and unions had the upper hand when workers possessed scarce skills that were not easily replaceable during strikes, when the work required labor to be delivered on demand (quickly, where surprise strikes left employers with little option but to settle), and/or when geographic isolation made acquiring strike replacements difficult. Conversely, employers had the upper hand when workers had little training and therefore were easily replaced, when employers could stockpile goods and/or arrange for replacement workers without haste, and/or when they had easy geographical access to replacement workers (replacements who are looking for work in the proximity of the workplace).

Skill levels constituted an important component of replacement costs in this period. Industries differed by skill levels, which we show in Figure 2.3. "Skill" is a contested concept, because it reflects workers' power or lack of

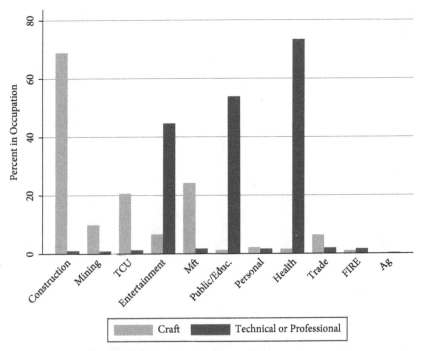

Figure 2.3 Unregulated period: Percent of the workforce characterized as craft or technical/professional occupations by industry, average for 1910–1930.

power, often in raced and gendered ways (Branch 2011; Steinberg 1990). We include both craft and technical and professional workers as high skill, as they held unique skills that required training and/or education, and could not easily be replaced with untrained workers. These workers, in theory, could have more readily formed unions, as they had disruptive potential; but as we will see, they didn't uniformly do so during this unregulated period.

Craft workers were mainly concentrated in construction, and to a lesser extent in manufacturing and TCU. By contrast, technical and professional workers were concentrated in entertainment, public administration/education, and health services. Public administration/education and health had large numbers of women workers, and for the most part, workers in these industries did not unionize during this period—though, unionization became prominent in these industries later in the century.

Industries that were highly unionized were dominated by white male workers, partly due to employers' and unions' exclusion of women and workers of color. As Figure 2.4 shows, white men (including European

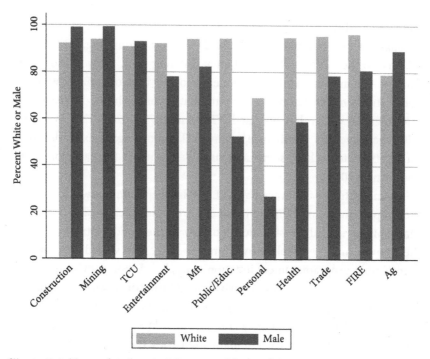

Figure 2.4 Unregulated period: Percent of the workforce characterized as white or male by industry, average for 1910–1930.

immigrants) made up the majority of the entire workforce. Women were clustered in entertainment and a few medium density industries, manufacturing (29 percent women) and public administration/education (47 percent), and low union density industries, personal services (72 percent), and health (46 percent). Workers of color, which included Black, Native American, Hispanic, and Asian and Pacific Islander, were also clustered in the low-wage, low union industries of personal services (32 percent) and agriculture (21 percent). Large numbers of foreign-born workers were present throughout all industries, including 25 percent or more in mining, manufacturing, and construction (not presented in Figure 2.4).

Skill Closure and Apprenticeship Programs

Through the 1930s, the AFL was mainly, though not wholly, a craft-based organization. Even early on (1897–1904), there were movements to include semi- and unskilled workers in AFL unions. Several long-standing AFL unions (e.g., what's now the Laborers International Union, HERE, and the United Mine Workers) consisted of workers with a mix of skill levels throughout our analysis (Cobble 2013). Since its founding, AFL unions adapted to their environments, albeit at different rates. Early on, some important AFL unions "exhibited a tendency to alter both organizing strategies and institutional structures to accommodate changes in the industrial environment in which they operated" (Tomlins 1979, 1024, 1026). When the CIO challenged its dominance, many AFL unions again expanded their jurisdictions to include semi- and unskilled workers (Stepan-Norris and Southworth 2010).

The main strategy embraced by AFL-affiliated craft unions was to increase their replacement costs through skill closure and apprenticeship programs. Many highly skilled construction workers in the building trades secured their power in the workplace by controlling access to skilled training (apprenticeship programs) in conjunction with closed shop provisions in collective bargaining agreements, which allowed hiring of only union members. In apprenticeship programs, socialization into union principles and the development of union solidarity could occur. Skilled workers built sizable power within the workplace. "In many industries, they collectively retained control of the shop floor, often hired their own assistants, and, . . . substantially influenced the recruitment of new skilled workers through their control of the apprenticeship system" (Bowles and Gintis 1976, 193). Many of these unions also regulated the number of new apprentices accepted and the ratio of apprentices to journeymen (Kimeldorf 2013; U.S. BLS 1926). Apprenticeship programs also helped union members transition to new technologies. In the printing industry, employers introduced new technology in the hope of reducing their need for higher-paid skilled workers, but the union was able to limit the effectiveness of this tactic, and even use it to their own advantage (see example earlier in this chapter).

Limiting some craft unions' ability to control the supply of skilled labor and adding to the generally weak apprenticeship programs in the United States was the fact that a substantial proportion of skilled U.S. workers were immigrants trained in their home countries, and hence, they skipped the local training altogether (Thelen 2004, 177–214). In addition, guild traditions were weak and rates of geographic and occupational mobility were high in the United States, preventing employers from investing heavily in training. Deskilling led to the collapse of apprenticeship programs in garment, boot and shoe, and textiles even before 1900. Still, about two-thirds of AFL unions had more or less successful apprenticeship programs by the turn of the twentieth century (authors' calculations based on Motley 1907).

Apprenticeship programs did not benefit all workers. Indeed, this form of closure ensured that the "labor aristocracy" continued to enjoy its advantages vis-à-vis both employers and semi- and unskilled workers (Parkin 1983; see Bonacich 1972 for a discussion of how this form of closure, or what she calls "split labor markets," also aligned with race/ethnicity). Using this strategy, unions developed trade- or industry-specific—but not working-class— union solidarity: "Each trade sought only its own material advantage and lost no time worrying about the others" (Bernstein 1972, 83).

Exclusionary practices based on race and gender were part of most apprenticeship programs. "As between the employer and the union, it is the former who takes the initiative and induces boys to enter the trade" (Motley 1907, 75). But unions also had important roles in selecting entrants to the trades, and some of the early union constitutions gave journeymen the right to teach the trade to "his son" or relative. When such practices were followed, racial and gender homophily resulted. Most apprenticeships were limited to boys between certain ages (normally teenage years through twenty-five) and training lasted from two to seven years (Motley 1907, 75, 80–89). In addition, many apprenticeship programs had informal mechanisms of exclusion, such as requiring a vote of existing members to include new members or requiring members to be of "sober" or "moral" character. Formal exclusions existed, too (U.S. BLS 1926).

Due to unions' (variable) influence on determining the number of apprentices, employers and employer associations became disillusioned with apprenticeship programs and unions' influence over them. Employers fought against workers' control over apprenticeship programs and skills training by spearheading "a largely successful attempt to destroy their unions," with the power of skilled workers "decisively broken in a number of major lockouts and unsuccessful strikes" (Bowles and Gintis 1976, 193–194). With the support of National Association of Manufacturers (NAM), the national trade school movement took off. Trade schools eliminated the need for employers' investments in apprenticeship training: "[S]quarely plac[ing] the expense of and responsibility for training upon the learner; they screened out those with little motivation; they achieved economies of scale; and perhaps most importantly, they removed control over the supply of labor from unions, thus helping to subdue the closed union shop movement" (Jacoby 1991, 893).

In the aftermath of World War I, school-based vocational training came into favor with employers (again with strong NAM support [Bowles and Gintis 1976]), gained some union support (in their weakened position), and was federally funded through the Smith-Hughes Act.[4] Employers favored vocational training because they didn't have to pay for it or guarantee outcomes for workers, and because unions were not directly in control. In addition, business leaders had sought for the teaching of job skills and "work values" to be under the control of management, which they felt could be achieved in school-based vocational training (Pincus 1980, 335). Unions clung to partial control through their membership on advisory committees and their ability to maintain training standards (Jacoby 1991, 904–906). By the 1930s, unions began to rethink their support for vocational training, observing that such programs tended to arise in industries where apprenticeship programs were active and not where they were absent. Moreover, the curriculum downplayed the roles of labor unions and labor legislation (Pincus 1980, 336).

We calculate which industries had substantial apprenticeship programs using two sources, Motley (1907) and the U.S. BLS (1926). We find that apprenticeship programs were most common in construction unions. Manufacturing unions had fewer apprenticeship programs than construction

---

[4] The Smith-Hughes Act (National Vocational Education Act) of 1917 provided states with aid to promote vocational education.

unions, but more than other industries, reflecting a transition period from higher to lower levels of craft work in manufacturing (see Motley 1907).

Employers Reduce Workers' Replacement Costs through Deskilling

In the early years of the century, employers arrived at a plan to consolidate their power in the workplace. Couched in the language of "efficiency," they adopted Frederick Taylor's scientific management methods, aiming to assert their control over the workplace (Braverman 1974). This managerial strategy "won acceptance just as World War I overturned the American labor market" (Bernstein 1972, 174–75). Employers spent many of the remaining years of the twentieth century mechanizing work processes, introducing technological developments, and automating (Braverman 1974); however, as some jobs were deskilled, some new jobs often required higher-level skills (Form 1987).

Craft unions in particular were confronted with new technology and work processes that made some of their members' skills obsolete. The construction industry, with the largest proportions of craft workers, experienced a drastic decline in its employment of craft workers, from 68.5 percent in 1910, to 58 percent in 1930, and 39.5 percent by the end of our study period in 2015. Likewise, while printers successfully used their skilled-based power to build successful unions, employers periodically introduced new technology that made some printers' skills obsolete and reduced the need for high-skilled workers. Introduction of the linotype machine and, several decades later, the teletype machine, changed the balance of employer/worker power and compelled negotiations.

Professional and Technical Workers and (Non) Union Identity

In the early 1900s, non-craft specialized workers began to appear in greater numbers, mainly in white-collar occupations and professions (Attwell 1987, 331). Professional associations (which we do not count among unionized workers) aspired to advocate for these workers, but not via class-based tactics. Instead, they appealed to the professional character of workers and were often in direct competition with unions. Professions require specialized training in a systematic theory, autonomy from employers, authority recognized by clientele and society at large, ethical codes emphasizing commitment to the public good, and a professional culture (Klegon 1978, 262).[5] They accomplish occupational closure by convincing the state and the public that due to their controlled training, they are the most (or only) capable practitioners of their work. This logic is orthogonal at best to union identification, which emphasizes increasing workers' position vis-à-vis the class divide. Employers, unsurprisingly, preferred dealing with professional associations.

In education and nursing, major battles between the two potential identities played out on a national scale. The teachers' case is illustrative. In this period, the National Educational Association (NEA) was a professional association focused on professionalizing education; it was dominated by a "small, male elite" of school administrators and college presidents (Murphy 1990, 51–53). Some dissatisfied teachers broke away from the NEA in 1916 to form a union that would focus on improving wages and gender equity, the American Federation of Teachers (AFT). The NEA vied with the new union over teachers' loyalties, launching the "100 Percent" campaign, which aimed at recruiting "these 'girls' to sign up with the NEA so that they could become more professional, unlike the increasingly feminist and socialist teachers of the AFT" (Murphy 1990, 91, 99). Superintendents enrolled entire staffs into the NEA, which cunningly framed membership in unions as "unprofessional." Meanwhile, the AFL's support for teacher unionization was timid at best. The AFL cut off the AFT's subsidy in 1921 and insisted that all public employee unions, including the AFT, adopt "no-strike" clauses in their constitution.

Similarly, health workers, particularly nurses, had strong professional associations in the early 1900s. The public service of care, and the deep-seated gender expectations for caregivers, pushed early health workers toward professional associations, such as the American Nurses Association (ANA) (Apesoa-Varano and Varano 2004). Police also had strong professional associations, though some unionized in the late 1910s. After the dramatic defeat of the 1919 Boston police strike, many police officers returned to their professional associations. By contrast, postal workers did

---

[5] Weeden (2002) outlines five institutionalized closure devices: licensing, educational credentialing, voluntary certification, association representation, and unionization.

not have professional associations but formed relatively strong unions in the early 1900s, with up to 70 percent union density by 1930 (Wolman 1936, 121).

Timing as a Source of Workers' Power

While skill was a major indicator of disruptive potential, even industries with fewer skilled workers had structural advantages if their industry was time-sensitive. Transportation, for example, had significantly fewer skilled workers than construction, but many transportation workers had timing on their side (Kimeldorf 2013). Their ability to create considerable disruption through strikes (or threats of strikes) was high, especially among railroad workers due to a combination of timeliness and workers' influence over the possibility and handling of sabotage of engines and tracks. Both railroad and maritime workers' power was enhanced because cargo shipments were necessary for a functioning economy, causing considerable pressure to settle disputes quickly. In the unregulated period, the state recognized the disruptive power of transportation unions: the Supreme Court held it evident "that Congress deems it of the highest public interest to prevent the interruption of interstate commerce by labor disputes and strikes" (quoted in Tomlins 1985, 121). The Railway Labor Act (1926), which sought to remedy the explosive situation in transportation, provided a model for the subsequent National Labor Relations Act. Other industries where workers enjoyed timing advantages included entertainment, public administration/education, health, and agriculture.

The music industry affords further insight into the importance of timing, as workers' skills there did not reduce over time, but the demand for their live performances varied greatly. Early on, musicians' power vis-à-vis employers was based on their scarce skills that were in demand at scheduled performance times. Musicians tended to work short-term "gigs" for multiple and distinct types of employers (e.g., bars, theaters, recording studios, orchestra halls). During the early period when musicians were the "sole source of music," they, like workers in the building trades, used the scarcity of their skills vis-à-vis numerous small and unorganized employers to successfully organize durable unions (notably, with racially segregated locals) to ensure their power in the workplace. Alongside their power to cause significant losses upon the withdrawal of their labor, musicians displayed strong solidarity that served them well and even extended to other entertainment workers via sympathy strikes.

But technological innovations changed the degree to which those skills were immediately necessary. While innovations in production reduced the skills necessary to perform certain jobs, in the music industry, they didn't do this. Rather, they changed the demand for live performances. Just before the beginning of our early period, one innovation drastically increased demand for musicians, which would last for thirty years: silent movies. During this time, theater owners introduced live orchestration to enhance the experience of silent movies, and audiences came to expect it. Yet the invention of the Vitaphone, then the Photophone in the late 1920s, which synchronized video and audio, replaced over twenty thousand musicians who worked in movie theaters with a few hundred jobs in Hollywood. Simultaneously, thousands of musicians were newly employed in live radio, which had come onboard during the early 1920s. But by the 1930s, changing corporate strategies, regulations, and inventions (the jukebox) moved the industry away (except for symphony musicians) from live and toward recorded music. These moves undermined musicians' power through timing (and skill) that had proved so effective in their early unions. Later, musicians fought back through recording bans and the like (Richardson 2009, 675–684).

Workplace Location as a Source of Workers' Power

During the unregulated period geographical location amplified replacement costs in the mining and agricultural/forestry industries. Of the workers in the mining industry, only 11 percent were skilled (craft, technical, or professional), but they were able to capitalize on their high replacement costs due to isolated workplaces. Although varying by state and type of coal mined, many miners, especially in bituminous operations, had to relocate with their families to sites where operators provided living quarters and community resources (Obenauer 1924, 12–13). When strikes occurred, employers had to import, house, and protect replacement workers. Isolation, cross-class alliances with local community leaders, and miners' occupation of the majority of dwellings in the location increased employers' replacement costs and the leverage of striking miners (see Kimeldorf 2013, 1042, 1048). Agriculture and especially forestry work also took place in isolated worksites. But unlike in mining, the AFL demonstrated little interest in organizing there, although the IWW had some success.

Especially important in our later periods, but relevant to some extent in this period, is employers' ability to move manufacturing production away from unionized and higher-wage to nonunion and lower-wage geographical locations. Even before the turn of the century, textile employers pursued a "combined strategy of spatial and technological fixes in an effort to resolve their labor-control problems" (Silver 2003, 87). The technological fix involved displacing certain militant skilled workers with machines; the spatial fix involved an aggressive mill-building program in the South to replace production in the unionized North.

Union and Employer Strategies: Making and Breaking Unions

AFL Unions Organize Workers Mainly Based on Craft Skills

The major union organizing strategy during this period—and that of the AFL—was based on craft skills. Early on, the AFL, founded in 1886, had a progressive agenda of broad social reform aimed at challenging dominant organizations and values. Wealth inequality and a distorted distribution of power in the workplace were among its main concerns. Building unions and pursuing legislation were the main strategies it used to accomplish these aims (Cobble 2013; Forbath 1989). The AFL turned in a more narrow and conservative direction in order to counter aggressive court use of injunctions against strikes and boycotts: "many in the AFL's rank and file and leadership had concluded that what worked was not radical reforms or inclusive unions but minimalist politics, craft unionism, and restrained but staunch strike policies" (Forbath 1989, 1149). The AFL's anti-injunction efforts were in fact successful; they helped pass the Clayton Act in 1914 and the Norris-La Guardia (anti-injunction) Act in 1932 (Forbath 1989, 1203, 1228).

Thus, during the unregulated period the AFL prioritized craft jurisdictions (keeping skills exclusive [tightening the labor market] and segregated by craft) and member union autonomy. It relied upon the strike, strike funds, and members' high replacement costs to force employers to address and rectify their concerns. It shunned reliance on either of the major unfriendly political parties or third parties to improve its members' conditions. It had little to do with the Republicans, who were mostly anti-union and the anti-union southern group that had a hold on the Democratic Party, but it did manage to work with some from both parties, including northern Democratic political machines and some progressive Republicans. It distrusted left-wing political parties and managed to stay clear of them, though it came close to adopting a Socialist plank in 1894.

The AFL's economic logic was to organize all workers who performed a specific set of skills (i.e., a "craft") into a union, control entry into the craft/union (Motley 1907), equip members with benefits and strike funds (based on high dues), and coordinate their strikes so as to win higher wages and better working conditions (Laslett 1984). But most crafts had ill-defined borders, and union jurisdictions became blurred as the production process evolved, leading to some compound craft unions (e.g., Amalgamated Iron, Steel, and Tin Workers). However, most craft unions ignored and some were even hostile to semi- and unskilled workers (including immigrants, women, and underrepresented racial minorities) because they lacked bargaining power vis-à-vis employers. For the AFL, then, solidarity was generated among skilled workers for the most part.

During the unregulated period, few union strategies were efficacious, but the one adopted by the AFL was fairly well suited to the context and this contributed to its success vis-à-vis other unions and employers. Yet over time, employers deskilled jobs, undermining craft power in some areas and employment grew in the mass production industries, putting a growing proportion of the workforce outside the AFL's purview. Still, the AFL clung to its predominantly craft strategy[6] until it began competing directly with the CIO (Stepan-Norris and Southworth 2010).

Later, the CIO made the industrial organizing logic a mainstay, targeting all workers in a workplace as potential union members. This logic expanded solidarity to include workers with a range of skills as well as women and workers of color. Earlier on and going forward, the industrial organizing logic was favored by socialists, Communists, and other radicals (Ulman 1961, 382–384) and gained some momentum through the formation of the IWW, founded in 1905. The IWW used a combination of industrial organizing logic and mass strikes to win concessions and organize unskilled workers into "one big union." But it suffered from internal divisions early in its history, split in 1908, and its dominant branch experienced its peak strength in 1917, with concentrations in lumber, metal mining, agriculture, maritime transportation, and some activity in bituminous coal (Bernstein 1972, 141–142).

---

[6] While most AFL organizing during this period was based on the craft logic, a few AFL unions organized less-skilled workers during the early 1900s, including AFL unions in coal and metal mining, maritime trades, and garment trades.

While the IWW advocated for solidarity among all workers (and criticized the ALF's pure and simple unionism), AFL leaders viewed the IWW as impractical and too radical. Employers and state officials agreed, and the IWW faced repression from all sides, especially during the Palmer Raids. Although it made a splash in the early 1900s, its membership dwindled to minimal numbers by the 1920s.

Communist participation in union organizing began with the formation of the TUEL in 1920, which chose to "bore from within" the existing AFL unions rather than form more radical "dual union" alternatives. Communist activists joined and worked within AFL unions in order to win workers over to their left-wing alternative to conservative AFL policies. Using this strategy, Communists "established themselves" in several unions (machinists, carpenters, miners, textile, clothing, fur, boot and shoe, Pullman porters, and seamen) (Bernstein 1972, 136–140). However, some AFL unions explicitly excluded Communists from leadership, and a few even excluded them from membership altogether. In these unions, Communist success was easily thwarted. In 1929, the TUEL disbanded and was replaced by the TUUL, which aimed to organize workers into industrial unions. While Bernstein (1972, 141) claims that TUUL "membership was either insignificant or evanescent; most of [the TUUL unions] proved to be little more than paper formations," Stepan-Norris and Zeitlin (1996) found TUUL organizing efforts to be consequential for whether Communists won leadership positions in the Congress of Industrial Organizations (CIO) unions that later organized in the same industries. While a few AFL unions adopted the industrial organizing logic, the AFL considered the IWW and TUUL (both of which used the industrial organizing logic), as well as the CIO, to be rival organizations, a designation that engendered anti-Communist sentiment in the AFL.

Unions' Use of Strikes, Boycotts, and the Union Label

Strikes were an unrivaled strategy for building union power during this period, and we return to discuss strikes in depth later in the chapter. However, boycotts and the union label were also important union strategies. Unions pursued boycotts as a "second weapon, but a less powerful one than the strike" (Millis and Montgomery 1945, 581). Often coordinated with strikes, boycotts were "highly effective in promoting union recognition" (Dubofsky and Dulles 2004, 184). But like strikes, boycotts became vulnerable to employer injunctions.

Union labels constituted a third tactic: labels identifying the union involved in producing the product were affixed to products, storefronts, and personal buttons to signify that an employer was in compliance with union terms. By 1909, over half of AFL unions used the union label, and the AFL founded a Union Label Trades Department. Although unions attempted to create a demand for union label products and services, they settled for boosting demand among fellow unionists (Spedden 1910). Later, union labels became symbols of quality and fair play, but their efficacy has remained uncertain.

Employers Organize to Break Unions

Employers formed employers' associations to coordinate their efforts. Starting in the late 1800s, they developed "negotiatory associations" (common in the building trades) to control prices. Beginning around 1901 and through World War I, employers' associations became belligerent, by combatting strikes, fostering trade schools, influencing the courts and political activities, and generally opposing union interests (Bonnett 1922, 25–26). Opportunities for great profit and increasing demand for labor during World War I tempered employer associations' union opposition during the war, but hostility (the stick) returned in full force in the postwar period (Bonnett 1922) along with the carrot: the development of new personnel policies (e.g., stock ownership programs, workers protections; Slichter 1929), welfare capitalism, and company unions. Employers in the new industries of automobiles, utilities, chemicals, and rubber were particularly anti-union, and several older industries (coal, textiles, hosiery) moved their operations to the unorganized and anti-union South (among the first examples of capital flight). In early 1921, at the instigation of the NAM, a large network of open shop organizations met to coordinate and then deploy the "American Plan"[7] to (very effectively) thwart unionism during the 1920s (Bernstein 1972, 156).

Employers used multiple tactics to disorganize unions. Combined, these dis-organizing tactics limited workers' ability to effectively disrupt

[7] The American Plan was a series of employer-organized strategies during the 1920s to label unions as un-American and to pursue the open shop.

production and to form unions. Through employers' associations, they co-ordinated blacklists, whereby they sought to encourage other employers to boycott hiring of union members and especially union leaders (or "agitators")—an effective tactic, as it was performed covertly and therefore beyond the gaze of public opinion (Millis and Montgomery 1945). Employers also organized the American Anti-Boycott Association, which aided in filing injunctions against union boycotts (Dubofsky and Dulles 2004). "Yellow-dog" contracts, whereby employers required workers to sign pledges to not join a union as a condition of employment, kept strong union supporters out of certain workplaces.

Employers also used industrial espionage against workers, which the La Follette Committee[8] found to be "a common, almost universal, practice in American industry" (quoted in Auerbach 1964, 2), private armies and po-lice (the latter mainly in isolated areas), industrial munitioning (tear and sickening gas, guns, and even machine guns), and, of course, strike breaking (Bernstein 1972, 88–89, 148–57). Existing and employer-initiated ethnic antagonisms among workers within labor markets kept workers from jointly opposing employers and ultimately harmed workers of color as well as overall working-class solidarity (Bonacich 1972). During strikes, it was not uncommon for employers to utilize and stoke ethnic and racial divisions by hiring strike breakers of different ethnicities/races than current workers (cf. Stepan-Norris and Zeitlin 1996).

To be sure, employers made extensive use of violence during strikes. Certain industries had especially violent employers. Over half (345) of the 685 strike deaths during this period occurred in extractive industries (mining and agriculture), followed by manufacturing (177), transportation (157), construction (5), and retail/other services (1) (Lipold and Isaac 2009).

After he was heavily criticized for his leading role in the 1914 Ludlow Massacre as well as other bloody industrial battles, John D. Rockefeller, Jr. initiated discussions among employers to develop welfare capitalism, which became the basis for the design of many company unions (with a peak of 1,547,766 members in 1928), the deployment of industrial rela-tions counselors, and the launch of industrial relations institutes within universities (Bernstein 1972, 157–169; 171). Other projects among this softer approach included workers' group life insurance plans, pension plans,

---

[8] The La Follette Committee (Committee on Education and Labor, Subcommittee Investigating Violations of Free Speech and the Rights of Labor), active from 1936 to 1941, sought to uncover the methods used by firms to avoid collective bargaining with unions.

housing assistance, stock ownership plans, and paternalistic programs like Ford's "Sociology Department," where company inspectors visited workers' homes to ensure that they lived in accordance with Ford's vision of American values (Stepan-Norris and Zeitlin 1996). Also on the softer side was the National Civic Federation (NCF) (1900–1950), which was the newly emerging corporate community's first national-level policy group. It convened industry leaders, the labor aristocracy (including AFL president Samuel Gompers, who participated until his death in 1924), and the public with the intention of easing labor/capital conflict. The NCF, opposed by both NAM from the right and the IWW from the left, lobbied, mediated disputes, and advocated for the acceptance of collective bargaining over wages, the number of apprentices, and other bread-and-butter issues, safer workplaces, workers' compensation, and the elimination of child labor.

The distribution of employers' associations across our industrial categories is difficult to ascertain. Systematic industry-wide information on the strength and character of employer organizations is not available. So we rely here on Clarence Bonnett's (1922) in-depth study of employers' associations (which lists all employers' associations in an appendix) to summarize their most noteworthy characteristics during this time period. We group by industry and identify thirty-one national and forty local employers' associations in construction; twenty-eight national and thirteen local associations in transportation; forty-one national and fifteen local associations in manufacturing; three national and seven local association in trade; and one national association in personal services. He also lists twenty-one national and sixty-one local associations that cannot be categorized by industry (due to membership across our industry categories; we list the NAM in this miscellaneous category). He also does not list any associations for mining, entertainment, public administration/education, health, agriculture, or FIRE—though his omission of these associations does not necessarily mean that there were none. And it is important to keep in mind that the publication date of the study precludes mention of new associations that may have formed between 1923 and 1934.

Construction stands out as the only industry in which employers' associations were more likely to organize at the local, as opposed to the national, level. In terms of coverage, we get a glimpse from Bonnett's observations of one large city. He mentions that in Chicago, the Building Construction Employers' Association covered less than 66 percent of builders. In terms of stance toward unions, he notes that some construction employers' associations were belligerent toward unions and others were negotiatory. So, overall, employers' associations in construction appear to have had a significant presence but were of mixed orientation.

In publishing (which is only a small part of our TCU category), employer associations covered a significant proportion of all employers: a very high percent of newspaper publishers were members of the American Newspaper Publishers Association, the United Typothetae had approximately five thousand members, and employers' associations also covered lithography, electrotype, and photo-engraving occupations. In terms of their orientation to labor unions, they, like construction employers' associations, were split between hostile and negotiatory stances.

Employers' associations in manufacturing stood out for being notoriously belligerent, organized, and capable of affecting a large and important sector of the economy. At the beginning of our period, the NAM took the lead in organizing the many employers' associations into a coherent anti-union and open shop drive (Griffin, Wallace, and Rubin 1986). The NAM represented a significant proportion of all employers (which employed more than six million workers; unfortunately, we do not have information on which of Bonnett's employers' associations belonged to NAM) and constituted a prominent and unified opponent of unionism. Employers' associations in manufacturing were infamous and effective, organizing a sophisticated propaganda and lobbying machine, and encouraging corporate leaders to participate in political and legislative efforts. "From 1902 to 1912, it successfully opposed the enactment of a federal eight-hour law applying to work done under government contract," and while it could not endure holding off "the passage of the law in 1912, it secured amendments to the law that limited somewhat the applications of the law" (Bonnet 1922, 308).

Strikes

In order to counter the often aggressive employer opposition to unions, workers had to be willing to strike and able to win. Without favorable laws or the right to elections, strikes constituted the major mechanism that workers used to form and defend unions.

Three data sources inform our calculations of the extent to which workers were involved in strikes. Coordinated by Florence Peterson (1937), the U.S. BLS reports strikes between 1880 and 1936 but does not systematically report all industry-level information for workers involved in stoppages until 1927.[9] Before 1922, the yearly numbers of workers involved in work stoppages by industry were only systematically reported by AFL unions (recorded in AFL yearly proceedings, 1900–1921). We have some information, but not consistent estimates for strikes outside of the AFL, including the IWW, TUUL, and independent unions. The IWW History Project collected information from the IWW newspaper, *Industrial Worker*, on four hundred IWW strikes between 1905 and 1920, including strike date, location, description, and source of information, but only sporadic information on the number of workers involved, the industry, the reason for the strike, or the outcome. We have two years (1933–1934) of information on the 169 TUUL-reported strikes (Devinatz 2005). These years overlap with the BLS data and are included in our strike analysis; we do not analyze them separately.[10]

How representative were AFL strikes of the total population of strikes? Using Peterson's (1937, 56) estimates, we calculate that for the early periods (1900–1905 and 1916–1921) almost 70 percent of strikes were associated with a labor organization. Between 1924 and 1932, 83 percent were associated with union organizations, of which 64 percent were led by AFL affiliates. So strikes associated with the AFL likely made up over half of all strikes during the period.

There were several strikes waves during the unregulated period. Most notably, there was an increase in the early 1900s, in the later teens, and again starting in 1933. The BLS did not report strike data from 1906 to 1915, but the AFL did report for its affiliates. The peak strike activity was in 1920, which culminated in over 4 million strikers or one out of every ten workers in the workforce, including 350,000 steel workers, 400,000 miners, Broadway workers, Boston police officers, and a general strike in Seattle (see Figure 2.5). But this period also marks the beginning of a series of losses, impacted by the first red scare and the stripping of wartime labor protections.

---

[9] Peterson includes the number of strikes, number of workers involved, causes, and results by year through 1905. She also provides industry breakdowns, but only for the aggregate period 1881–1905. For 1914–1926, she provides the number of strikes by industry by year. For 1927–1936, she reports the number of strikes, number of workers involved, and man-days idle by major issues for each industry by year, but no breakdowns on strike outcomes by industry.

[10] The basic pattern is that the TUUL's affiliated unions won 45 percent, lost 5 percent, and reported no outcome for 49 percent. For the thirty-nine strikes with information on the cause of the strike, the vast majority (89 percent) concerned wages and 28 percent included union recognition as a goal. Of the twenty-four victorious strikes with information on specific outcomes, Devinatz reports that 87.5 percent of TUUL strikes won increased wages and 29 percent won union recognition.

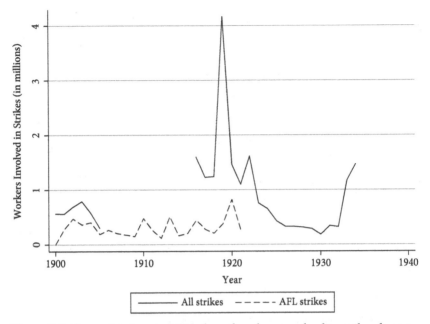

Figure 2.5 Unregulated period: Number of workers involved in strikes, by year.
Note: "All strikes" are data from the Bureau of Labor Statistics. AFL strikes are data from AFL reports. The AFL numbers of workers involved in strikes are sums of the industry totals. Aggregate AFL reports are slightly different than overall numbers.

How do losses impact the number of strikes? We argue that workers (and leaders) are more likely to strike when the conditions are favorable and they see other workers successfully winning strikes. Major strike losses often have chilling effects on workers' willingness to strike. One way to evaluate this argument is to assess whether high numbers of strikes are associated with higher win rates. U.S. BLS data on win rates, 1916–1936, supports this argument. A strike was reported as successful when "the employees succeeded in enforcing full compliance with all of their demands; partly successful, when they succeeded in enforcing compliance with a part of their demands, or partial compliance with some or all of their demands" (Peterson 1937, 33). Figure 2.6 shows the relationship between union wins (full or partial wins) and the number of strikes reported as ended.

Win rates and the number of strikes were high in the late teens, with upward of 60 percent of all strikes won and over 2,000 strikes ending each year. This record changed quickly, with a string of large, high-profile strike defeats, including the Boston police strike which ended with the police being fired and replaced with new recruits, the Great Steel strike with 365,000 workers

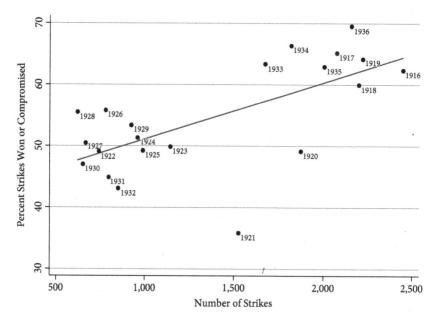

Figure 2.6 Bivariate relationship between number of strikes ended and strike outcome, 1916–1936.

involved, and the violent Blair Mountain miners' strike, where local police, deputized vigilantes, and the National Guard killed sixteen workers. The 1920s was a challenging decade for workers and the labor movement. The strike win rate plummeted in 1920, reaching a low of 36 percent in 1921. Not surprisingly, the remaining years of the 1920s had far fewer strikes, with a low of 620 strikes ending in 1928. Armed with new industrial organizing tactics, strike numbers surged again by 1933, and the win rate rebounded to over 63 percent.

Some industries were more strike prone than others.[11] Construction, TCU, mining, and manufacturing had at least a few hundred work stoppages a year. Manufacturing saw a large spike in the teens, when employment was high.

The number of strikes, however, is not standardized by employment size. Strike rates, the number of workers involved divided by employment, provide standardization. Figure 2.7 presents strike rates for each industry in the three

[11] The BLS data reports on aggregate strikes from 1900–1905 and 1916–1921, including all stoppages (AFL, independent, and IWW). The BLS began reporting detailed industry level strike data in 1927, which also includes all strikes (AFL, independent, and TUUL). The AFL provides yearly strike data beginning in 1900 for AFL affiliated unions. We do not have systematic industry level strike data for IWW or independent unions for the early 1900s.

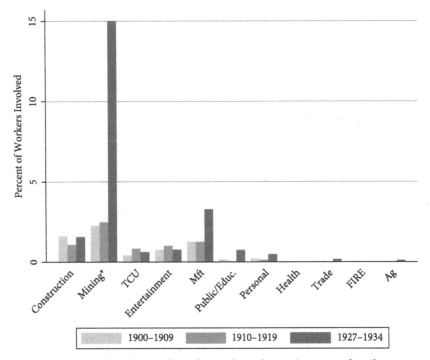

Figure 2.7 Unregulated period: Strike rate by industry (percent of workers involved in strikes), average by subperiods.

Note: Rates are underestimated before 1919 because we do not have industry-specific data on IWW and independent union strikes for those years. Industry-level data from 1900 to 1919 include only AFL affiliated unions. Non-AFL manufacturing, forestry, and mining workers, especially, had strikes during those years, so rates are likely higher than these data suggest. In addition, because industry employment was not collected by the census until 1910, we use 1910 as an employment base for 1900–1909. This likely underestimates strike rates during 1900–1909. The 1927–1934 period includes all strikes and uses the 1930 census for employment estimates. We cap the y axis at 15 percent of workers on strike so that the variation is observable. The mining strike rate is higher than 15 percent during 1927–1934.

subperiods, with strike data from AFL unions (1900–1910 and 1911–1921) and BLS data on all strikes (1927–1934). Mining had very elevated strike rates, with upward of 3 percent involved in strikes annually. Manufacturing and construction also had relatively high levels of strikes, with over 1 percent of workers involved in each period. Several other industries had more moderate levels of between .5 percent and 1 percent of workers on strike or higher, including entertainment, transportation, and public administration/education (the personal service industry is just below the .5 percent threshold).

Within the context of the unregulated period, workers had to routinely strike in order to make gains. But union presence also enabled strikes—strike funds, support from a national organization, and union leaders' experiences all helped workers execute strikes. Examining this period, Edwards (1981) cautions not to reduce strikes to a function of union density, as it is unclear what the driving factors are. Regardless, striking was a key feature of union life, and consistent strikes were fundamental to forming and defending unions in this period with few institutional supports for unionization.

Winning strikes also mattered for unionization. Successful strikes led to more opportunities to organize workers into unions (union recognition was often the main union demand) (Peterson 1937). In general, to achieve high union density during this period, workers not only had to strike, they also had to win often—at least 60 percent of the time. Figure 2.8 shows the percent of strikes that AFL workers won by industry from 1900 to 1921 as reported by the AFL (the BLS did not collect strike outcomes by industry). Of the high strike industries, most had over 60 percent win rates. Manufacturing had slightly lower win rates, reflecting its mismatch with craft organizing approaches.

Mining stands out with its extremely high percentage of workers that engaged in strikes during this period along with relatively high win rates (about

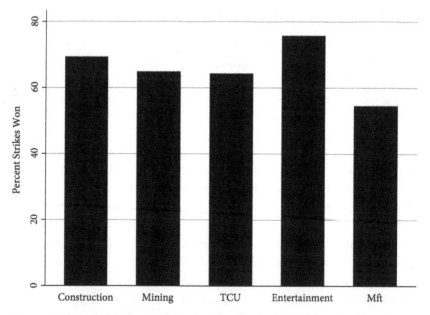

Figure 2.8 Unregulated period: Strike win rates for AFL affiliated unions in high-strike industries, average for 1900–1921.

65 percent). As discussed earlier, mining work was geographically isolated, which made miners difficult to replace during strikes (i.e., a structural advantage). In addition, miners' union leadership decided to pursue an industrial organizing strategy that was beneficial to their organizing efforts. All mine workers were eligible to be union members, not only craft workers. This decision generated solidarity among workers and empowered miners to stop production fully when striking. During the beginning of this period, the United Mine Workers' vast anthracite strikes in 1900 and 1902 established their presence in that industry, and the 1912 strike resulted in the resumption of the interstate conferences (and union presence) in the bituminous industry.

But they did not always win, and the price of losing was steep. For example, eleven thousand miners struck the Colorado Fuel and Iron company, owned by John Rockefeller, with demands including union recognition, an eight-hour day, safety enforcement, higher wages, and the right to live and shop outside of the company-owned town. Both sides were armed, and violence ensued. To break the strike, the company brought in strike breakers (mostly Black men from the South) and the notoriously violent Baldwin-Felts Detective Agency, which patrolled the perimeter of the tent colony with a machine gun mounted to an armored car nicknamed the "Death Special." The strike culminated in the 1914 "Ludlow Massacre," after the National Guard lit the tent colony ablaze and opened fire with machine guns, killing twenty-five people, including children (Zinn et al. 2002). Still, mining strikes continued—including a 1922 strike that successfully targeted nonunion fields in West Virginia and Pennsylvania (Wolman 1924, 46). During this unregulated period, the miners succeeded in achieving high union density by striking and winning often.

But did early successful strikes lead to sustained industrial peace? If this were the case, workers who struck and won may not have had to strike continuously to realize gains. If unions with sustained histories of winning strikes earned reputations as formidable opponents, they may also have developed a "threat" effect, which would require only the threat of a strike rather than actual strikes. Though we do not present yearly strike rates here, we found little evidence that successful strike waves resulted in sustained labor peace at the industry level during this era. Rather, strikes were relatively continuous over the period. There were ebbs and flows for each industry, but in general, to form and defend unions—and to improve or maintain working conditions—workers had to routinely strike and win during this period.

Race and Gender

Women and workers of color had less power, especially at the beginning of the unregulated period. Women did not have the right to vote until 1920 and were considered unfit for many jobs. The Fifteenth Amendment (1870) prohibited denying the right of males to vote based on race, yet discriminatory practices, especially in the South, were used to prevent Black people from exercising that right.

Many AFL unions either formally or informally excluded women and workers of color. The U.S. BLS (1926) reports that nine of forty (22.5 percent, our calculations) AFL and independent union constitutions explicitly excluded members on the basis of race or relegated them to second-class auxiliary organizations; four of forty (10 percent) excluded on the basis of sex as of the mid-1920s. No union explicitly included all workers regardless of race and seventeen of forty (42.5 percent) explicitly included both sexes. At this formal level, then, union constitutions were more exclusionary with regard to race than to sex. Within industries, transportation was the most exclusionary by race. Seven of its fourteen unions, all railroad unions, only admitted white members. And apprenticeship programs, as noted, sometimes refused entry to nonwhite and women workers. In effect, these exclusionary practices pushed low-status workers into industries that required less training, had lower replacement costs, and lower pay (Milkman 2016). Even when unions admitted women and workers of color, they faced additional barriers. The AFL often placed unskilled and low-status workers who were ineligible for craft union membership into Federal Labor Unions (Wolman 1936, 59–64) or segregated locals, both of which had less support and autonomy than national unions.

Labor force patterns and social norms created additional hurdles for women and workers of color. Especially during the early period, nonparticipation in the labor force, the inability of women to vote in elections, and occupational segregation by gender reflected the status and social expectations of women. Protective laws, pushed by middle-class reformers, prevented women from certain types of work while prevailing social expectations that married women keep house during child-bearing years limited their chances for employment. Women and girls were constrained by educational programs that limited their job options and their expectations: "First- and second-generation immigrant women sought jobs in domestic service or in the factories of northeastern and mid-Atlantic states.

Native-born white women of native parentage preferred the employments of smaller towns with less heterogeneous populations. Black women sought domestic work in southern and northern communities" (Blackwelder 1997, 34). This period saw the feminization of office work, with women relegated to the low-pay and low-status positions with little opportunities for upward mobility (Strom 1989). In sum, "women found jobs in labor markets segregated by gender and by race or nativity" (Blackwelder 1997, 35).

Although the first Civil Rights Act of 1866 was designed to prohibit racial employment discrimination, it completely lacked enforcement. During this early period, workers of color experienced severe discrimination and were relegated to jobs at the bottom of the occupational hierarchy—jobs that were not unionized. Waves of opportunity for workers of color (and women) came with wartime economies (both World War I and World War II). With the exit of much of the white male workforce to join the armed services, openings for others materialized. While these were temporary advances, they enabled visions of what the occupational structure might be like. But it was not until the Civil Rights Act of 1964 prohibited employment discrimination on the basis of race that workers of color had some recourse to discrimination.

Jim Crow laws and companies' paternalistic policies against married women's participation in the workforce conspired to form obstacles to collective action, while legacies of racism, sexism, and violence created barriers to cross-race and cross-gender solidarity. Thus, even if they had high replacement costs, women and workers of color faced substantial barriers to unionization. The outcomes in health services and public administration/education highlight the mutual implications of skill, gender, and unions in this period. Both industries had high replacement costs—they were high skill (technical and professional, not craft) and time-sensitive. They also both had large numbers of women workers. During this period, unions did not achieve high density in either industry (though in later decades they did). The workers in these two industries did not decisively turn to unions for support. Workers in public administration/education accomplished moderate union density, mainly within its male occupations (e.g., mail carriers). Health workers accomplished very little. This lack of unionization was partially due to the competing forces of professional associations, which often had gendered underpinnings. These associations encouraged professional identities and actively worked to thwart union orientations. Educators and nurses followed the quest for professional status during this early period, to little avail in terms of bettering their status and income. Some women did strive to unionize, especially in semi- and unskilled manufacturing work. Our earlier example of the 1912 "Bread and Roses" strike, with over ten thousand women textile workers representing forty nationalities testifies to this. These women were militant unionists: they picketed, fought security and state militiamen, and sabotaged mill machinery to stop production.

Union Density Analysis

We summarize our factors to enable comparative analysis in Table 2.1. We reduce our variables to trichotomies, with higher numbers representing more pro-union opportunities: 1 indicates the presence of each factor, .5 indicates a moderate presence, and 0 indicates it is minimal or absent. Codes of 1 are favorable for workers' power; 0 for employers' power; .5 in between. We don't present density for the years 1900–1909 because the census did not yet begin industry-level employment counts. However, our estimates suggest that density was generally lower in this first decade. Note that we include a measure for protective laws. However, all industries are coded as 0. Laws were not protective of workers' rights in any industry during the unregulated period.

Features of Relatively High Union Density Industries

Four industries achieved union density of over 20 percent by 1930: construction, mining, transportation, and entertainment. All industries in our high-density category had at least one (but most had two) feature(s) associated with high replacement costs—timing, isolation, or skill. The one industry in this category whose high replacement cost was based solely on craft skill (construction) also had robust apprenticeship programs. And workers in one industry (entertainment) acquired their high skills through artistic technical training, rather than in craft-based apprenticeship programs. These (mostly) structural advantages, however, were not sufficient to achieve high union density. We see, for example, that public administration/education and health had high skill but not high density, and manufacturing had moderate skill and medium density. Workers had to enact their power, which occurred mainly through work stoppages—by striking and winning. Thus, two additional factors that contribute to our explanation of high union density during this period are strike proneness and success. All of the high-density

Table 2.1 Unregulated Period: Characteristics of Industries with High, Medium, and Low Union Densities

	Union Density	High Replacement Costs			Strikes		Race and Gender	Laws
	1910s/1920s	Timing or Isolation	High Skill	Apprenticeship Programs	Strike Prone	High Win Rate	White and Male	Protective
High Density								
Construction	26/31	0	1	1	1	1	1	0
Mining	32/39	1	.5	0	1	1	1	0
TCU	17/27	1	.5	0	.5	1	1	0
Entertainment	39/36	1	1	0	.5	1	1	0
Medium Density								
Manufacturing	10/12	0	.5	1	1	.5	1	0
Public Admin.	8/10	1	1	0	.5	1	0	0
Low Density								
Personal Serv.	2/3	0	0	—	0	—	0	0
Health	<1/<1	1	1	0	0	—	0	0
Trade	<1/<1	0	0	—	0	—	1	0
FIRE	<1/<1	0	0	—	0	—	1	0
Agriculture	<1/<1	1	0	—	0	—	0	0

Notes: High density = >20 percent; Medium density = <20 to 5 percent; Low density = <5 percent.

Timing or Isolation: Codes are drawn from Kimeldorf (2013) along with our own assessments for industries he omits (based on Motley 1907).

High Skill: Coded 1 if census data indicate that the percent of craft or technical/professional workers is greater than 40 percent; .5 for between 10 and 40 percent; 0 for less than 10 percent skilled craft, technical, or professional workers.

Apprenticeship Programs: Calculated only for industries that are moderate or high skill (.5 or 1 for the *high skill* measure). Coded as 1 if at least 60 percent of unions in the industry have partial or complete apprenticeship programs; less than 60 percent is coded as 0. Dashes indicate they did not have high or moderate skill and therefore are not included in the measure.

Strike Prone: This is based on strike rates, or the number of workers involved in work stoppages divided by employment. Industries are coded as 1 if the strike rate averages 1 percent or greater; .5 if between .5 and .99 percent of workers are involved in strikes; and 0 for those with less than .5 percent involved. See Figure 2.7.

High Win Rate: Calculated only for AFL unions in industries with high or moderate strike rates (.5 or 1 for *strike prone* measure). Coded as 1 when success rate is over 60 percent of their strikes; .5 when they win 40–60 percent of their strikes, and 0 if they win less than 40 percent. Dashes indicate they did not have high or moderate strike rates and therefore are not included in the measure.

Race and Gender: Coded 1 if workers in industry were at least 60 percent male and 90 percent white; 0 if they were not.

Protective Laws: During this time, no industries had substantial laws to protect workers' rights, and therefore all are coded as 0.

TCU, Transportation, Communication, and Utilities; Public Admin, Public Administration and Education; Health, Health Services; Personal Serv, Personal Services; Trade, Wholesale and Retail Trade; FIRE, Finance, Insurance, and Real Estate; Agriculture, Agriculture, Forestry and Fishing.

industries had high (construction and mining) or medium (TCU and entertainment) proportions of workers who struck and their strikes achieved high win rates. We also note that all of the industries that achieved high density were primarily comprised of white men.

Features of Medium Union Density Industries

Two industries had medium density levels: manufacturing and public administration/education. The manufacturing industry did not have structural advantages in terms of timing or isolation, but it had moderate levels of skilled craft workers, along with apprenticeship programs for skill closure. Still, manufacturing unions were unable to gain traction largely because the dominant craft organization logic of the times was at odds with the industry structure. While manufacturing did have a substantial minority of skilled workers, the large workplaces with considerable numbers of semi- and unskilled workers begged for an industrial organizing strategy, which was not to gain significant traction until the 1930s. While the AFL's rivals, the IWW and TUUL, did adopt an industrial logic and contributed to the eventual emergence of industrial organizing, they failed to significantly penetrate the manufacturing sector in this early period. In addition, some of these manufacturing workers were located in what would become "basic industries" that were more economically concentrated, and thus dominated by a few deep-pocketed employers with the power to resist unions. Workers were only able to penetrate them when, following the introduction of the assembly-line mass production model, small groups could disrupt an entire line of production (Edwards 1979).

It is not that manufacturing workers did not try to form unions—they had among the highest strike rates of the period. But they had less success in winning these strikes. With the exception of some crucial operations, most manufacturing workers did not have the right timing to boost their power during strikes, and they faced a well-organized, belligerent employers' association, the NAM. They also faced organizational issues: efforts that focused on industrial organization were often undermined by powerful AFL leaders, who championed a craft orientation. Efforts that focused along craft lines were ill-fitted to the industrial settings. The result was that AFL led manufacturing strikes were successful little more than half of the time.

Public administration/education traversed a different path to modest unionization. Workers in this industry had favorable structural features, including time sensitivity and skill closure. When they struck, they tended to win. However, they were not particularly strike prone. A combination of gender composition of the workforce and professional identification was crucial in shaping strike proneness as well as union organization. Where workers considered themselves professionals, and/or when they had a sense of duty to the public or patients they served, they were more likely to eschew union membership and direct action through strikes. As mentioned above, professional status won over workers in teaching, a female-dominated occupation. Yet in male-dominated public administration occupations, such as postal work, workers tended to lean toward unions. In fact, postal workers had extremely high union density, upward of 70 percent, according to Wolman (1936). Combined with teachers and other public workers, however, the public administration/education category averaged to medium union density.

Features of Low Union Density Industries

Unions had minimal presence in several industries during this period: personal services, health services, retail and wholesale trade, FIRE, and agriculture, forestry, and fisheries. While some of these industries had features that increased replacement costs, strike rates were low. High replacement costs occurred in health services, with timing and technical skill to their advantage, and in agricultural work, with timing and isolation on their side. However, these seeming advantages were undermined by other social forces. Similar to teachers, health workers had professional associations which competed for their loyalties. Unions showed little interest in organizing them, and they remained unorganized. In addition to family farm workers, agriculture had large numbers of formerly enslaved Black workers, who faced multiple barriers to unionization. Many mainstream AFL unions formally or informally excluded workers of color, and white workers were not quick to show solidarity. A combination of racism, anti-unionism, and violence kept agricultural workers from forming unions in this period.

The remaining industries that were low density had low replacement costs as well as few strikes. While workers in retail and wholesale trade had unions

affiliated with the AFL (and later in the CIO), those unions made little progress in organizing the large workforce there. FIRE was largely white collar
and sales, and, for the most part, outside the imagination of AFL organizing
plans. Personal services workers were mostly women with a higher percent
of nonwhite workers than other industries, who also tended to work alone
or separated from other workers. Unions showed little interest in organizing
them, apart from the male-dominated and skilled corners of the industry,
such as barbers. Barbers, along with bartenders, benefited from a non-strike
tactic: they displayed union labels in windows and called for consumer
boycotts of nonunion establishments. Overall, the workers in these industries
did not benefit from organizational support; the AFL, at least, was uninterested in workers who had not demonstrated that they could win strikes.

Conclusion

We began this chapter with a question: Why did unions in some industries
accomplish high union density while others did not? We find that industries
with high union density shared three features during this period: high replacement costs (based on skill, timing, isolation), their workers struck often
and won, and they were composed of primarily white male workers. This
chapter illustrates how structures and agency interacted in this early period.
Structures, we argue, are fluid and able to be acted upon. Workers had structural advantages in some industries. But they fought to secure and extend
those advantages, using tactics such as apprenticeship programs and developing policies on the introduction of technologies to maintain their skill and
timing advantages. To realize these structural advantages, they also had to
disrupt businesses, which they did through repeated strikes throughout the
early period. In turn, employers did not passively allow workers to gain an
upper hand. They deskilled, relocated, automated, and sometimes deployed
ruthless tactics. They lobbied for employer-friendly politicians, courts, and
the National Guard. And they aggressively dis-organized unions and broke
strikes, often by using violent means and by stoking race, ethnic, and gender
divisions.

Neither unions nor employers sat idly by during this period. In the absence
of government regulations, both groups actively tried to tilt the terrain of
struggle to their favor and to win real outcomes. Our findings are consistent
with Kimeldorf's analysis of union density in this period—replacement

costs matter. We extend his findings by considering the lack of organization by high-skill workers such as technical and professional workers, the role of race and gender, and the actual behaviors of workers (striking and winning).

By the early 1930s, tensions reached a tipping point. With the unemployed workers' movement gaining steam, hundreds of thousands of workers on strike, and escalating tensions over the craft versus industrial model of organizing, union dynamics were poised to change.

3

Union Density in the Regulated Period
(1935–1979)

After struggling to make their mark during the first three decades of the twentieth century, workers and unions encountered a more favorable set of conditions during what we call the regulated period. Significant economic changes driven by the Great Depression incited massive worker and unemployed protests. These uprisings were met with substantial political and legal changes aimed at containing worker disruption, which in turn generated a new set of opportunities for union organization and, down the road, new constraints for workers.

This chapter shows how these conditions led to changing patterns of unionization by industry. As in the unregulated period, workers in some industries were more successful than others in building and maintaining unions. While only a handful of industries had gained substantial density in the early 1900s, unionization grew exponentially during the regulated period—even spectacularly in some industries. But, by the 1970s, many of these same industries had already begun to see union density decline, except in public administration/education.

The industries in which unions were already established in the earlier period—mining; construction; transportation, communication, and utilities (TCU); and entertainment—all saw large upswings in union density, reaching over 50 percent during the peak of this period. With the exception of the entertainment industry, strike rates also soared. This impressive growth can be attributed to their continuing use of power based on high worker replacement costs and enacted through strikes, use of the new National Labor Relations Board (NLRB) protections, the boom in industrial organizing, and existing unions' impulse for competition with the new industrial unions (Stepan-Norris and Southworth 2010). But union density began to fall in these industries before the end of this period, foreshadowing the long decline that continued well into the 2000s.

Union Booms and Busts. Judith Stepan-Norris and Jasmine Kerrissey, Oxford University Press.
© Oxford University Press 2023. DOI: 10.1093/oso/9780197539859.003.0003

The regulated period saw explosive unionization growth in manufacturing and later in public administration/education, both of which had medium union density of around 10 percent in the earlier 1900s. During the 1930s and 1940s, manufacturing, with extensive use of new industrial organizing drives, strikes, and NLRB procedures, grew to almost 50 percent density. Similarly, after substantial worker pressure for relief among public workers, high-profile strikes, and a Democratic president, the 1962 Executive Order allowed federal worker union organization. State and local workers were not to be left behind, and after a public sector strike wave in the late 1960s, subsequent state laws loosened regulations on other public workers' right to organize. By 1979, organization within the public administration/education industry had grown to nearly 35 percent.

Industries that had almost no unionization in the unregulated period—including personal services and health, and to some extent wholesale/retail trade—now saw modest increases. Workers in these industries used strikes in moderation, with some gains, while unionization remained minimal in agriculture and finance, insurance, and real estate (FIRE), even in this explosive period. Figure 3.1 shows average union density by industry and decade from the 1930s through the 1970s.

Again, we address the national state and macro context (legal, political, and economic), replacement costs, union and employer strategies, and race and gender dynamics to understand industrial differences in union density during this regulated period. As we demonstrate, the context evolved as employers and unions developed new strategies to enhance their positions.

Subperiods

While we address the mid-century period as a coherent and unique set of legal, economic, and political conditions that shaped the prospects for unionization, we also note considerable shifts within this period. We recognize these shifts by considering three subperiods. The first subperiod, 1935–1946, began with mass worker and unemployed demonstrations, the implementation of the New Deal (namely, the National Labor Relations Act [NLRA] and the creation of the NLRB), the birth of the Congress of Industrial Organizations (CIO), sit-down strikes, and the explosion of industrial unionism, especially in manufacturing. These conditions were sustained throughout the U.S. entry into World War II, when wartime brought

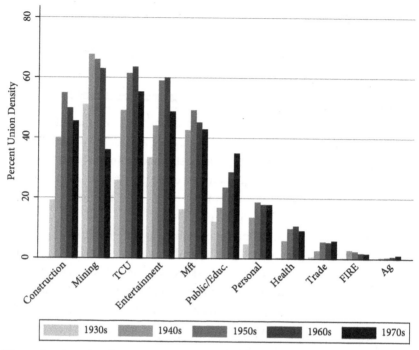

Figure 3.1 Regulated period: Union density by industry, average by decade.
TCU, transportation, communication, and utilities; Mft, manufacturing; Public administration/
Educ, public administration and education; Health, health services; Personal, personal services;
Trade, wholesale and retail trade; FIRE, finance, insurance, and real estate; Ag, agriculture, fisheries,
and forestry.

higher demand, government boards, and labor force shortages. Our second
subperiod, 1947–1954, begins with pent-up worker discontent within the
postwar economy, which gave way to a massive strike wave. This worker militancy afforded employers a rationale for their successful attempt to pass the
anti-union Taft-Hartley Act, thereby scaling back legal rights, restricting
Communist involvement in unions, and opening the way for the passage of
state right-to-work laws. Here, we see the first manifestations of the so-called
capital-labor accord wherein unions and workers traded the promise of industrial peace for a larger piece of the pie. The third subperiod, 1955–1979,
begins with the American Federation of Labor (AFL) and CIO merger and
the expansion of strike-reducing measures like restrictive contracts and
arbitration. Here we see the beginning of the long-term decline in private
sector unionism accompanied by a substantial rise in public sector union
organization.

The State and Macro Context

By 1935, the terrain for labor struggles had shifted in seismic ways. The lack of union and employer regulations in the early unregulated period yielded to the articulation, enactment, and enforcement of a substantial set of workers' (and later, employers') rights. On the eve of the regulated period, sweeping unemployment during the Great Depression sparked historic unemployed and worker protests. Also key was a breakthrough in union organizing strategy: finally, industrial organizing took off in a major way. These advances led to significant state actions that limited employer power and supported workers' right to join unions. All of these factors established the context within which workers formed and operated their unions, shaping their ability to maintain current members and to organize new ones. Large numbers of workers were successful in unionizing, while corporations that dominated workplaces began to experience constraints on their power, which they later reasserted.

Pro-Labor Legislation

The United States did not begin to develop a unified national labor policy until the early to mid-1930s, in the wake of the Depression, which stirred social upheaval and united the working class (Domhoff 2020). Prior to this period, the Railway Labor Act of 1926 attempted to regulate labor relations on the railroads (and by 1936 included airlines) by replacing strikes with government mediation and grievance resolution.[1] But in the 1930s, for the first time, workers' and unions' rights in most industries and sectors were articulated in legislation.[2]

Arguably, the most important pro-labor legislation of the twentieth century was the NLRA of 1935. Also known as the Wagner Act, the NLRA replaced the National Industrial Recovery Act of 1933, which was deemed unconstitutional in May 1935. A central rationale behind the NLRA was that unequal power between employers and workers injured the economy in several ways. First, an unequal playing field kept workers disenfranchised at the workplace and their wages so low that overall demand for goods and

[1] The Railway Labor Act was later amended to further strengthen workers' rights.
[2] As discussed below, agriculture, along with home-based domestic service workers, was conspicuously omitted from coverage, as were public workers.

services was suppressed. Second, this imbalance led to wasteful idle time during strikes, which benefited neither employers nor workers. The act intended to institutionalize collective bargaining to remedy these problems. Indeed, its passage meant that "collective bargaining was guaranteed to play a major role in the regulation of employment practices in a wide range of industries . . . bringing this hitherto private activity fully within the regulatory ambit of the administrative state." For the AFL, this state-regulated model introduced a challenge to its primary organizing principle of exclusive jurisdiction (Tomlins 1985, 147).

The NLRA bestowed most private sector workers the right to organize, strike (except under certain conditions), and collectively bargain using representatives they chose. The act empowered the NLRB, an independent government agency, to supervise secret ballot union elections and enforce U.S. labor law with regard to collective bargaining and unfair labor practices.[3]

The NLRB and its predecessors "hammered out the essentials of a labor policy on a case-by-case basis in a series of turbulent and dramatic conflicts with employers and unions, President Roosevelt, Congress, the National Recovery Administration (NRA), the Department of Labor, the National Association of Manufacturers, the Liberty League, the press, and the Department of Justice and the federal judiciary, including the Supreme Court of the United States" (Gross 1974, 2). But before it could be effective, blatant employer violations of workers' civil rights (through the use of spying and provocateurs, strikebreaking, private police, and munitioning during the unregulated period) had to be addressed. In 1936, the U.S. Senate initiated the La Follette Civil Liberties Committee, which exposed, "with sensational impact, the grim underside of corporate labor relations policies—like lifting the lid of a garbage pail to permit light to reach the decaying organic matter in which maggots bred" (Bernstein 1969, 451).

The NLRB did not assume full jurisdiction over all industries. Fully covered industries included manufacturing and mineral extraction. Some parts of the following industries were covered: TCU (water transportation, telephone, and telegraph, and radio transmission were fully covered while truck and bus transportation, taxi, and railroad were not), trade (wholesale was

---

[3] The NLRB acts through many field offices located in major cities throughout the country. Unfair labor practices by employers include the following: interference with workers' right to organize into unions of their own choosing; interference with any labor organization (no company unions); discriminatory hiring based on union membership (no yellow-dog contracts); discrimination based on workers testimony under the act; and refusal to bargain in good faith (Rifkin and Rifkin 1979, 4-17–4-22).

fully covered, but retail was not), and agriculture (fishing was the only fully covered subindustry). Construction was mostly uncovered, though after the 1947 Taft-Hartley Act was passed, the NLRB changed its position on its jurisdiction. Largely omitted were the agriculture and domestic workers in the service industries, which at the time were disproportionately comprised of women and Black workers. Completely outside of NLRB jurisdiction were workers covered under the Railway Labor Act (who had different applicable laws and infrastructure) and public workers, who had no similar laws and infrastructure at this time (NLRB yearly reports).

The NLRB, a once powerful and pro-union agency, was significantly altered through employer actions, subsequent legislation, and court decisions. By 1947, it had become a "conservative, insecure, politically sensitive agency preoccupied with its own survival and reduced to deciding essentially marginal legal issues using legal tools of analysis exclusively" (Gross 1981, 4).

Other major legislation during this period also supported workers. In 1938, the Fair Labor Standards Act included provisions for a federal minimum wage, a forty-hour work week, and overtime pay for most workers. The legislation restricted children from working in certain industries, limited their maximum hours of work, and prohibited most work for children under fourteen years of age. The 1960s ushered in race and gender equity reforms, including the Equal Pay Act in 1963, the Civil Rights Act in 1964, and the establishment of the Equal Employment Opportunity Commission (EEOC) in 1965. National worker safety legislation first covered workers with the passage of the Occupational Safety and Health Act in 1970. Its operational arm, Occupational Safety and Health Administration (OSHA), enforces workplace standards and led to a decline in workplace fatalities (from 18 per 100,000 in 1970 to 13 per 100,000 in 1980).

Bargaining rights came to the public sector in the 1960s. Despite their exclusion from the NLRA, public workers had significant union membership, especially postal workers, as did teachers in some locations (namely, in cities with strong private sector unions) prior to legal protections. As Goldfield (1989b) and others argue, these workers ramped up their organizing prior to the early 1960s. In 1962, President Kennedy signed Executive Order 10988, extending the right to organize to public federal workers (but their right to strike remained limited). Kennedy's executive order came after a series of strikes among skilled trades workers in the National Aeronautics and Space Administration's (NASA) Kennedy Space Center (just as the space race was heating up). A bill previously introduced in Congress created concern that resulting legislation might give public workers too much power. The AFL-CIO unsuccessfully advocated for a stronger order. Not surprisingly, the National Association of Manufacturers (NAM) and Chamber of Commerce (COC) opposed conferring public workers the right to collective bargaining and supported the Labor Law Reform Group's unsuccessful attempts to change the NLRA to further employers' advantage. Corporate moderates sponsored reports calling for public officials to discuss with their employees their right to remain union-free as well as to contract work out to private firms to avoid unionism (Domhoff 2020, 168–177). Despite objections from both sides, Kennedy signed the executive order, which, along with the passage of subsequent state laws for state- and municipal-level workers, signaled a new era for public sector organizing.

Several large strikes among state and local workers occurred in the late 1960s. Educators spearheaded this wave, including shutdowns in 1968 by 47,000 teachers in New York, 26,000 in Florida, 20,000 in Pennsylvania, and 14,000 in Oklahoma. Laws subsequently passed in many states that allowed state and local public workers to organize and collectively bargain. These laws were designed to reduce workplace conflict and were constraining in some ways, but they also helped to expand union density in the public sector. By 1969, ten states had pro-bargaining laws for public workers, a number that had increased to twenty-five by 1984 (Valletta and Freeman 1988).

Labor's political clout reached a peak in the 1960s, with the more politically oriented unions coordinating their efforts with the Democratic Party. In regions where unions were dense and strong (such as in Detroit, Michigan), they were sometimes able to assume a dominant role. Still, they never amassed enough national political power to repeal the Taft-Hartley Act (Zieger and Gall 2002, 230–231).

Pro-Employer Legislation

Workers' pent-up frustrations around rising prices and frozen wages led to a postwar strike wave, which impacted the public and gave employers ammunition to move the country toward legislation that would limit workers' right to strike. Although corporate pushback began earlier (Gross 1981), employers made major advances with the Taft-Hartley Act (Labor-Management Relations Act), passed in 1947. The Taft-Hartley Act rolled back many of the advantages gained by labor in the NLRA, shifting power back toward employers. It also included multiple anti-union measures related to strikes and politics. In particular, the Taft-Hartley Act held unions legally responsible for their collective bargaining agreements (especially agreements not to strike), prohibited unions and corporations from expending funds on political campaigns, banned the closed shop (the highest level of union security), released employers from bargaining with supervisors' unions, outlawed the dues check-off system (whereby members agree to have their dues automatically withdrawn from their wages), and required unions to file annual financial reports. The Taft-Hartley Act also gave employers and individual workers protections vis-à-vis unions, allowing unfair labor practices cases to be filed against unions.[4]

The Taft-Hartley Act also banned Communists from union leadership. With the Communist unions' decision to diverge from the larger CIO's political position (by supporting a third political party in 1948) a few years later, and in accordance with this prohibition, the CIO expelled all "Communist-dominated" unions from its midst, effectively eliminating those unions most successful in fighting for workers' rights and power on the shop floor (Stepan-Norris and Zeitlin 2003). Significantly, McCammon (1994) notes that the courts only moved to restrict strikes—and especially those over workplace control—in the early 1950s, after the Communist unions were expelled.

The Taft-Hartley Act, as interpreted by subsequent court cases, requires unions to honor arbitration agreements (which placed arbitration as the method of dispute resolution instead of strikes) and allows suits to be brought to federal courts in cases of contract violations. As might be expected, this measure depressed unions' use of the strike—and gave the NLRB the quasi-judicial power to issue injunctions during strikes, which was used more frequently against unions than employers (about fifty-eight times per year, on average [Adams 1995]).

Importantly, the Taft-Hartley Act also changed the administrative structure of the NLRB and created the Federal Mediation and Conciliation Service (FMCS), with the explicit aim of reducing strikes.[5] FMCS responsibilities

---

[4] Unfair labor practices by labor organizations include coercion of employees in their right to organize or of employers in their right to select representatives for bargaining; causing employers to discriminate against any employee; refusing to bargain collectively; inducing persons engaged in commerce to engage in secondary or sympathy strikes or boycotts; charging excessive initiation dues or fees; charging fees to employers, except for services; and picketing for union representation under certain conditions (Rifkin and Rifkin 1979, 4-22–4-29).

[5] With the creation of the Department of Labor in 1913, the federal government set up the U.S. Conciliation Service to intervene in industrial disputes (a separate mediation service was earlier established for railroads and later, in maritime), but the commissioners had "no power of coercion or

include using mediation and conciliation to help settle labor disputes; helping to prevent labor disputes; and encouraging the voluntary use of arbitration. According to the FMCS, the decade following the Taft-Hartley Act "has seen much modernization in labor-management joint relationships as well as in the respective fields of operation [. . . such that they] have become more stable" (FMCS 1958, 388). All of the following increased during this decade: long-term contracts without reopening clauses (which reduced the number of negotiations), multiunit bargaining, wage and benefit compensation packages, cost-of-living clauses, and arbitration clauses, which have "undoubtedly contributed to peaceful relations" (U.S. FMCS 1958, 389–391).

The establishment of the FMCS was consequential in its own right. Whereas the NLRA failed to deliver on its intended design of reducing strikes, the FMCS acted directly to do so. Its purpose is to prevent labor-management disputes substantially affecting interstate commerce (except for rail and air) from developing into strikes and to mitigate the impact of existing strikes. Mediation is requested by one or both parties to a conflict and entails voluntary and impartial help in arriving at settlements. In 1955, the FMCS handled over fourteen thousand cases (about half through formal and half through informal mediation) and encouraged voluntary arbitration for all cases that failed to settle. About two-thirds of states also offered mediation services (U.S. BLS 1958, 2:04).

A Bureau of Labor Statistics (1958, 2:03) analysis of grievances brought to arbitration by one union, the United Steelworkers Union, CIO, at fifteen plants of Bethlehem Steel between 1942 and 1952 revealed that more than half of the 2,400 grievances were disposed of prior to the arbitrators' decision. Of the remaining disputes, almost half were over wages/job classifications; and about one-third were over seniority in layoffs, promotions, and so forth. Regarding outcomes: 20 percent were decided in favor of workers; 12 percent were granted in part; 50 percent were decided in favor of the employer; and 18 percent were dismissed (due to lack of jurisdiction, untimely, or already settled) or remained to be settled. Unions bring forward grievances when workers deem a situation to be unjust and the union determines it to be a violation of the collective bargaining contract. Because unions expend resources in pursuing grievances, we expect them to pursue only (or mostly) those they

means to enforce their recommendations" (Peterson 1945, 239). It was seldom used until the war and postwar years of 1918–1919, when it intervened in over 2,500 disputes. During the 1920s, the number of yearly cases averaged 383 and in the 1930s, 818.

expect to be decided in their favor. But at least this union's efforts to solve disputes through arbitration doesn't seem to have paid off for workers.

Finally, the Taft-Hartley Act opened the door for states' passage of right-to-work laws (Foley 1947). As of 1979, twenty-one states (predominately in the South) had passed right-to-work laws limiting union security agreements, which govern the extent to which unions may require membership or dues payment as a condition of employment. Right-to-work laws tend to be synonymous with other business-friendly policies; indeed, states with such laws tend to have better outcomes for business and lower average wages and benefits for workers (Dixon 2020). Notably, these laws are rooted in racial and ethnic divisions stemming back to the nineteenth century (de Leon 2015).

By 1959, Congress had passed an additional act restricting unions. Following several years of congressional investigations into union corruption and the AFL-CIO's expulsion of two unions for corruption, Congress passed the Landrum-Griffin Act (Labor-Management Reporting and Disclosing Act), which established a "bill of rights" for union members and added strict standards for labor leaders' handling of funds, including requiring detailed annual reports. The act also expanded the NLRB's injunction powers, dampening workers' incentives to strike (Wallace 2007, 775).

The Courts

During this period, the courts made several rulings limiting the protections enshrined in the NLRA; and later they severely restricted workers' legal right to strike.

Regarding hiring replacement workers during strikes, the Mackay Radio Supreme Court decision (1938) ruled as follows: An employer "is not bound to discharge those hired to fill the places of strikers, upon the election of the latter to resume their employment, in order to create places for them. The assurance by respondent [the employer] to those who accepted employment during the strike that if they so desired their places might be permanent was not an unfair labor practice, nor was it such to reinstate only so many of the strikers as there were vacant places to be filled" (U.S. NLRB 1952, 764). While this doctrine contradicts the NLRA's protection of workers' right to strike, it has remained in place mainly because Congress has "implicitly agreed over fifty years that it is consistent with the NLRA" (LeRoy 1995a, 5–6).

A year later, in 1939, the Supreme Court banned sit-down strikes—which had been successfully used by CIO unions—thereby eliminating a powerful tool for industrial organizing.

Over time, Supreme Court cases solidified the shift of the terminal point of labor-management disputes from strikes to arbitration clauses. With this shift, workers "achieve a measure of job security through 'just cause' and seniority protections . . . as well as a fixed pay and benefit package." Employers, for their part, get "a prohibition against strikes during the life of the contract, a regularizing of day to day labor relations at the workplace and predictable industrial discipline" (Boone 2010, 131). But employers also received a major boon: now the collective bargaining agreement, as interpreted by the (usually fair-minded) arbitrator, was the final word on items specified in the agreement and employers were now free to act on anything not specified in the agreement. In other words, management was given a "right which it did not have, the right to take action without being faced with a possibility of a strike" (Feller, qtd. in Boone 2010, 119). In this way, workers necessarily forfeited much of their right to strike, formally protected by the Wagner Act, thereby rendering labor relations more predictable and significantly less combative (Klare 1981). While the 1930s and 1940s were characterized by union power "generated by collective mass action . . . [which] requires understanding, commitment, creativity and courage by individual workers and masses of workers" (Boone 2010, 133), now unions and labor relations became more predictable and bureaucratic (service, rather than activist, oriented). By 1962, 94 percent of collective bargaining agreements and 96 percent of workers covered were subject to arbitration (Boone 2010, 116–117), which implied no-strike clauses even when they were not articulated in the contract.

The courts also systematically eroded the NLRB's expectation that employers have a "duty to bargain." A 1949 court decision determined that to avoid the duty to bargain, employers had to demonstrate doubt (regarding union authorization cards or other supporting evidence) that justified their refusal to bargain. In 1966, the burden of proof shifted to unions, requiring unions to document employers' bad faith through a "course of conduct." In addition, the penalties to which unions are subject (e.g., with regard to damages under secondary boycotts) are proportionately much greater than those to which employers are held (e.g., with regard to back pay due to illegally discharged workers, which are only fully paid when workers have not earned wages in the meantime) (Brody 2004, 13–14).

The Borg-Warner (1958) decision distinguished among mandatory, permissive, and illegal bargaining issues, the first of which requires both parties to bargain, while permissive issues may be a subject of bargaining if both parties agree, and illegal bargaining is prohibited. The issues of mandatory bargaining include wages, hours, terms, and conditions of employment. Illegal issues include the closed shop, wages below the legal minimum, policies involving racial discrimination, and the like. Permissive bargaining covers all other topics, including workplace control (how production is organized and the use of technology), financial decisions and marketing, and plant closings (but their effects are subject to mandatory bargaining). Importantly, workers are not protected if they strike over permissive issues (unless otherwise attributed; the above paragraphs on NLRB case law rely primarily on Budd 2008).

A series of decisions upheld employers' right to hold captive meetings with workers to explain their opposition to unions and restricted union organizers' right to solicit workers on company property and surrounds. Because employers control entry and exit points to their workplaces, it's difficult for organizers to approach workers to make their case for the union. The NLRB's answer came in the form of the Excelsior list decision (1966), which requires employers to deliver the names and addresses of eligible workers so that union organizers have a chance to contact them. Employers are allowed to undertake all-inclusive, highly developed, aggressive campaigns in the workplace, and they regularly take advantage of this opening.

The courts also supported workers' rights in a 1975 decision that gave union members the right to union representation during a meeting with employers where the worker expects that the employer intends to discipline them (Weingarten Rights).

Government Boards

World War II had major implications for labor relations. Both the AFL and CIO agreed to suspend strikes for the duration, and employers agreed to wage and price freezes. The tripartite National War Labor Board (WLB) and its regional offices were charged with resolving disputes to keep wartime production moving. Whereas the Wagner Act secured workers' right to strike, the WLB, which ruled on wartime disputes, preferred arbitration clauses along with a form of union security—called maintenance of membership—in the interest of ensuring labor peace.[6] But labor peace was elusive—strikes rose steadily after 1942 and especially in the immediate postwar period. After the war, many WLB staffers took positions as professional labor arbitrators, further embedding arbitration in labor relations (Stone 2004, 9, 28). In the long term, the increasing presence of arbitration clauses in union collective bargaining contracts contributed to a decline in strikes.

As in World War I, increased wartime production demand, in combination with the new labor legislation, translated into significant gains for unions in both federations. Total union membership rose from under nine million in 1941 to close to twelve million in 1945. Whereas in the unregulated period, employers sought to make work process decisions unilaterally, World War II government boards encouraged joint committees on which employers and workers discussed best practices. In the postwar period, the AFL and CIO remained committed to joint committees while employers remained cautious (U.S. BLS 1958, 2:07).

The war also changed workplace demographics. With the enlistment of multitudes of workers into the armed services, industrialists recruited women, using the government's "Rosie the Riveter" campaign, and southern Blacks, by conducting their own recruiting drives.

Political Context

During the regulated period, the Democratic Party occupied the White House for twice the number of years that Republicans did and controlled the House and Senate for all but four years. Yet, overall, Democratic Party labor influence in politics was not as powerful and successful as their contributions might suggest.

In comparison to the unregulated period, and especially after World War II, U.S. presidents and governors intervened in labor disputes less often. The use of the National Guard in labor disputes remained high in the early to mid-1930s (with an average of ten interventions per year) and then declined to fewer than one per year until 1969 through 1983 (when the average rose to 5.5 per year) (Adams 1995, 205).[7] Violence surrounding strikes declined

---

[6] "Maintenance of membership" specifies that workers who opt to join a union must remain as members until a yearly (or other specified term) opt-out period.

[7] After World War II, the target of internal U.S. military interventions shifted from labor to other disturbances (like urban rioters).

considerably during the regulated period. Whereas 685 deaths occurred during the unregulated period (an average of 17.5 per year), 26 (3.2 per year) occurred between 1940 and 1947 (Lipold and Isaac 2009).

The Great Depression ushered in a new political reality. As workers moved decisively toward the party more friendly to labor, they helped usher in two consecutive decades of Democratic rule. Franklin D. Roosevelt, elected in a landslide in 1932, shortly thereafter moved toward the New Deal and friendly labor legislation. Representatives from employers' and workers' organizations participated in extended discussions with Roosevelt's appointees to develop New Deal labor legislation and agencies. The most controversial sticking point concerned a clause stipulating that labor has the right to bargain collectively through representatives of its choosing. Roosevelt decided to include it (Domhoff 2020, chapter 2), which made a significant difference for labor unions and became a bone of contention between the AFL and the soon to be formed CIO.

The two federations approached politics differently. Although the AFL began to abandon its voluntarism in 1932 by endorsing funding for unemployment compensation, throughout the 1930s it clung to "detachment from day-to-day political activities, a limited view of the state's proper role, and suspicion that government activity would, in the long run, work against union interests" (Zieger and Gall 2002, 94). It launched its Nonpartisan League in 1936 to help with the upcoming elections; but when the new CIO unions inserted their more Democratically affiliated policies, the AFL withdrew. The AFL centralized its efforts and created a new political action department in 1947 called Labor's League for Political Education, which remained cautious and nonideological. Some AFL union leaders, especially in construction and transportation, held onto their ties with the Republican Party.

In contrast, the CIO embraced political action. CIO leaders recognized that because industrial workers were more easily replaced during strikes, "the political environment, from the behavior of local police all the way up to the attitude and policies of the chief executive, were of central importance." And because their ability to create private welfare systems (like those of many craft unions) was limited, they opted to support the development of a national social welfare system. In 1943, the CIO formed a political action committee to translate workers' support into electoral strength. With FDR in the White House, the CIO sidelined third-party hopes to enthusiastically contribute to his reelection by blitzing precincts with canvassers. It also engaged in a host of other Democratic campaigns and social causes, including civil rights, social welfare, and a more progressive foreign policy (Zieger and Gall 2002, 94).

In the face of the Cold War and growing anti-Communism, the CIO abandoned hopes of a third political party (though the CIO's left wing clung to it, supporting Henry Wallace in 1948); and both federations integrated their political operations with the Democratic Party. The AFL and CIO unsuccessfully fought against the passage of the Taft-Hartley Act and, after its passage, for its repeal.

The CIO offered important help on legislation that broadly benefited workers, and both federations developed "extensive research, information, and lobbying arms" and helped to resist right-to-work laws in some states (Zieger and Gall 2002, 165–166). With the AFL-CIO merger in 1955, the two political arms combined to form the Committee on Political Education (COPE), which continued to endorse and bring labor's resources to bear in progressive, mainly Democratic, candidates' campaigns. In all but one presidential election (1972) between 1944 and 1976, the majority of union members voted for the Democratic Party presidential candidate, and in all of those elections, they registered a higher percent Democratic Party vote than did nonmembers. Yet AFL-CIO organizational support was uneven, sometimes leaders failed to accomplish internal agreement, and outcomes were not always as expected. Moreover, candidates' party affiliations often failed to predict pro-labor policies once elected (Form 1995, 270–279). The zenith of labor influence came in the 1960 election when the Black vote was critical to electing pro-labor candidates (Quadagno 1992).

Organized labor's political efforts to amend the Taft-Hartley Act, to stop and reverse right-to-work and other anti-union legislation, and to contain employers' power were largely unsuccessful. Labor's inability to influence labor policy in its favor was largely due to its political incorporation first within the New Deal coalition, and then into the Democratic Party. Here, labor was one of several "special interests" groups that had to vie with other Democratic Party constituents (including southern racists) to prioritize pro-labor legislation and labor regime change. Given these conditions, the labor position mostly failed to prevail (Eidlin 2018).

Employers' influence in Congress crossed party lines: southern Democrats played a pivotal role, sometimes aligning with Republicans (mainly representing corporate interests) to form a conservative coalition (to fight unions and to limit social benefits and business regulation); at other times joining the spending coalition with urban Democrats (to support agricultural and urban renewal subsidies, redevelopment grants, and roads) (Domhoff 2020). Despite this influence, employer power was checked in the 1930s. Injunctions, which were an important employer tactic in the early period, were checked by the Norris-La Guardia Act along with subsequent state-level laws.[8] And of course, the NLRA severely restricted employer power. In response, employers embarked on their most impactful political actions of this period: their efforts to revise the NLRA culminated in the passage of the Taft-Hartley Act, which swung the contextual tide back in favor of employers in many ways. Among them, it allowed the president to issue temporary (sixty-day) injunctions on strikes affecting national health and safety and held unions responsible for damages resulting from unlawful strikes and boycotts (Woytinsky et al. 1953, 114).

Following President Kennedy's appointments of pro-labor members to the NRLB, the Board moved quickly to reinforce workers' and unions' rights. Employers utilized delays and backlogged cases began to accumulate. With financial support from both NAM and COC, the Labor Law Reform Group, founded in 1965, sought to influence public opinion in employers' interest and to introduce new legislation to reshape the NLRA. Though their early efforts fell flat, they later prospered under the Nixon administration (Domhoff 2020).

The Economy

The Great Depression wreaked havoc on the nation. Unemployment, malnutrition, and evictions were widespread. Millions were in need of relief. Desperate people "took to the road," postponed marriages, and even took their lives (Zieger and Gall 2002, chapter 2). Workers' and unemployed people's protests, an upsurge in strike activity, and worker mobility were early reactions. Until 1932, the AFL opposed relief and welfare legislation; but as the depth of the troubles began to hit in 1932, it broke with its voluntarism policy (Zieger and Gall 2002, 62).

The prices workers faced for daily necessities in this period fluctuated significantly. Deflation characterized the early Depression Era, followed

---

[8] The Norris–La Guardia Act (Anti-Injunction Bill) of 1932 declared that yellow-dog contracts (where workers agree not to join a union as a condition of employment) are not enforceable in federal courts, that workers are free to form unions without employer interference, and that injunctions cannot be issued when worker violence is absent.

by attempts to address it with the National Recovery Act of 1933 (which introduced wage and price controls, but was deemed unconstitutional in 1935). Prices fluctuated through the beginning of World War II, and by then, prices were still significantly below pre-1929 levels (Reed 2014).

Wartime conditions, which began in 1941 with foreign purchasing and ramped up during full wartime production with the U.S. entry into the war in December 1941, led to extraordinary new demand and labor shortages. Inflation was sharp with the onset of World War II (9.8 percent increase in consumer price index [CPI] per year between January 1941 and May 1943), modest during the later years of the war (1.2 percent per year between May 1943 and February 1946), and even more extreme in the postwar period (12.8 percent between February 1946 and August 1948). The 1960s through 1979 saw high inflation, even during a sluggish economy. Between 1968 and 1979, CPI increased to 7.3 percent annually (Reed 2014).

Following the massive unemployment of the early 1930s, the labor force grew through World War II, followed by an immediate postwar drop, and then back to gradual growth. Its demographic composition changed considerably during this period: both children and aged workers declined, women workers increased, and Black workers, who were earlier essentially barred from skilled jobs, were hired and sometimes upgraded. Many of the workers who entered the labor force to aid the war effort found themselves out of work after victory over Japan, especially women (Milkman 1987; Woytinsky et al. 1953, chapter 23).

The labor force also drastically shifted across industries during this period. Of note, agricultural employment declined, while employment rose sharply in several industries—including manufacturing, trade, public administration/education, and health services. Manufacturing dominated employment during the period, but by 1979 retail and wholesale trade had nearly caught up (see Figure 3.2).

Replacement Costs

How did the relative replacement costs of striking workers line up during this period? Traditional powers to which workers in some industries had become accustomed faded toward the end of this period, as new sources of worker power rose in other industries.

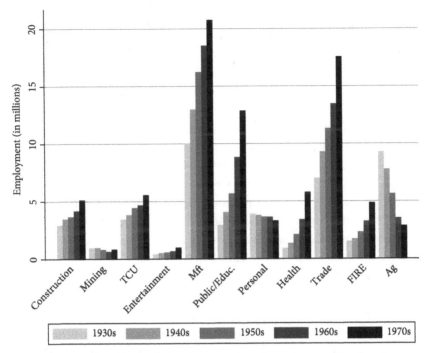

Figure 3.2 Regulated period: Employment by industry, average by decade.

Employers Deskill and Centralize

Following World War II, transportation and communication technology made enormous strides. Computers along with global communications systems allowed centralized control of worldwide production operations. The extension of the assembly line to more industries, advances in numerically controlled machine tools, and micro-computerized sewing machines combined to enable capital flight, first within the United States and then abroad. This technological and spatial reorganization of production followed growing centralization and concentration of control over production in many industries. Bluestone and Harrison (1982, 116–121) find that concentration of ownership grew, sometimes dramatically, in manufacturing, metal mining, petroleum and gas extraction, and retail trade between 1947 and 1972.

The Decline of Unions' Traditional Skill Closure and New Approaches

Recall that the early 1900s saw craft-based unions build their power, in part, through apprenticeship programs and skill closure. The nature and delivery of apprenticeship training programs changed during the regulated period with the rise of new joint employer-union programs, the weakening of union selection rights, and the increase of community college-based programs.

The National Apprenticeship Act (1937 and its amendments) regulate apprenticeship programs through the Department of Labor (DOL). It provides technical assistance, registers, and monitors apprenticeship programs, but it provides little direct funding. Under the Nixon administration, DOL Secretary George Shultz worked to reduce union power by removing their power to select new apprentices (Domhoff 2020, 195).

There are two types of apprenticeship programs. Joint programs are run by unions and employers/employer associations. Apprentice wages and apprenticeship-worker ratios are specified in collective bargaining agreements. Since the 1950s, collective bargaining also often included the specifics for financing trust funds that paid for the programs. Decisions concerning curricula, admissions, and advancement are handled by joint committees with equal representation by unions and employers. Union hiring halls normally place workers who complete the programs. Common in the building trades, hiring halls give unions a unique form of control over access to union jobs. The second type of apprenticeship programs is employer-only run programs, which are run by individual employers/employer associations without any union involvement (Glover and Bilginsoy 2005).

Like in the unregulated period, some industries continued to have higher proportions of craft workers, technical, or professional workers. Figure 3.3 shows that construction stands out as the industry with the highest proportion of craft-based skilled workers during this period, at just over 50 percent, followed by moderate proportions of craft workers in TCU, mining, and manufacturing (close to 20 percent each). These industries continued to be dominated by white workers, who were, for the most part, male. Technical and professional workers continued to be concentrated in public administration/education, health services, and, to a lesser extent, entertainment. Two of the industries with large technical and professional workers, public administration/education and health, also had large numbers of women workers.

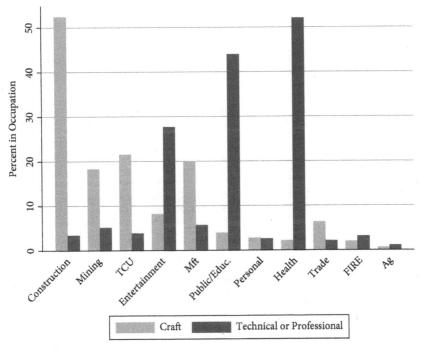

Figure 3.3 Regulated period: Percent of the workforce characterized as craft or technical/professional occupations by industry, average for period.

Race and gender continued to be linked to employment trends associated with skilled work and unionization. As shown in Figure 3.4, white men continued to make up the majority of the workforce. Even given their brief move into manufacturing production during World War II, women continued to be clustered in the same industries: personal services (70 percent), public administration/education (46 percent), health (66 percent), and FIRE (42 percent). Workers of color, which included Black, Native American, Hispanic, and Asian and Pacific Islander, also continued to cluster in personal services (33 percent workers of color).

The skill closure strategy became increasingly strained during the regulated period. The number and proportion of apprenticeship training programs declined drastically in all but TCU, where it remained the same. In 1929, 70 of 141 unions studied (49.6 percent) had apprenticeship programs. By 1946, only 47 of the 177 unions (26.5 percent) had one (Summers 1946). Although experiencing decline, construction continued to have the highest percent of apprenticeship programs. In 1946, 9 out of 15 construction

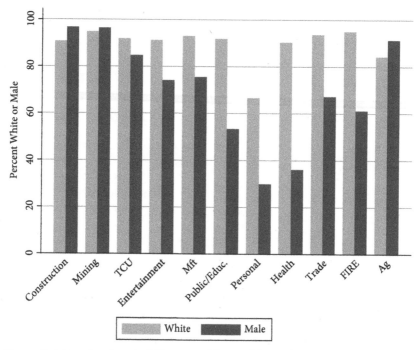

Figure 3.4 Regulated period: Percent of the workforce characterized as white or male by industry, average for period.

unions (60 percent) had robust apprenticeship programs, down from 14 of 15 (93 percent) in 1929. Manufacturing had the most numerically, with programs in 22 of 78 unions (28 percent) in 1946.[9]

Skilled labor is costly. Employers emphasized that runaway inflation in the late 1960s along with ramped-up international competition required U.S. firms to modernize their plants and equipment, but that the cost to do so was prohibitively high. Employers' associations identified escalating union wages, especially in the construction industry, as the cause of inflation, the crippling economy, and their inability to modernize. This, they argued, legitimized their call for scaling back unions in the public interest (Domhoff 2020).

[9] The number of apprenticeship programs in the mining, entertainment, service, FIRE, and trade industries were all fewer than ten. Their programs are as follows: in Mining, 1 of 6 unions (17 percent); in Entertainment, 1 of 4 (25 percent); in Service, 2 of 6 (33 percent); in FIRE, 0 of 2; in trade, 0 of 2.

In the late 1960s, several central employers' associations established the Construction Users Anti-Inflation Roundtable (CUAIR). CUAIR aimed to suspend the Davis-Bacon Act (this would remove the requirement that federal contractors pay all workers the prevailing wage), provided aid to firms that faced strikes to resist excessive wage demands, and encouraged construction companies to double breast (when a firm has one company under a union agreement and creates an additional site that operates union-free). This, along with the blow to construction workers' apprenticeship programs, put building trades unions on the defensive. In 1969, CUAIR joined with other prominent employer organizations to initiate the highly influential Business Roundtable, which absorbed CUAIR as a committee and the Labor Law Reform Group's leaders (Domhoff 2020). The Business Roundtable, which represents the majority of the largest U.S. corporations through its taskforces, high-level research efforts, and legislative work, has been a major actor on behalf of employers during the end of the regulated and throughout the dis-regulated periods.

Routes for acquiring craft labor skills were changing in other ways as well. In the 1960s and early 1970s, federal government job training policies aimed at Black workers, particularly Black youth, became a core feature of the civil rights movement and the war on poverty.[10] As these programs trained young men, they increased the pool of skilled labor. A series of executive orders targeted minority hiring in government contract work, which were in part a response to pressures from Black workers inside and outside of the unions during the 1960s and 1970s, demanding accountability from unions and employers on delivering good (skilled) jobs to Black workers (Hill 1985). The Kennedy and Johnson administrations (1961–1969) focused on racial equality, and the Nixon administration (1969–1974) focused on reducing housing costs and high wages in construction. Nixon's policies controlled wages by increasing the labor supply through vocational training that was independent of union control and also by mechanizing parts of the building process. The result was a precipitous decline in craft unions' long-held control over apprenticeships and hiring, especially in the building trades. The Comprehensive Employment and Training Act (CETA), which brought together the major training programs in 1973, grew quickly to a $10 billion budget with three million annual recently unemployed participants.

---

[10] President Johnson's war on poverty aimed to reduce poverty by improving poor people's living conditions and providing them new access to economic opportunities. Federal expenditures on job training expanded from $200 million in 1964 to $1.4 billion in 1970.

Unemployment in construction was in double digits from the mid-1950s through 1965; overblown manpower projections led to an increase to 12 percent in 1974 (Quadagno 1992).

Clearly unions' roles in apprenticeship programs, which used nepotism and workers' social networks to control labor supply during the early part of the century, were already in decline before their more systematic dismantling began in the 1960s. The continuing intraclass struggle within the AFL-CIO (between conservative and often racist craft unions and more progressive industrial unions) collided with the contentious politics of the civil rights movement, exposing the craft unions' role in fostering racial injustice by denying workers of color access to skilled jobs.

Simultaneously, public community college enrollments increased quickly after World War II. By 1978, half of all first-year college students were enrolled there. In this way, vocational training replaced some on-the-job training, thereby transferring a portion of training costs away from employers, and moving access to training from unions toward the state. The unions that relied on apprenticeship programs to reduce labor supply and increase replacement costs lost one important source of power with these developments.

At this time, professionals in several other industries opted into the union framework. Professionals—for our purposes, workers that command high replacement costs—include nurses and teachers but also potentially doctors, dentists, engineers, librarians, college instructors, social workers, and scientists. In the early 1900s, many professional workers instead chose to mainly organize as professionals, but unions increasingly won over professionals during the regulated period. This shift was perhaps due to failed attempts at professionalization or de-professionalization and served as an avenue to address workers' dissatisfaction with salary and working conditions as well as to protect their professional commitments. Interestingly, their prior professional identifications carried student, patient, or client interest-based loyalties into their collective bargaining goals—a framework that remains intact today. Befitting their prior professional identities, nurses and teachers telegraphed that, when they leveraged their power of disruption (by engaging in strikes and winning those strikes), doing so was not only for their own edification but also to protect and enrich the people they served.

Professional training had never been under union control. Once trained, nurses and teachers had been torn between defining themselves as unionists or professionals. In both occupations, training became more formalized within higher education during the regulated period. Required nursing training transformed significantly after the mid-1960s: bachelor's degree and associate's degree programs replaced hospital diploma programs and credentialing (Thelen 2004). Teaching credentialing, which had been subject to demands from multiple sources (governments, education professionals, unions, employers, and the public), transitioned from local control to more centralized credentialing control throughout this period. Teacher training now occurs in colleges and universities, with required credentialing.

Importantly, during the regulated period both the American Nurses Association (ANA) in the mid-1930s and the National Education Association (NEA) in the 1970s moved toward union orientations (the American Federation of Teachers [AFT] had long been affiliated with the AFL). Both of these organizations rescinded their long-standing "no-strike" policies in the 1960s and contributed to substantial union density gains in their respective industries.

AFT membership surged with the union organizing wave of the 1930s, and it won collective bargaining rights in many cities during World War II. Just after President Kennedy's 1962 Executive Order, which gave federal public workers the right to organize and enter into collective bargaining agreements, New York City teachers engaged in an important strike. While they faced serious legal constraints, including the threat of injunction and jail terms, they ultimately succeeded. In 1963, the AFT repealed its "no-strike" policy. As the AFT continued to grow, the NEA began its slow drift toward collective bargaining, and teachers entered a season of militancy spurred on by competition between the two organizations. While it never joined the AFL-CIO, the NEA began collective bargaining in 1962. Regardless of their continuing divisions—NEA maintaining its professional identity even in the midst of its transition toward collective bargaining and the AFT fully in the union camp—by the end of the 1970s, 72 percent of public teachers belonged to a union (Murphy 1990, 209–210; Nass 1977, 367–368).

While higher education training lacks some of the attributes that make union-controlled apprenticeship programs helpful to unions, these training programs do control the labor supply through credentialing. Provided that workers choose union affiliation rather than solely professional associations, professional skill closure added to union strength by raising replacement costs. Evidence suggests that professional workers were more successful in winning NLRB elections. In the private sector, professionals in the service and health sectors—and to a lesser extent, manufacturing and TCU—engaged in and won NLRB elections, at higher rates than nonprofessionals (Aronson 1985, 352–358).

Timing Continues To Be a Source of Workers' Power

Similar to the early 1900s, workers in time-sensitive industries were better able to leverage their timing to fortify their positions. Their ability to create considerable disruption through strikes and the threat of strikes remained high. This continued to be true among railroad, airline, and maritime workers, mainly because cargo shipments were urgent and necessary. Workers in TCU, including longshore and seamen, as well as workers in health services (doctors and nurses), public administration/education (teachers and mail carriers), and entertainment continued to have the advantage of timing.

Spatial Issues: The Decline of Isolated Workplaces and the Emergence of Capital Flight

As the world became more interconnected, isolation became less of a factor for replacement costs during the regulated period. With new transportation systems, few U.S. workplaces were truly isolated. The union that most benefited from geographical isolation during our first period—the United Mine Workers (UMW)—prospered and then severely declined during the regulated period. Crucial in these developments was the 1950 Bituminous Coal Wage Agreement, which accomplished nationwide bargaining but allowed mechanization in coal mining operations and a virtual end to strikes for two decades. These circumstances provoked a drastic drop in coal mining employment from over 400,000 at the beginning of the contract to 130,000 by 1965 (Fink 1977, 231–232).

During this period, employers embraced an additional technique to challenge union strength: geographical movement away from union strongholds. In the unregulated period, employers' decisions on plant location mainly relied on access to raw materials, transportation routes, and labor supplies. But as union strength grew, they increasingly considered moving existing (often aging) plants to non-union areas, first to the South, and then abroad.

Capital flight, along with its deleterious effects on unions, is illustrated by an early case in the auto industry, involving the single largest production facility in the nation, located just outside of Detroit, Michigan. Henry Ford ran the River Rouge plant with an iron fist, engaging in some of the worst labor rights violations uncovered by the La Follette Committee along with paternalistic and intimidating practices in the surrounding communities where Ford workers lived. Since its beginning in the late 1920s, it was a comprehensive and very large operation. It employed 83,000 in 1941 and swelled to over 100,000 when the plant shifted to wartime production. Designed to manufacture vehicles from the ground up, the plant included operations to produce the steel, rubber, glass, and plastic materials which were then stamped, crafted, and molded for use in the final assembly of Ford vehicles.

It took many years before organizers finally succeeded in organizing the Ford Rouge plant in 1941. The union local, similar in size to a medium-sized international union, maintained a democratic political culture with a mix of right, left, and center leaders across the plant's many subunits; it was also very militant. With the signing of the contract, the Ford Motor Company moved from the violent anti-unionism of the earlier period to collective bargaining and more bureaucratic methods. Still, it preferred to be free of the large and powerful local union at the Rouge. By the late 1940s, Ford began planning the Rouge plant's "geographical decentralization," otherwise known as capital flight. Once apprised of the situation, United Auto Workers Union (UAW) Local 600 formed a committee and requested a meeting to discuss the company's plans, which it estimated would impact half a million people (workers and their families) in the Detroit area. But answers to their questions were not forthcoming. In 1950, while the local was assembling a response to what the local union called "operation runaway," the international union signed a five-year contract with Ford, over the local's objection. The local sought to halt the capital flight through the courts by seeking an injunction. Its suit made the novel argument that when Ford entered the five-year agreement, it made an implicit commitment to maintaining normal employment in its plants. Capital flight in the immediate aftermath of the contract perpetrated fraud on the local that should require either the prohibition of the move or the nullification of the agreement. If the courts made any concession to the local, it would have been a great gain for labor in its fight against capital flight. But because it was the international union that signed the contract, and its president, Walter Reuther, refused to participate in the suit (due to the bad relations between the left-leaning and highly democratic local and the international), the courts remained doubtful of the fraud complaint and ruled that the contract had no implied commitment against capital flight, given the managerial prerogative clause.[11] Employment at the plant declined to sixty-five thousand in 1950 and to fewer than thirty thousand by 1960, mostly due to the relocation of Ford plants (Stepan-Norris and Zeitlin 1996).

This example illuminates two important points. First, although some re-location of textile mills had occurred earlier, capital flight became a new and important employer strategy to diffuse powerful centers of worker power in the postwar period. Second, managerial prerogatives clauses in contracts mattered. The courts referred to the UAW's inclusion of the clause (which the local opposed) as a basis of its decision. In the early-to-middle CIO years, left-wing unions had fought against including managerial prerogatives clauses in their collective bargaining agreements, but with their expulsion, these clauses became commonplace.

Union and Employer Strategies: Making and Breaking Unions

Employers and unions aimed to shape the legal and political arenas as well as to influence replacement costs, but they did much more to secure their positions. Unions aimed to build solidarity among workers, and in many industries, workers used strikes to win unions and better workplaces. They also now had the opportunity to use NLRB elections to form unions and the ability to file unfair labor practices (ULPs) cases against employers. Similar to the unregulated period, employers did not sit idly by to let workers or-ganize and strike. Many joined employers' associations and used their own strategies to break unions and reduce workers' power.

Depression-Era Organizing and Upsurge

The 1930s was a time of great action and innovation on the part of American working people. Protests in the streets over unemployment, anti-eviction

[11] In managerial prerogatives clauses, unions cede the right to manage. A common clause reads: "management has the right to hire, the right to discharge for just cause, the right to discipline, the right to plan production, the right to change the process of production, etc." (California Institute of Technology, cited in Stepan-Norris and Zeitlin 2003, 139).

actions, radical political organizing, and the successful push for industrial organizing, along with new tactics such as the sit-down strike, culminated in an enormous influx of new union members.

Unemployed workers took to the streets during the Depression. The University of Washington's Civil Rights and Labor History Consortium documents seven hundred unemployed workers' protest events in the early 1930s, most of which were organized by the Communist Party (as reported by the *Daily Worker*). In 1933, various unemployed organizations had perhaps one hundred thousand members. These organizations raised unemployed workers' trade union consciousness and promoted interracial solidarity (Rosenzweig 1983). Unemployed workers were important to the massive upsurge in protests and strikes that would come to define the 1930s.

The CIO Organizing Challenge

Earlier in the century, the AFL minimized industrial organizing within its ranks. However, by the 1930s, the workforce had been steadily moving toward more employment in mass production, and the AFL's few industrial unions brought the issue to a head within the federation. Further gains in the quickly growing UMW hinged on the organization of the steel industry, which owned unionized mines. The AFL convention delegates responded by supporting new industrial union charters as well as a major organizing drive in steel. But the AFL old guard failed to forcefully act on the new context. The president of the UMW, John L. Lewis, met with the leaders of seven other unions to form the Committee for Industrial Organizations to force the issue. The AFL's attempt to squelch industrial organizing by ordering the dissolution of the committee was useless: workers' response was already dramatically favorable. The AFL leaders' attachment to their jurisdictions and fears of losing control in the face of many new semi-skilled and unskilled recruits held sway, and in 1936 it suspended ten unions working with the committee, charging them with dual unionism (which is considered to be destructive of union solidarity). These unions fled to the transformed rival federation, now called the Congress of Industrial Organizations (CIO).[12] Altogether, fourteen AFL unions and four groups of workers from AFL federal labor unions

---

[12] Several of these of these unions, including the International Ladies Garment Workers Union, eventually returned to the AFL.

(FLUs) seceded from their AFL international unions/FLUs (the latter often joined with other units) to form new CIO unions.

The CIO upsurge infused enthusiasm, energy, and resources into union organizing. The established leader unions, especially the UMW, contributed large sums to new CIO organizing campaigns and introduced many new organizing committees that flooded workplaces with organizers (Fink 1977, 65–71; Zieger and Gall 2002, 82 ff). Twelve of the formal organizing committees later became CIO member unions (Stepan-Norris and Zeitlin 2003). Still other CIO unions were formed through amalgamations of new and existing units (from independent unions and AFL locals or FLUs). To varying degrees, the AFL unions that remained in the AFL experienced new-found and compelling competition for workers' loyalties. Stepan-Norris and Southworth (2010) find that this competition between AFL and CIO unions, although sometimes caustic, benefited overall growth in union density. The 1930s and 1940s saw an uptick in both strikes and NLRB elections, especially in industries that had strong CIO influence.

The CIO's membership was concentrated in the core of the workforce, with 86 percent of its members enrolled in manufacturing unions. In 1946, just ten years after its initial formation as a committee, the CIO came to represent 56 percent of all union members in manufacturing, compared to the AFL's 37.5 percent and independents' 6 percent.[13] In trade, the CIO represented 36 percent, compared to the AFL's 64 percent. The CIO made only a minor dent in TCU (9 percent), enrolled less than 1 percent of construction workers, and even fewer workers in the other industries. The proportion of miners in the CIO (represented by UMW and the Mine, Mill, and Smelter Workers) depended on the then-huge UMW's current affiliation. While its president, John L. Lewis, was a founder of the CIO, he withdrew the UMW from the CIO in 1942 (over the 1940 Roosevelt election endorsement) where it remained independent until he led it back into the AFL for two short years in 1946 and 1947, and then back to independence.

Whereas the AFL had succeeded in preventing Communists from gaining positions of authority in its unions during the unregulated period—a policy it effectively extended into this period—the CIO cautiously opened itself to their help. With the paucity of organizers during the 1930s upsurge, the CIO hired experienced organizers with roots in the Trade Union Unity League and other left-wing organizations. Lewis planned to limit their power within

---

[13] Independent unions are ones that chose not to affiliate with a larger labor federation.

the new organizing committees. For example, in steel, the committee's head office hired, fired, and moved around organizers, thereby preventing them from gaining bases of support that would lead to their election to leadership positions and in this way limited local autonomy (Stepan-Norris and Zeitlin 2003, 42). Nevertheless, Communists succeeded in winning leadership of nearly half of CIO unions representing approximately a third of its membership. Their leadership there made a difference for union democracy, workers' power on the shop floor, and racial and gender inclusion.

Most of the left-led unions themselves were eventually destroyed: they either merged with other unions, were decimated, or completely disappeared. Disintegration began with the Taft-Hartley Act's non-Communist affidavit, with the expulsion and raiding of the "Communist-led" unions, and culminated in the AFL-CIO merger in 1955. By the early 1950s, many of the gains made by the CIO, especially those prioritized by its left wing, were severely diminished. With the left wing no longer a force in the CIO, it was poised to merge with the AFL.

In sum, while the rise of the CIO sparked organizing enthusiasm in many ways, nowhere was it more important than in manufacturing. The CIO's core organizing focus was on manufacturing, the largest industry in terms of employment. Although attempts to organize manufacturing had been made in the earlier 1900s, not until the CIO, with its commitment to industrial organizing, militancy, and use of the NLRB protections, did unionization grow substantially in manufacturing. The orienting logic of the CIO expanded solidarity from skilled only to semi-skilled and unskilled workers, in turn, opening up avenues for greater participation from women and workers of color. This expansive solidarity, paired with other factors, helped to build unions.

The Stalwart AFL

While the CIO embraced the NLRA, the AFL was conflicted about it. Its own reluctance to organize the mass industries was based on its necessary encroachment on existing AFL union jurisdictions,[14] which the AFL

[14] Consider a mass production plant, with a combination of skilled, semi-skilled, and unskilled workers. Different AFL unions claimed jurisdiction over various groups of skilled workers employed there. A craft union might want to organize, say, skilled pipefitters into a nearby local union of pipefitters, while a different craft union might organize other skilled workers into its local. But if an industrial union were to organize there, it would argue to include all workers (skilled, semi-skilled,

considered to be an internal union matter that the board should avoid. But the NLRB exercised its unrestricted authority over jurisdiction in union elections, causing the AFL to claim interference and bias in favor of the CIO (Tomlins 1985, 164–165). According to Gross (1981, 2–3), the AFL went so far as to enter a coalition with anti-NLRB conservatives and employers to weaken the NLRB.

As we demonstrated in the previous chapter, AFL craft unions benefited from high replacement costs, which allowed them to wield power in strike situations. Despite losing some unions to the CIO and suffering secessions in many others (Stepan-Norris and Zeitlin 2003), AFL unions continued to use their power to organize skilled workers throughout this period. But they also added a new strategy: the AFL slowly ramped up its use of NLRB elections to organize semi-skilled and unskilled workers into its unions. During 1942, the AFL was involved in slightly fewer NLRB elections than the CIO (1522 vs. 1723), with less than half of the workers eligible to vote (206,442 vs. 560,815). By the merger in 1955, the AFL was involved in over twice the number of NLRB elections as the CIO (1721 vs. 804), which covered more workers eligible to vote (138,636 vs. 123,320) (NLRB Reports, various years). As a result, most AFL unions moved away from strictly craft membership toward mixed membership.

Use of NLRB Protections

The NLRB dramatically changed the landscape for unions. The NLRB supports workplace relations by designating appropriate units for elections and bargaining, holding secret ballot elections to determine outcomes for union certification and decertification, and adjudicating unfair labor practices (ULP) claims on the part of unions beginning in 1936 and employers beginning in 1947.[15] Many unions seized this opportunity to grow—especially in manufacturing.

The relative load of election and ULP cases is instructive of the board's activities. In 1936, with employer offenses still relatively unchecked, election

and unskilled) in that workplace into the same industrial union, thereby conflicting with AFL unions' jurisdictional claims and intended organizing plans of the skilled unions.

[15] The Postal Recognition Act of 1971 added coverage for postal workers, and an amendment to the act in 1974 added coverage for privately operated healthcare institutions (Rifkin and Rifkin 1979).

cases constituted only 20 percent of the overall NLRB case workload and 80 percent of ULPs. The NLRB welcomed the surge in ULPs filed against employers, seeing the agency as an alternative to strikes. The Third Annual Report of the NLRB explains: "Industrial unrest, particularly where the right to organize is an important issue, finds two main outlets—strikes and appeal to the Board" (1937, 3).

By 1941, the La Follette Committee Hearings were complete, and union organizing began to rise. Elections constituted the bulk of the cases (80 percent) by 1945. Between 1945 and 1979, employer opposition rose again, as reflected in the growing proportion of ULPs (of overall NLRB activity) to 75 percent.

Union Elections

Union elections became a main avenue for forming new unions during the regulated period. In addition to elections, workers were also able to use a form of card check in the early years of the fledgling NLRB, which authorized a bargaining unit if the majority of the workers on payroll signed a card. Employer pressure led the NLRB to abandon this approach (Logan 1999). Workers, especially in the 1930s and early 1940s, continued to use strikes as a way to gain union recognition, too. Still, over time, union elections became a major way that non-union workers established unions in their workplaces.

The total number of NLRB elections rose from only 31 in 1936 to 6,920 in 1947, the year the Taft-Hartley Act was passed. The number of elections rose to a high of 9,369 in 1973 and ended our period in 1979 with 8,043 elections (with a drop in 1948, due to new requirements on participating unions). However, analyzing election numbers alone only tells a partial story. The number of workers eligible to vote in NLRB elections, which represents the number of possible new union members, is also revealing. The number of workers followed a different pattern than number of elections, with the war years having almost double the action: over one million workers were eligible to vote in elections during each year of World War II (and the decade yearly average was almost nine hundred thousand). By contrast, the number eligible to vote in the 1950s, 1960s, and 1970s averaged around half a million per year. In other words, after the initial spurt of activity, decline set in. While the number of elections remained reasonably high, the number of workers covered fell dramatically.

We find an even steeper decline if we look at union success in these elections, or the percent of voting workers in elections won by unions. During the 1950s, 68 percent of workers who voted were in units won by unions, compared to 51 percent in the 1960s, and 42 percent in the 1970s. Another way to look at these data is that during each year of the 1950s, unions won an average of 397,222 potential new union members annually; in the 1960s, that yearly average dropped to 276,521, and in the 1970s, to 238,984. NLRB elections were bringing in fewer and fewer new union members each decade—even in this period of relative growth.

The lion's share of election activity was in manufacturing. Figure 3.5 depicts the mean number of workers eligible to vote per year in two different time periods. Although reports on total NLRB activities begins in 1936,

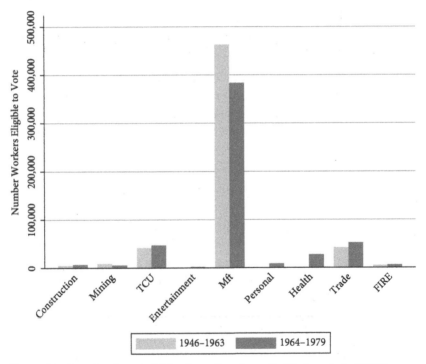

Figure 3.5 Regulated period: Number of workers eligible to vote in NLRB elections by industry, average by subperiods.

Note: These data represent election cases closed. Public administration/education and agriculture are excluded because they are mostly not covered by the NLRB. In 1964, the NLRB changed several aspects of its yearly reports. It included several additional industries (entertainment, personal services, and health) and began to include decertification elections in their industry-level election counts.

systematic industry-level data on NLRB elections only starts in 1946 for most industries, though several industries do not have data until 1964 (entertainment, personal services, health services). Manufacturing stands out as having elections that covered hundreds of thousands of workers. For most years between 1946 and 1979, between 2 and 4.5 percent of all manufacturing workers were involved in an election. For example, in 1950, nearly seven hundred thousand manufacturing workers were part of NLRB election campaigns, out of roughly 15.2 million manufacturing workers. Mining and TCU hovered around 1 percent of workers involved in an election per year during this period. Other industries typically had less than 1 percent of their workers involved in elections. Trade had a fairly large number of workers involved, but the rate was below 1 percent.

Overall, election success for unions was relatively high, as Figure 3.6 shows. For industries that had substantial NLRB activity, union wins were the norm, with often well above 50 percent win rates. However, the percentage of successful elections declined for all industries for which we have election data from the first part of the regulated period to the last. For example, in manufacturing—which saw the bulk of election activity both in absolute numbers and in rates of workers involved compared to total employment—election success declined over time, from about two-thirds of elections won, or 67 percent in 1942–1963, to 54 percent in 1964–1979.

Unions enjoyed considerable success and gained many new union members through NLRB elections during the earlier years of the regulated period. But several developments served to reduce union success after this initial organizing spurt. First were new employer rights, embodied in the Taft-Hartley Act. Second were increasing rights for replacement workers both embodied in the Taft-Hartley Act and in subsequent court decisions. These included permanent rights to their jobs, their right to vote in NLRB elections in the aftermath of strikes, and the withdrawal of replaced strikers' right to vote in those elections (Landrum-Griffin Act restored strikers' right to vote, but only for twelve months from the strikes' beginning [McCammon 1990]). Third was the realization by employers that committing unfair labor practices (which carried only small penalties) could be effectively used to prevent union election wins. Fourth, with the left wing of the union movement purged, the social movement energy experienced in the earlier decades had begun to wane (Stepan-Norris and Zeitlin 2003). Finally, NLRB elections became increasingly difficult for unions to win, in part due to delays in elections after the union had filed. Prosten (1979) shows

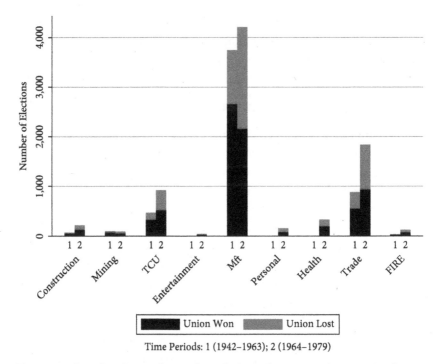

Time Periods: 1 (1942–1963); 2 (1964–1979)

Figure 3.6 Regulated period: Number of NLRB elections and union wins by industry, average by subperiods.

Note: Public administration/education and agriculture are excluded because they are mostly not covered by the NLRB. Several industries only begin data in 1964: entertainment, personal services, and health services.

that between 1962 and 1977, elections held more than a month after filing had lower win rates and that election delays increased over that time.

Unions also began to face the potential of losing members through de-certification elections, made possible through the Taft-Hartley Act. In 1948, unions faced 97 decertification elections with nearly 9,000 workers eligible to vote. By 1979, they faced 777 decertification elections with nearly 40,000 workers eligible. Unions lost well over half of these elections.

Unfair Labor Practices

NLRB protections also covered ULPs. NLRB remedies for employer violations included posting notices of violations in the workplace and reinstating workers with backpay. The bulk of ULPs before World War II (which were all filed by unions) resulted in reinstating strikers and workers who were discriminatorily discharged and eradicating company unions. During World War II, far fewer strikers were reinstated (due in part to the "no-strike pledge") (12th NLRB Report 1947, 88). In 1979, unions (as opposed to employers) filed nearly 70 percent of ULPs; of these, illegal discharge was the most common ULP complaint (59 percent), followed by refusal to bargain (30 percent). Employers filed 29 percent of ULP complaints. Of these, 69 percent alleged illegal restraint and coercion of employees and 20 percent claimed illegal secondary boycotts (NLRB Annual Report 1979, 10).

An increase in NLRB decisions requiring employers to provide backpay to workers reflected employers' increasing aggression, especially starting in 1965. Our data show a ten-fold increase in backpay between 1965 and 1980. Between 1939 and 1947, decisions mandating backpay ranged between an annual total of $659,000 and $2,260,000. In 1965, backpay was a little over this range, at $2,782,360, but it grew steadily to $17,724,850 in 1979 and to over $32 million by 1980 (NLRB Annual Reports 1979, 1980). While inflation accounts for some of this increase,[16] we see that, after 1965, more employers came to assess violations of the NLRA as a viable strategy for preventing unions from forming or continuing in their workplaces. They simply paid the fines and continued the practice.

Industry-level data on ULPs are more limited. We present the number of ULPs filed in each industry, differentiating by union- versus employer-filed cases. The clear pattern of increasing numbers of cases over time holds across all industries. By far, the most ULPs were within manufacturing. Construction, TCU, and trade also rose to a moderate level of activity later in the period (see Figure 3.7).[17]

The character of unfair labor practices also changed over time. The NLRA gave unions the right to file ULPs, and unions used them to limit employer anti-union abuses. For example, in 1941, at the onset of the ULP program, manufacturing unions filed 3,386 ULPs against employers. Once allowed by the Taft-Hartley Act, employers slowly began filing cases and, over time, picked up the pace. Employers in certain industries opted to file NLRB ULPs more often than others. A very large percent of ULP activity was on the

---

[16] Inflation accounted for some of this gain: the 1965 amount of $2,782,360 is equivalent to $6,412,677 in 1979 and $7,278,300 in 1980.

[17] We are unable to standardize ULPs by industries, as we do not have data on the number of workers covered.

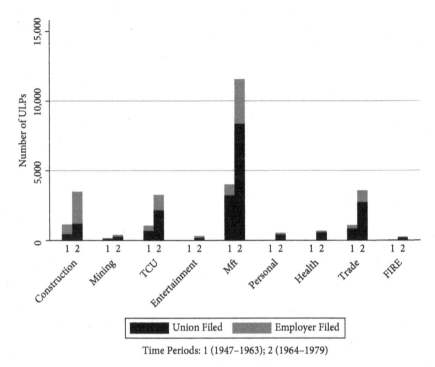

Time Periods: 1 (1947–1963); 2 (1964–1979)

Figure 3.7 Regulated period: Number of unfair labor practices filed by unions and employers by industry, average by subperiods.

Note: Public administration/education and agriculture are excluded because they are mostly not covered by the NLRB. Several industries only begin data in 1964: entertainment, personal services, and health services.

part of employers in construction (over 60 percent of ULPs in construction were employer filed), with lower proportions in entertainment (over 40 percent), TCU (34 percent), trade (28 percent), and manufacturing (27 percent). Employer ULP cases have been shown to be associated with a decline in union density, while union-filed ULPs do not seem to help unions much (Stepan-Norris and Southworth 2010). By the end of the regulated period, both union and employer filed ULPs probably reflected the employer opposition to unions that grew during the regulated period.

We also have standardized data for workers covered by ULPs, but only for 1941 (which we report in the summary table). Although the number of ULPs filed by unions has been considered a measure of employer aggression, we also see union ULP filings as a strategic effort on unions' part to defend themselves and help to enforce the newly legislated NLRA.

Employers' Efforts to Dis-organize Unions

Employers were active in maintaining and extending their positions vis-à-vis workers during the regulated period. Employers lost the leverage they had over injunctions, and professional workers' decided to affiliate with unions rather than professional associations, as they had done in the early period. Employers continued to apply new labor-saving technology to the work process, automating in order to wrestle production away from skilled workers and their union strongholds and seeking to dramatically revise the NLRB to their benefit.

A foremost goal of employers' organizations in this period was to revise the Wagner Act to weaken union protections. After reorganizing itself to give large employers more voice as well as more financial responsibility in the organization, the NAM took the lead in organizing against unions, hiring specialists and setting its sights on acquiring WLB appointment power as well as influencing public opinion in its favor. Meanwhile, the other main management organization, the Chamber of Commerce, was initially less aggressive toward unions once it installed a president who advocated acceptance of the New Deal. With the AFL and CIO in conflict, and internal state department disagreements (between the Department of Labor and National War Labor Board), NAM was prepared to set the agenda for change: "Management was portrayed as having a reasonable plan for industrial peace which would eliminate most strikes. The key was to make unions appear to be selfish and irresponsible, even criminal, for refusing to go along with the moderate proposal" (Workman 1998, 313). The NAM corralled a rough business consensus to limit union power and largely forged the business plan that it carried into the fight for the Taft-Hartley Act. "In sum, NAM's actions were conditioned by a complex interplay of intra-organizational forces and competition with other groups. The ideology of NAM and other business groups, coupled with the balance of political forces, made the success of the postwar ascendancy of business possible; the internal dynamic by which these business groups, particularly NAM, developed and projected their program explain why this postwar resurgence took the shape and character that it did" (Workman 1998, 317).

With the onset of regulations in this period, strike violence declined. During the years 1940–1947, the extractive industries (mining and agriculture) experienced the most strike-related deaths (13), followed by manufacturing and transportation (each with 5), retail/other services (2) and construction (1) (Lipold and Isaac 2009).

More Restrictive Contracts

Employers also aimed to disempower unions through more restrictive contracts. Managerial rights clauses specified those functions specifically relegated to management and outside the purview of the workers' negotiations with management, rendering some issues illegitimate in collective bargaining discussions. Functions normally specified in such clauses include authority over employment, promotion, transfers, suspensions, discharge, layoffs, discipline, and planning or changing production. When contracts excluded such clauses, those functions were interpreted to be legitimate topics for negotiations.

Research by the Conference Board (cited in Woytinsky et al. 1953, 267–268) demonstrates the movement toward more restraint on unions (through the "no-strike" clause) and more freedom for employers (through management prerogatives clauses) in collective bargaining agreements. The study compares clauses in 114 contracts in 1939 and 212 in 1945. While strikes were prohibited in only 38 percent of the 1939 sample, they were prohibited in 78 percent of those negotiated in 1945. In 1945, contracts reserved more authority for management than they did in 1939. With regard to functions related to employment, for example, 33 percent of the 1939 contracts in the sample reserved authority for management as opposed to 49 percent in the 1945 sample. A similar increase in management prerogatives among contracts negotiated in 1939 and 1945 contracts was found for each of the other functions listed by the study: promotion (4 percent in 1939 to 36 percent in 1945), transfer (29 to 41 percent), suspension (29 to 41 percent), discharge (38 to 45 percent), and layoff (29 to 42 percent).

Stepan-Norris and Zeitlin (2003, 143) found that left-led CIO unions were more likely to refuse to cede managerial prerogatives clauses than were center- or right-led CIO unions. Their sample of 236 California collective bargaining agreements negotiated between 1938 and 1955 found that Communist-led unions refused to cede managerial prerogatives in 59 percent of their contracts, compared to 41 percent of the center unions and 22 percent of the anti-Communist unions. Managerial prerogatives clauses became the norm as time progressed, a development that left unions powerless in the face of capital flight (runaway shops), which increasingly became a contributor to declining union density toward the later decades of the twentieth century.

Strikes

As in the unregulated period, in order to realize their power, workers in this period had to be willing to strike to present themselves as a force. New Deal legislation protected most workers' rights to strike, but these rights were severely curtailed with the passage of the Taft-Hartley Act in 1947. And, after the defeat of the CIO left, subsequent legal intervention beginning in the 1950s restricted strikes that posed the most challenge to employer authority—those over union organization and work rules. Meanwhile, strikes over wages and more negotiable issues remained legal. Likewise, spontaneous and unpredictable strikes yielded to more predictable forms (McCammon 1994, 1038). Although arbitration began to replace strikes as the primary means of negotiating workplace disputes, strikes continued to constitute a major mechanism that workers used to form unions and to renegotiate contracts during this period, though they reduced sharply in the 1980s.

Workers in all industries significantly increased their strike activity during the mid-1930s, and this set of worker actions is key to understanding corresponding growth in overall union density. These worker actions are also key to understanding legislation, including the NLRA, which was designed to curb strike activity, and subsequently the Taft-Hartley Act, which capitalized on increasing strike disruption to argue for its curtailment.

The number of work stoppages fluctuated, reaching peaks of 5,000 per year in the mid-1940s through mid-1950s, followed by a trough that ended with a dramatic rise during the mid-1960s, with yearly peaks nearing 6,000. The period ends with just under 5,000 strikes in 1979, followed by a steep decline in the following years. With regard to numbers of workers involved in strikes, the immediate post–World War II period had by far the highest (with 4.6 million workers involved in 1946), followed by 1970, with 3.3 million workers involved. By 1979, the number had declined to 1.7 million workers.[18]

When labor-friendly laws and institutions first guaranteed workers' right to strike and limited employers' ability to replace striking workers, unions

---

[18] Work stoppage data from this period come from annual BLS Work Stoppage Reports. Here, work stoppages include strikes and lockouts, though the vast majority of stoppages were strikes.

were empowered in industries in which they had previously been easily replaced. But, as in the earlier period, these workers still had to rely on both their solidarity and maintaining high replacement costs to disrupt business and thus win and maintain union recognition. They mostly did so through strikes.

But this time around, a new and growing group of workers (unskilled and semi-skilled) entered into the action with an extremely effective new tactic: the sit-down strike. Here, workers locked themselves in their work facilities and sat down at their individual work stations to defend their jobs from possible replacement workers. If employers were to attempt to replace them, either employers or each replacement worker would have to remove each striking worker from their work station. The first year with significant sit-down activity was 1936, with 48 sit-down strikes involving nearly 88,000 workers. The peak came the following year in 1937, with 477 strikes and 398,117 workers involved in the sit-downs, representing roughly 20 percent of all striking workers that year.[19] This effective tactic was banned by the Supreme Court in 1939.

Once a wave of new organizers who joined the CIO—many of them with radical political views—set their sights on industrial organizing, and various government initiatives began to control employer excesses, workers in mass production industries responded with aggressive and effective strikes. Despite its considerably smaller size, in 1942, the CIO led 34 percent of all strikes with 45 percent of all workers involved, compared to the AFL's 53 percent of strikes and 40 percent of workers involved (the first year we have such data). Alongside the AFL action (and spurring it along), semi-skilled and unskilled workers utilized industrial organizing to claim a successful source of power of their own. During the postwar period, through the merger in 1955, the AFL accounted for more than half of strikes in most years (with a range of 42–61 percent), and a yearly average of 32 percent of workers involved (with a range of 14–45 percent). AFL unions continued to utilize their traditional strategies to enhance workers' replacement costs (closure on access to skills and utilization of time sensitivity and isolation) and to act on that power through successful strikes.

---

[19] This figure excludes sit-down strikes that lasted only a few hours. It includes only strikes where workers remained at their machine/place of work for a full day or shift after stopping work (U.S. BLS Analysis of Strikes in 1938).

Some industries were more strike prone than others. Figure 3.8 reports the average yearly number of workers involved in work stoppages by industry for three substantive subperiods of interest: 1935–1946, 1947–1954, and 1955–1979. In terms of absolute numbers, manufacturing workers accounted for the majority of workers involved in work stoppages during the regulated period. The mid-1930s through 1950s often saw over a million manufacturing workers a year on strike. But most of the other high union density industries also had substantial numbers of workers involved in strikes, including construction, mining, TCU, and later public administration/education. Notably, similar to the unregulated period, entertainment, which had much lower employment, had far fewer strikes. The lower union density industries had minimal strike activity, with the exception of trade.

Interestingly, Figure 3.8 also reveals that, contrary to the commonly held perception about the explosive strikes that occurred prior to the Taft-Hartley Act's passage, work stoppages actually increased directly after its passage for several major industries that had relatively high union density, including manufacturing, construction, mining, and TCU, at least until the mid-1950s.

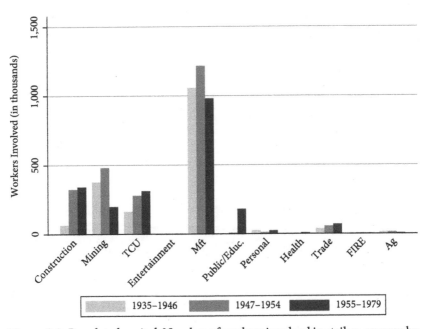

Figure 3.8 Regulated period: Number of workers involved in strikes, average by subperiods.

A way to capture the importance of strikes across industries is by considering rates, or a standardized measure that divides the number of workers involved by industry employment. Figure 3.9 shows several trends in strike rates across industries. Mining is by far the most strike-prone industry. Similar to the early 1900s, mining workers struck regularly, often with substantial percentages of the workforce in any given year (25–50 percent). Other industries with high union density also tended to have high strike rates. Manufacturing (4–8 percent), construction (1–8 percent), and TCU (4–6 percent) all had substantial annual numbers of striking workers during this period. Several of these strike-prone industries saw a reduced strike rate from 1955 to 1979 compared to earlier years, including construction, mining, and manufacturing. While their strike rates remained high, this trend marked the beginning of a long decline in strike rates.

The entertainment industry unions, which organized talent professions with high barriers to entry, continued to be anomalous with regard to their union success with few strikes. Public administration and education also

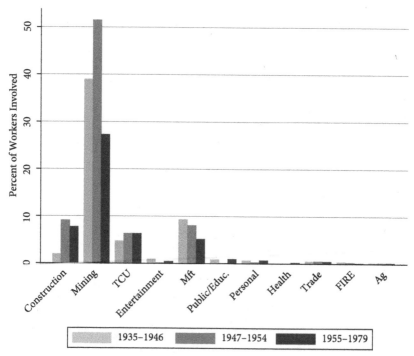

Figure 3.9 Regulated period: Strike rate by industry (percent of workers involved in strikes), average by subperiods.

had a different strike trajectory. The beginning of the regulated period saw some strikes, especially by workers with Works Projects Administration (WPA), a New Deal initiative to provide employment for public works projects from 1935 to 1943. The biggest surge came in 1939, when at least 123,000 workers were out for at least one day to protest budget cuts to the WPA (this surge is reflected in the 1930s strike rate of public administration/ education workers). With the exception of the late 1930s, however, public administration and education had low strike rates during the early years of the regulated period. This rate jumped dramatically by the later years of this period, reaching 2 percent of workers involved in strikes. From 1967 to 1979 every year saw between 143,000 and 335,000 public administration/education workers on strike (in comparison, the late 1940s and 1950s saw under 10,000 workers involved in strikes).

In the earlier 1900s, workers had to strike often in order to form and maintain unions. In the regulated period, strikes continued to be a key part of the labor movement story. Once unions were on the scene, their presence made resources such as organizing committees, strike funds, and—most importantly—experienced leaders available to help workers plan and win strikes.

Industries in our medium union density category, personal services and health, both experienced mostly low strike proneness, with personal services only gaining moderate strike levels in one of the three subperiods. Two of the three industries in our low-density category, agriculture and FIRE, had uniformly low strike proneness. Trade had medium strike proneness in two of the three subperiods. Our takeaway from this period is that striking was just as important for union life and maintenance as it was in the unregulated period.

What exactly were the stated aims of strikes? More often than not, better wages and hours were key demands. However, especially in the early regulated period, many strikes concerned union organizing. As one might expect, strikes over union organizing spiked when an industry was in its early upward trajectory toward higher union density. Strikes over new organizing peaked at 2,728 in 1937, which constituted 58 percent of all strikes, dipped below 20 percent during World War II, rose again in the immediate postwar period to 32 percent, and then slowly declined to a mere 5 percent by 1980. Looking at reasons for strikes by industry, this pattern holds for all except public sector unionism, which hit its peak later, in the late 1960s. This pattern demonstrates that the union movement's attention toward bringing new workers into the union fold peaked during the CIO's initiation period.

How do these strikes align with the legal right to organize and to strike? As discussed above, Goldfield (1989a, 1989b) argues that these strike surges in the 1930s in manufacturing and the 1960s in the public sector began before legal changes, and in fact helped push elected officials to reconsider their positions on workers' rights. Industry-level strike data support these arguments.

In manufacturing, the key legal passage came in 1935 with the NLRA. As Figure 3.10 shows, strikes began to surge in 1933 and 1934 with upward of 750,000 workers on strike. However, this figure also suggests that not all strike surges lead to more protective laws. The sharp increase in the wartime strikes was followed by the passage of the anti-union Taft-Hartley Act in 1947.

Similarly, the key public sector changes occurred in 1962, with the Executive Order for federal workers, and in the late 1960s for various state laws allowing for public sector collective bargaining rights. Figure 3.11 shows

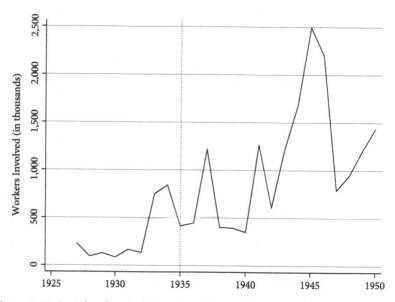

Figure 3.10 Regulated period: Number of manufacturing workers involved in strikes, 1927–1950.

Note: Dashed line for the year 1935 to mark the passage of the NLRA.

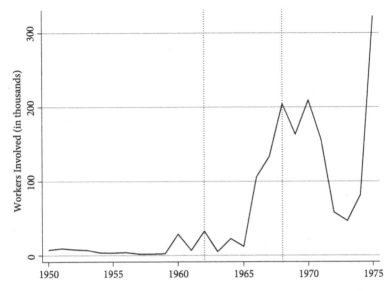

Figure 3.11 Regulated period: Number of public administration and education workers involved in strikes, 1950–1975.

Note: Dashed lines for the years 1962 and 1968 to signal legal changes.

that in 1966 and 1967 over 100,000 public sector workers struck; by 1968 that number had increased to 200,000 workers.

Winning strikes also mattered—and by all known accounts, workers were winning during the early years of this period. As in the unregulated period, strikes by workers with high replacement costs inflicted higher costs on employers, thereby enhancing the chances that employers would capitulate. But, with the NLRA, workers experienced greater state support, including the right to strike. The NLRA reduced employers' opportunities to suppress workers' collective actions, which was also clearly beneficial to unions. Unfortunately, we only have a few years of data on strike results (because the BLS stopped collecting this information after 1942). In the early 1930s, workers won (partial or substantial) gains in around half of all strikes; by 1936, the percent of strikes that workers won rose to 72 percent and continued its upward trajectory, hitting peaks of 81 percent in 1937 and 1941.

To supplement this partial information, we collected information on very large strikes, with over 10,000 workers involved, beginning in 1936. BLS reports on these large strikes and their outcomes through 1980 (after which we used secondary sources to determine whether unions were successful). Of the 880 large strikes during the regulated period, we have outcome data for 660 strikes, the vast majority of which had either substantial or partial union wins. Very large strikes tended to end in favor of unions. In the 1940s, unions fully or partially won 40 percent of these large strikes, only to see an increase in the next decades, winning 79 percent in the 1950s, 82 percent in the 1960s, 83 percent in the 1970s. Win rates began to drop in the dis-regulated period. These relatively successful outcomes are consistent with the win rates for all strikes compiled by the BLS from 1916 to 1941.

Overall, strikes and positive outcomes for unions were necessary to building and maintaining union strength throughout the unregulated and regulated periods. But developments after the NLRA "diminished the effectiveness of the strike, reduced the likelihood of its occurrence, and limited its legitimate forms" (McCammon 1990, 206). As we will see, the downward strike trajectory and the decoupling of strikes from workers' economic gains was to become even more prominent in the next period (Rosenfeld 2006), along with substantial decline in union density. Common factors were at work: legal changes, including greater employer rights and post-strike security for replacement workers, were important. Also crucial were increasing contractual strictures that made arbitration a major substitute for strikes. Coupled with managerial prerogatives clauses and explicit or implicit "no-strike" clauses in collective bargaining agreements, arbitration led to a more constrained terrain of bargaining issues, and increasingly removed worker participation from the grievance process. And within-contract strikes were largely prohibited, making the strikes that did occur (between contracts) more predictable (McCammon 1993). Predictability gave employers more opportunities to plan; they knew when to stockpile, secure replacement workers, and so forth, in order to make their outcomes more successful. Strikes in manufacturing migrated toward greater focus on wage and hours issues rather than organizing or workplace control issues (Wallace 2007).

Importantly, striker replacement rights are only effective when employers can locate appropriate substitutions in a timely fashion. Employers in industries that continued to have higher percentages of skilled or professional workers, or where timing was an issue, were comparatively disadvantaged in this regard. Among industries subject to NLRB jurisdiction and in which replacement costs remained high (like in TCU, and for part of this period, in construction and mining), employers continued to have difficulty hiring replacement workers, and unions continued to strike. But with the enhancement of replacement worker rights, strikes in manufacturing began to decline.

Race and Gender

Although the New Deal legislation generally favored workers, it still left ample opportunity for race and gender inequities. The Wagner Act failed to protect workers of color and women workers in several ways. First, it excluded agricultural laborers and domestic servants, who were disproportionately women and workers of color. And, second, it neglected to address race-based exclusions from unions. Black leaders, especially in the National Association for the Advancement of Colored People (NAACP), were concerned that the act would entrench AFL racial exclusion—but their efforts to amend the Wagner Act were overpowered by AFL and southern lobbying (Dubofsky 1994, 129).

It was not until 1964 that Congress passed the Civil Rights Act, which forbade employment discrimination based on race, color, religion, sex, or national origin,[20] and initiated the EEOC to investigate and adjudicate claims. Subsequent court decisions weakened the original act; but in 1991, Congress updated and strengthened it. Black workers continue to suffer twice the rate of unemployment (Boone 2015) and still have not obtained parity in the job hierarchy. Still, the Civil Rights Act opened the doors for workers of color and women, pushing employers toward more equitable hiring and promotion practices. As employment segregation began to recede, women and workers of color gained new opportunities to unionize (Windham 2017).

In 1963, Congress passed the Equal Pay Act, which mandated employers to pay men and women conducting the same work equal pay. This act did not eliminate pay differentials, and during the regulated period, it did not even reduce them: in 1960, women earned 60.7 percent of men's earnings; in 1979, they earned 59.7 percent. During this time, women's participation in the labor force moved steadily upward from 35.5 percent in 1960 to 47.5 percent in 1979. In sum, while some laws began to better protect women workers and workers of color, gaping inequities persisted.

---

[20] Later amendments made it illegal to discriminate on the basis of pregnancy, age, and disability, and explicitly forbade gender discrimination in education programs (Title IX). Also, presidential executive orders followed, including those requiring affirmative action.

Unions, the Civil Rights Movement, and the Women's Movement

The civil rights movement energized and mobilized large numbers of working people around their basic rights and equal treatment. What was the impact of this movement on labor militancy? Research has demonstrated that the "civil rights movement fueled an expanded militant worker culture that challenged management and sometimes union leadership," resulting in reinvigorated militancy, new tactical options, and leadership attention to racial equity. In particular, civil rights movement organizational density, protests, and urban rebellions all increased labor militancy in the public sector. Only rebellions also led to increased militancy in the private sector (Isaac and Christiansen 2002, 722, 731–734).

In the early part of the century, women and workers of color faced occupational segregation, exclusion by many craft unions, and other barriers to organization. But, as the demographic characteristics of the workforce changed, union doors began to open for women and workers of color, at least in some industries. And importantly, the CIO brought industrial organizing to the mainstream, with more inclusiveness for semi-skilled and unskilled workers as well as for women and workers of color. Still, even with these changes, tensions over race and gender continued to rear their heads, at times coming from workers themselves.

As discussed earlier, World War II brought many women and Black workers into traditionally white male occupations and industries. But, when the war ended and servicemen reclaimed their jobs, many women and non-white workers (but proportionately, more women) were laid off and forced to seek lower-paying jobs (Milkman 1987). Three and a half million women were union members in 1944 (Summers 1946, 77), a little over two million women were members in 1954, and then back to over three and a half million by 1978 (U.S. BLS Directories 1955–1979). Thus, the number of women union members increased during the war, dipped after, and then increased again as women's labor force participation rose mid-century.

The Women's Trade Union League (WTUL) was the main organization operating on working women's behalf, continuing to fight for their inclusion in unions. Alongside unions, WTUL fought sex-based wage differentials, which were lessened by the War Labor Board's decision to support equal pay for equal work. Later, in 1974, women organized the Coalition of Labor Union Women (CLUW) to forcefully argue that women's issues are union issues (Boris and Orleck 2011). By the late 1970s, some unions, especially in the public sector, had allied with women's rights groups to push for "comparable worth," arguing that gender devaluation had pushed down women's wages (Acker 1989).

While AFL unions were slow to support women, CIO unions sought to include them. In the unregulated period, women made up substantial proportions of only a few AFL unions, namely, women's garments and retail clerks. But when CIO unions came on the scene, they proclaimed their aim to organize working men and women. Still only a few women were present at its founding convention, and women's interests were not specifically addressed there except to provide for women's auxiliaries. In 1944, the CIO adopted a program to address women's equity, but adherence to the program was uneven (Stepan-Norris and Zeitlin 2003). In the postwar period, many CIO unions added women and workers of color to their membership, and some industrial unions established women's caucuses and/or pursued labor-feminist agendas.

Integrating women into AFL craft unions was a much slower process. In 1954 (BLS Directory 1955), forty unions (25 AFL, 2 CIO, and 13 independents) still reported no women members. At the other extreme, six unions (three AFL,[21] three CIO,[22] and no independents) reported over 100,000 women members. By 1978 (BLS Directory 1979), five of the twenty-five AFL unions listed above with no women members still had none, and only one of these (letter carriers) listed over 10,000.

Unions were also slow to incorporate women into leadership positions, although the CIO left-leaning unions were the most successful here (Stepan-Norris and Zeitlin 2003, 198). Of the six unions with over 100,000 women members in 1954, only two reported any woman officers/officials (garment had one officer and clothing/textile had two officers), and three reported women governing board members (8 of a total of 116 positions among the six unions: one in retail clerks, six in clothing/textile, and one in communications). By 1978 (the last year we have this data on gender), women made up less than 5 percent of AFL-CIO union officers and about 7 percent of their governing boards. Independent unions were a bit more inclusive, with almost 10 percent women officers and almost 8 percent women governing

---

[21] Electrical workers, ladies garment workers, and retail clerks.
[22] Amalgamated clothing, communications workers, and textile workers.

board members (BLS Directories 1955 and 1979). The AFL-CIO executive board included its first woman in 1980 (Boris and Orleck 2011).

Many AFL unions continued to either formally (in their constitutions) or informally (through exclusion from apprenticeship programs) exclude women and workers of color. Summers (1946) reports that, by the mid-1940s, 32 of 147 (21.8 percent, our calculations) AFL and independent union constitutions explicitly excluded members on the basis of race (or relegated them to second-class auxiliary organizations) and 33 of 147 (22 percent) excluded on the basis of sex. Not a single CIO union excluded membership on the basis of race or gender. Eight AFL/independent unions of 147 (5 percent) explicitly included all workers regardless of race, and 27 of 38 (71 percent) CIO unions did. Women were explicitly included in 19 of 147 (13 percent) AFL/independent unions and 19 of 38 (50 percent) of CIO unions. At this formal level, then, union constitutions differed in their racial and gender inclusion. The railroad unions and skilled crafts remained the most exclusionary.

Although the industrial unions had a better record on racial equity, especially the left-leaning CIO unions (see Stepan-Norris and Zeitlin 2003; Zeitlin and Weyher 2001), inequities persisted. A prominent issue was how collective bargaining agreements codified seniority, job assignments, and promotion procedures that privileged white workers over Black workers. Black workers, who had been among the most energetic supporters of the new CIO, pushed back against these policies. Hill (1985, 24) recounts a typical action taken by steelworkers: a petition sent to national headquarters. Dated 1958, the petition read "all the undersigned are employed at the Atlanta Steel Company Plant in Atlanta, Georgia, and are members of the Steelworkers Union. For many years we have been denied the right to be upgraded and promoted . . . all the colored workers are kept in laborer jobs while the whites with less seniority are promoted over us." The national union failed to respond.

In the non-southern states between 1940 and 1950, CIO union density was a source of movement toward racial equity in unemployment rates. States where the CIO had the strongest hold had more equal reductions in unemployment rates of white and Black workers (Zeitlin and Weyher 2001). The CIO realized that the lack of union presence in the South, where racial inequalities were the starkest, posed a serious challenge to overall U.S. union density. Organized labor's absence there "left both a political and economic bastion of reaction (represented by the control of the Senate and House committees by openly racist southern Dixiecrats) and helped to stabilize a section of the country that represented both a source of cheap labor and an area of lower-than-union wages" (Goldfield 1987, 238–239). The CIO's campaign to organize the South, called "Operation Dixie," encompassed numerous union organizing drives there but failed to produce the desired results. Red-baiting, racism, and anti-union propaganda were fierce, and ultimately Operation Dixie leaders excluded left-wing organizers and overlooked opportunities to ally with the left-liberal community of the South (Honey 1993, 448). Operation Dixie was unable to overcome the many external and internal challenges it faced, and it ceased in 1953. The AFL launched its own southern organizing drive in response to the CIO efforts, but it was even less successful and short-lived (Honey 1993, 228). The South continued to be largely union-free, remaining a beacon for cheap labor for U.S. employers seeking to relocate to business-friendly terrain.

With the failure of Operation Dixie, domestic capital flight from union strongholds to union-free geographies would remain a major union avoidance tactic by employers for decades to come. Unencumbered by unions, wages remained low in much of the South and contributed to the stark racial wage inequities that persisted over the twentieth century.

Unions' internal tensions over race and gender endured. The civil rights movement's integrationist demands created divisions between liberals and labor about how to act in response. The AFL's long-standing weakness on racial equality continued to direct its path: it opposed legislation that would curb member unions' racial exclusionary practices (Domhoff 2020, 122), leaving lingering anti-union sentiment among many northern Black workers. But several leaders of industrial unions lent union support, encouraged member participation in the civil rights movement, and supported civil rights legislation, although they often had internal struggles to manage. Some of the unions that were able to deal effectively with either member or leader opposition to race or gender inclusivity include teachers in New Orleans (Chanin 2021), agricultural workers in Hawaii (Jung 2006), Ford auto workers in Michigan (Stepan-Norris and Zeitlin 1996), some public sector unions (Isaac and Christiansen 2002), and farmworkers (Shaw 2008). On the other hand, according to Boyle (1998), the "struggles fought—and lost" by one international union, the UAW, to unify white and Black workers behind an expanded welfare state failed due to some white members' increasing reluctance to support integration and, in turn, Democratic Party presidential candidates. Not only did large numbers of UAW members in some locals support Nixon in 1968, but in certain regions, they also supported the openly racist George Wallace (Boyle 1995). Despite its inability to get all of its members onboard with the cause of racial equality, the UAW made considerable contributions to the goal of racial equality (Stepan-Norris and Zeitlin 2003).[23] Nevertheless, when unions could not deliver voting coalitions, their political clout declined and election outcomes were less likely to go their way.

These dynamics illustrate how race and gender are intimately linked with replacement costs, strikes, eligibility for union membership, and—ultimately—union density. Whereas in the unregulated period, industries with high replacement costs and a high proportion of women workers (health and public administration/education) failed to achieve high union density, in the regulated period they advanced considerably. This is because nurses and teachers as well as other professionals trained outside of union apprenticeship programs abandoned their strict adherence to their professional identities and embraced collective bargaining and union status. Women with lower levels of skills also entered the union ranks, as industrial organization allowed for organizing in industries (mainly in manufacturing) with higher numbers of women and workers of color.

Overall, unions considerably changed their orientations toward race and gender in the regulated period. Women and workers of color had more opportunities for work in different industries. Unions were more inclusive, with the new CIO unions (and, in slow response, existing AFL unions) bringing them in through industrial (and mixed) organizing strategies. In addition, important professional women's organizations pivoted toward unions and away from professional organizations. And, finally toward the end of the regulated period, the legal and cultural context had changed considerably, with the Civil Rights Act and vibrant social movements that pushed for greater equality for women and people of color.

Analysis of Union Density

As favorable conditions proliferated, manufacturing unions ran high while previously successful unions grew in tandem, yet workers in some industries

---

[23] Stepan-Norris and Zeitlin (2003) find that the left-led unions, especially the United Electrical, Radio, and Machine Workers Union (UE), made the most consistent contributions to the goal of racial equality. The UAW was not a right-wing union, but in their "uncertain and shifting" political camp.

still struggled to form unions. The explanatory factors discussed above combined to produce a high (above 20), medium (5–19), and low (below 5) percent of workers organized in various industries. Again, we use trichotomous variables to indicate the presence of each factor, with 1 indicating a strong presence, .5 indicating a moderate presence, and 0 indicating a low presence. Codes of 1 are favorable for workers' power; 0 for employers' power; .5 in between. Two tables present summary indicators. Table 3.1 includes variables similar to the unregulated period: replacement costs, strikes, and race and gender composition. Similar to the first period, replacement costs and strikes contribute to union density. Race and gender continued to be related to union density and interrelated with our other factors, with high-status workers dominating industries that had high replacement costs and strikes.

However, the regulated period (see Table 3.2) also ushered in a new set of opportunities and constraints for workers. The second table adds new indicators important for this period: industrial organizing, the use of NLRB elections and ULP filings, and new legal protections for workers' rights. These features are particularly important to the largest sector of the time—manufacturing—but also impact the growth of unionization in multiple industries. These factors relate to replacement costs. The strategies used by the early CIO—industrial organizing and sit-down strikes—made it harder for employers to replace workers, as did the new NLRB protections to form unions and to strike. And NLRB elections provided a new route to unionization, which proved to be an effective tool for workers during this period.

Features of High Union Density Industries

Four industries achieved over 20 percent density in the unregulated period: construction, mining, entertainment, and transportation/communication/utilities. These same four industries increased their density during the regulated period. Their peak density hit during the middle of this period and declined beginning in 1955, with the exception of TCU, whose union density continued to grow through the 1960s and 1970s. Workers in three of the four industries continued to strike at high rates, with mining continuing its especially high strike rate and entertainment continuing its earlier pattern of a lower strike rate.

Table 3.1 Regulated Period: Characteristics of Industries With High, Medium, and Low Union Densities—Indicators From the Unregulated Period

| | Union Density 1935–46/ 1947–54/ 1955–79 | High Replacement Costs | | | Strikes Strike Prone 1935–46/ 1947–54/ 1955–79 | Race and Gender White and Male |
		Timing or Isolation	High Skill	Apprenticeship Programs		
High Density						
Construction	24/50/42	0	1	1	1/1/1	1
Mining	59/66/48	1	.5	0	1/1/1	1
TCU	50/61/66	1	.5	0	1/1/1	1
Entertainment	33/54/49	1	.5	0	.5/0/0	1
Manufacturing	32/47/43	.5	.5	0	1/1/1	1
Public Admin.	15/22/28	1	1	0	.5/0/1	0
Medium Density						
Personal Serv.	9/18/19	0	0	—	.5/0/0	0
Health	5/9/9	1	1	0	0/0/0	0
Low Density						
Trade	2/4/6	0	0	—	.5/.5/0	1
FIRE	2/3/2	0	0	—	0/0/0	0
Agriculture	.2/.4/.8	1	0	—	0/0/0	0

Notes: High density = >20 percent; Medium density = <20 to 5 percent; Low density = <5 percent.

"*Replacement Cost*" variables: *Timing or isolation:* Following Kimeldorf (2013) as in Chapter 2. We include manufacturing as .5 due to war production demands.

High skill: Coded as 1 if census data indicate that the percent of craft or technical/professional workers is greater than 40 percent; .5 for between 10 and 40 percent; 0 for less than 10 percent skilled craft, technical, or professional workers.

Apprenticeship Programs: Coded as 1 = >60 percent have partial or complete apprenticeship programs; .5 = 20–59 percent have programs; 0 = <20 percent have programs. We use dashes if data are missing for an industry. Source: Summers (1946).

Strike Prone: This is based on strike rates, or the number of workers involved in work stoppages divided by employment. Industries are coded as 1 if the strike rate averages 1 percent or greater; .5 if between .5 and .99 percent of workers are involved in strikes; and 0 for those with less than .5 percent involved.

Strike Win Rate is not available for all strikes by industry in this period. We do examine large (10,000 + worker strikes) only. In the text, we note that there appears to be little variation in win rates by industry for this group of strikes. The majority of these large strikes are won by unions.

Race and Gender: Coded as 1 if >90 percent white and >60 percent male.

TCU, Transportation, Communication, and Utilities; Public Admin, Public Administration and Education; Health, Health Services; Personal Serv, Personal Services; Trade, Wholesale and Retail Trade; FIRE, Finance, Insurance, and Real Estate; Agriculture, Agriculture, Forestry, and Fishing.

Table 3.2 Regulated Period: Characteristics of Industries With High, Medium, and Low Union Densities—Emergent Indicators Important for the Regulated Period

	Industrial Organizing	Laws	NLRB Elections			ULPs
	CIO Presence	Protective	Election Effort 1946–63/1964–79	Election Success 1942–63/1964–79	ULP Effort 1941	Percent Union-Filed ULPs (as Opposed to Employers)
High Density						
Construction	0	1	0/0	1/.5	*	0
Mining	.5	1	0/0	.5/.5	1	1
TCU	.5	1	0/.5	1/1	1	.5
Entertainment	0	1	–/0	–/1	1	1
Manufacturing	1	1	1/1	1/.5	1	.5
Public Admin.	0	.5	*	*	*	*
Medium Density						
Personal Serv.	0	.5	0/0	–/.5	0	—
Health	0	.5	0/0	–/1	0	—
Low Density						
Trade	0	1	0/0	1/.5	0	.5
FIRE	0	1	0/.5	.5/.5	0	1
Agriculture	0	0	*	*	*	*

(continued)

Table 3.2 Continued

Industrial Organizing and CIO: Coded as 1 if > 50 percent of unionized workers were CIO members; .5 if > 50 percent of union members were CIO members; 0 if < 50 percent of union members were CIO members.

Protective Laws: Coded as 1 if industry workers were mostly covered by protective laws; .5 if partial coverage or coverage comes late in the period; 0 if the bulk of the industry remains uncovered. We consider several sets of laws. The Railway Act (1926); the NLRA; and public sector laws, including Executive Order and state laws regarding public workers, which were established later during this period (1960s and 1970s). By the end of the period, about half of states had laws allowed state public workers to collectively bargain. Many public workers continued to be barred from striking. Therefore, we designate public administration/education as .5 and health (which had some public workers) as .5. We designate personal services as .5, because some were covered by the NLRA while others were not. We designate agriculture as 0, although some workers in this broad category were covered by the NLRA (e.g., some forestry workers).

NLRB Elections: The NLRB covers private sector workers and therefore is not applicable to public administration/education or agriculture, which we mark with "*". Not all of construction was covered until after 1941. We use dashes if data are missing for an industry.

Election Effort: This is the percent of workers involved in yearly elections. 1 = 1 percent or more; .5 = .5 to .99 percent; 0 = < .5 percent were involved in elections.

Election Success: This is the percent of NLRB elections won by unions. High = 60 percent or greater; .5 = 50 to 59 percent; Low = < 50 percent of elections were won. We only include data on election success if the industry has at least ten elections a year and reports include election outcome. We use dashes if an industry does not meet this standard.

ULP Effort: We only have data for 1941 on percent of workers involved in ULPs. 1 = 1 percent or more; .5 = .5 to .99 percent; 0 = < .5 percent or so low that it is was not reported. Construction is excluded.

Percent ULPs filed by unions (as opposed to filed by employers): Coded as 1 = > 75 percent; .5 = 50 to 75 percent; 0 = < 50 percent. This measure considers the years 1947–1979. We use dashes if data are missing for an industry.

CIO, Congress of Industrial Organizations; TCU, Transportation, Communication, and Utilities; Public Admin, Public Administration and Education; Health, Health Services; Personal Serv, Personal Services; Trade, Wholesale and Retail Trade; FIRE, Finance, Insurance, and Real Estate; Agriculture, Agriculture, Forestry, and Fishing.

As the years passed, unions' ability to keep striker replacement costs high in these industries suffered blows. In construction, union apprenticeship programs collapsed in favor of skill training mostly outside of the unions' control, which resulted in an oversupply of skilled workers without a union orientation. In mining, the 1950 industry-wide bituminous coal agreement included restrictions on certain strikes, leading to a great reduction in strikes through the beginning of the 1970s, and it also provided for technological changes that led to massive job loss in the mining industry. In entertainment, technological developments reduced the demand for live performances. Musicians countered with an effective recording ban and initiated a Music Performance Trust Fund to help displaced musicians, but the passage of the Lea Act (also known as the anti-Petrillo Act, after the musician union's president) along with the Taft-Hartley Act restriction on secondary boycotts rendered these strategies ineffective and their numbers declined drastically (Richardson 2009).[24]

Two industries moved into the high-density category in this period, after having only moderate success in the unregulated period: manufacturing and public administration/education. Manufacturing unions struck often, and their strikes involved the largest number of workers throughout the period. Public administration/education had only moderate strike rates on average, with fewer in the beginning of the regulated period and a sharp spike toward the late 1960s.

Unions in all high-density industries utilized NLRB protections (except for public administration/education, which was not covered), with construction using it the least. Most experienced a peak in election success just after enactment of the NLRA, followed by decline over the period.

But, of all industries, manufacturing unions stand out as participating the most in NLRB elections and ULP filings. They were involved in the overwhelming majority of elections, with hundreds of thousands of workers eligible to vote in elections in most years, sometimes representing 2 to 4 percent of all manufacturing workers. Manufacturing industry workers also filed many ULPs, though a moderate percent were filed by employers. Federal-level public workers used the Federal Labor Relations Authority (FLRA) protections, which are similar to those of the NLRB.[25]

---

[24] The Lea Act of 1946 amended the Communications Act of 1934 to outlaw some of the practices of the union, including compelling broadcasters to hire more musicians than necessary and to pay more than once for services performed for a broadcast.

[25] Because federal workers are a small fraction of all public administration/education workers, we do not include data on their activity with the FLRA.

The explosive strikes and relative legal protections we saw at the beginning of the regulated period weakened over time. A main aim of the NLRB was to tame labor–capital relations within the collective bargaining regime in order to reduce industrial strife. In that regime, unions and employers exercised their power to arrive at agreements that codify relations for several years. Presumably, industrial peace would follow, at least during contract terms. But it did not. Strike rates remained high, even throughout World War II. Within the CIO, the left-wing unions were more likely to refuse to surrender their contractual right to strike during the term of the agreement. They were also more likely to refuse to cede management prerogatives and included grievance procedures that were more effective and involved workers in the process. Yet with the passage of the Taft-Hartley Act (and the courts increasingly pro-employer interpretations of it) and the expulsion and decimation of the CIO's left, more conservative collective bargaining set in, with agreements that prohibited strikes in favor of bureaucratic grievance procedures with compulsory arbitration. With these developments came the beginning of the devastating long-term decline in union density as well as strikes. Unions' ability to utilize their most powerful weapon, the right to strike, had been decimated. Collective bargaining agreements increasingly included longer terms (such as the five-year term in the 1950 UAW-General Motors contract known as the "Treaty of Detroit"), both collective bargaining agreements and laws increased restrictions on unions' right to strike, and the courts increased replacement worker rights, further diminishing unions' source of power. Accompanying these developments was a reduction in NLRB union election success in manufacturing, which began its decline in 1952. All unions filed substantially more ULPs over time, reflecting growing employer opposition to unionization. Construction stands out as also having high numbers of employer-filed ULPs.

Change in union density in the public administration/education industry came with strike activity and new laws allowing public workers to organize and with more teachers transitioning to the union model. Teachers subsequently relied on their professional closure through licensing/credentialing and a large spurt of strike actions to accomplish an influx of new union members and increase in density. In 1961, the year before the Executive Order to protect federal workers' rights, roughly 6,610 state and local public workers struck. Public workers' strikes escalated over the decade, with 105,000 striking in 1965, 202,000 in 1968, and over 333,000 in 1970—or about 3 percent of the eleven million workers in the industry. With these strikes came new legislation, workplace protections, and a sense of union identity. Workers in the public sector faced less aggressive anti-unionism than in the past, which helped them in this period—and especially in the next.

As in the unregulated period, high replacement costs alone were not sufficient to achieve high union density. But a combination of factors did yield higher union density: strikes paired with factors such as high replacement costs, use of state election protections, and a more expansive solidarity that included a broader swath of the labor force. The effects of strikes, however, began to ebb over time. When strikes were constrained, made more predictable, and rendered less effective, density declined.

In this regulated period, white men continued to comprise the vast majority of the workers in high-density industries. While women and workers of color had made key gains within the labor movement during this period, especially with the more inclusive vision of the CIO and the expansion of industrial organizing, they still were often employed in industries or jobs that were not unionized or not covered by the NLRA. Public sector organizing, however, began to draw in workers who had previously been excluded in large numbers. As we see in the next chapter, women and workers of color expanded their organizational power in the subsequent decades.

Features of Medium Union Density Industries

Two industries had medium density levels: personal services and health services, both of which saw an increase in union density compared to the early 1900s. However, they did not break the 20 percent threshold that we designate as high union density. Personal services continued to have little leverage in worker replacement costs and moderate-to-low strike proneness. They were also outside of the core organizing targets of the CIO and were less likely to be covered by the new protective labor laws. Accordingly, they had low rates of NLRB elections. The moderate surge of strikes at the start of this period was accompanied by a leap in union density (from 9 percent to 18 percent). Subsequent lower strike rates accompanied density stagnation. The health industry experienced quite different conditions. Like teachers, health workers (especially nurses) transitioned to union affiliation during this period and continued to utilize their professional skills to press for unions along with better wages and working conditions, but their strike proneness was low during this period.

Features of Low Union Density Industries

Unions had minimal presence in three industries during this period: trade, FIRE, and agriculture. These industries had few factors that increased workers' replacement costs. Workers in FIRE and agriculture did not use the NLRB regularly (agriculture was exempt) and did not strike often. Despite their exclusion, farmworkers did make some spectacular, if temporary, gains in California with the United Farm Workers, after widespread boycotts and strikes (Shaw 2008). While trade remained largely unorganized, its density crept up over the period. Trade had mainly white male workers, and workers engaged in slightly more NLRB elections than in other industries with low density. They also maintained moderate levels of strike proneness (they hovered near .05 percent of workers on strike for each subperiod, though the 1955–1979 subperiod fell just under .05 and is therefore coded as 0). By the last years of the regulated period, they had reached a density of nearly 6 percent.

Conclusion

The regulated period experienced substantial growth in overall union density—but some industries grew much more than others. What accounts for the different patterns? Industries with high union density fit into two categories. First are those that continued to prosper based on the features that made them strong during the earlier period, especially high worker replacement cost and high strike rates (except for entertainment): construction, mining, TCU, and entertainment. These workers were also aided by the new NLRB protections and the momentum of the times. Second were the newly ascendant high-density industries. Those in manufacturing entered the high union density category when they dramatically used mass worker insurgency (industrial organizing and sit-down strikes—which were very effective strategies given the structure of their work), the resources and mission heralded by the CIO, and the NLRA legislation that gave them the opportunity to hold secret-ballot elections. Workers in public administration/education grew their unions toward high density on a later timeline using closure through their professional status, new legal changes, and dramatic strikes. As we see in Chapter 4, they continue to prosper.

In the traditionally skilled industries, workers' bases of power rooted in limiting the labor supply during strikes declined over the period. Skills themselves were subject to deskilling through technological advancements and automation, and union-controlled apprenticeship programs declined, as did isolated workplaces. Among manufacturing workers, union breakthroughs came with considerable worker unrest and innovation (sit-down strikes) as well as restrictions on employers' aggressive union-busting tactics (NLRA). But shortly thereafter, employers were instrumental in writing and passing the Taft-Hartley Act, which, along with subsequent court decisions, limited workers power as manifested in the strike, and consequentially, the effectiveness and reach of collective bargaining. In all, while pro-labor laws addressed important worker concerns, such as job safety and security, and provided a system for addressing grievances, later legislation presented an institutional context for arbitration in lieu of most strikes (Wallace 2007, 792).

Unions innovated by solidifying a place for the industrial union approach. They made good use of the new NLRB protections. They succeeded in accomplishing an incredible boom in mass production union organization, along with an accompanying invigoration of AFL craft unions. The CIO had a more progressive and inclusive orientation, but in the end, its downfall was its excision of its most progressive wing in 1949–1950, which had fought the hardest against the slow accumulation of employers' power vis-à-vis unions. The Achilles heel of the stalwart AFL, which affected it especially in later years, was its relentless pursuit of exclusion even as the economy changed and, in particular, its complicity in upholding racism.

Employers innovated to avoid unions: they gained important rights that enabled them to disrupt union organizing and strikes, began to move their operations to non-union areas, and developed more sophisticated anti-union approaches. As the regulated period's decades wore on, unions filed more and more ULPs against employers, which reflects the anti-union tactics that many employers used during elections, strikes, and negotiations. These union-thwarting actions were well worth employers' efforts. With the exception of public administration and education, union density had dropped by the 1970s, compared to earlier decades. This union erosion foreshadowed the widespread decline many industries would experience in the dis-regulated period.

The regulated period also sheds light on the relationship between new organizing, strikes, and protective laws. New laws accompanied both manufacturing (NLRA) and public administration/education union growth surges (President Kennedy's Executive Order and state collective bargaining laws). Scholars have pointed to the causal role of the Executive Order for federal workers and to the accumulation of state laws (covering collective bargaining of state and municipal workplaces) in growing union density there. But the beginning of the rise precedes those legal changes in both the manufacturing and public administration/education industries (Goldfield 1987, 1989a, 1989b). Federal workers had been slowly organizing for decades, and many state and local workers struck prior to winning union rights. Still, the new legislation was beneficial in propelling continued organization in both manufacturing and in public administration/education.

For overall union density trends, these new public sector rights came just in time. Private sector union density already showed signs of trouble as the two main federations merged in 1955. But the new laws regarding public workers helped unions in public administration/education and to some extent health industries. With the onset of the 1980s and the dis-regulated period, the troubles for many unions worsened as employer power consolidated and workers in many industries lost key strike leverage.

4

Union Density in the Dis-Regulated Period (1980–2015)

Following the mid-century boom came the big bust. Since 1955, overall union density moved steadily downward. And, since 1979, absolute numbers of union members declined, moving from over twenty-one million members in 1979 to under fifteen million in 2015. Even in industries with the traditionally strong ability to maintain high worker replacement costs (construction; transportation, communications, and utilities [TCU]; mining; and entertainment), membership drastically waned. Likewise, manufacturing, which began its impressive ascendency in the 1930s, significantly flagged, as did the industries with already low density (trade; finance, insurance, and real estate [FIRE]; and agriculture; and to a lesser extent, personal services). Only the public administration/education and health sectors avoided a similar fate. The trend of reversing fortunes between the public and private sectors that began in the 1970s progressed to the point where public sector unionism outpaced the private sector not only in density, but by 2015, public sector workers accounted for roughly half of all union members.

These developments occurred in the context of new legal, political, and economic conditions, which were met with a combination of new and old employer and union strategies. Prominent among the changing conditions was the new economic paradigm, including financialization (a shift of power from manufacturing to banks and investment firms). Globalization, too, along with new competition (especially from Germany and Japan), new trade deals, and increased production in China and Mexico also contributed to this shift in power, although these global trends may have a smaller impact on the fate of unions than is commonly believed (Mishel, Rhinehart, and Windham 2020; Piazza 2005). Bipartisan efforts to deregulate some industries, especially transportation and utilities, benefitted some employers at the expense of workers and other employers.

Employers embraced anti-union activities, this time with a higher degree of sophistication. They pressed to pass more right-to-work laws in the

Union Booms and Busts. Judith Stepan-Norris and Jasmine Kerrissey, Oxford University Press.
© Oxford University Press 2023. DOI: 10.1093/oso/9780197539859.003.0004

private sector, resulting in the demise of the so-called capital-labor accord, if there ever was one. Now workers were asked to accept a smaller piece of the pie going forward and even to "give back" previous advances (also known as concession bargaining). These maneuvers took place while they endured strong restrictions on their right to strike and decreased returns when they chose to strike.

We call this period "dis-regulated" to capture the extent to which workers' rights were dismantled. Protections enshrined in the National Labor Relations Act (NLRA) were eroded, shifting the playing field even more in favor of employers. Workers' "right to strike" had become hollow, due to the shift toward the rights and use of permanent replacement workers during and after strikes, contract language regulating strikes, and the role of arbitration. The regulations guaranteeing workers' rights put in place under the NLRA, including in National Labor Relations Board (NLRB) union elections, were slowly chipped away to the point that organizing new union shops through elections had become fraught for many unions. The regulations that workers had fought for in the 1930s—and then benefited from in the mid-century— were shadows of their former selves by the twenty-first century.

A more mild erosion of collective rights came to the public sector later. A wave of favorable state laws had passed decades earlier. But, by the 2010s, laws that placed restrictions on public sector unions had replaced many of the more union-friendly laws, along with more aggressive opposition to public sector unions. Still, the public sector held steady, and as of 2015, it had not experienced decline similar to the private sector.

Union decline in the dis-regulated period was largest in industries that had made the most gains during the regulated period. Mining, TCU, construction, entertainment, and manufacturing had all reached high levels of unionization by mid-century, with some reaching over 50 percent density. Each of these industries dropped precipitously in the dis-regulated era. Recall, two industries rose to high unionization from the early 1900s to the mid-century: manufacturing and public administration/education. These industries experienced different outcomes in the dis-regulated period: manufacturing declined by almost half, but public administration/education remained steady (at around 36 percent).

Unions in industries that secured medium density in the regulated period (personal services and health services) also had mixed outcomes in the dis-regulated period: personal services declined moderately and health services slightly grew its density. And unions in the low-density category during the regulated period (agriculture, FIRE, and trade) also declined. Notably, in 2015, the three industries in which unions saw the most success in maintaining density during the dis-regulated period (public administration/education, health, and to a lesser extent, personal service) were those with the highest percent of female workers and workers of color (though the public administration/education is just around the mean on the latter). Figure 4.1 shows the drastic union density declines that occurred in all industries except public administration/education and health services.

We attribute this drastic overall decline to unions' flagging ability to keep worker replacement costs high, oppositional employers who had perfected successful ways to avoid unions, a state that was unwilling or unable to temper employer power, a changed NLRB that was no longer fitted to the workplace structures or employers' actions, the lack of active progressive

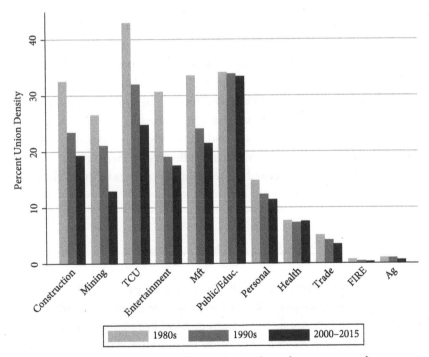

Figure 4.1 Dis-regulated period: Union density by industry, average by subperiod.

TCU, transportation, communication, and utilities; Mft, manufacturing; Public administration/Educ, public administration and education; Personal, personal services; Trade, wholesale and retail trade; FIRE, finance, insurance, and real estate; Ag, agriculture, fisheries, and forestry.

union leadership (Stepan-Norris and Zeitlin 2003) until the revitalization efforts beginning in the mid-1990s, and finally, as both a reaction to the new terrain and a contribution to creating it, unions' inability to enact successful strikes (indicated by an overall decline in the strike rate).

Membership declines led unions to pursue mergers, which oftentimes resulted in struggling unions joining stronger ones. With more union mergers and fewer new union foundings, the number of federated unions hit their lowest mark since 1900. At the beginning of the last century, there were 82 American Federation of Labor (AFL) unions; by mid-century (1957), there were 139 AFL-CIO affiliates; and by 2015, the AFL-CIO had only 56 member unions and its new rival, Change to Win, had 4 affiliates. As mentioned earlier, the lack of competition between unions is associated with lower union density (Stepan-Norris and Southworth 2010).

The dis-regulated period constitutes a coherent set of legal, political, and economic conditions that began to develop in the mid- to late twentieth century. This chapter describes the state and macro context, replacement costs, union and employer strategies, and race and gender dynamics that elucidate industry differences in union density during this period. As it demonstrates, the upper hand gained by employers in the postwar period (especially with the passage of the Taft-Hartley Act in 1947) accumulated employers' power, with drastic outcomes for workers and unions. In response, union efforts devolved to mainly defensive and fairly unsuccessful strategies to protect their positions. By the end of this period, some union revitalization occurred, though these efforts barely moved the needle on membership numbers. By then, union density had receded to levels similar to those of the unregulated period of the early 1900s.

The State and Macro Context

This section details how during the dis-regulated period, 1980–2015, the state, prompted by employers, acted to dismantle a series of workers' and unions' legal and economic protections that had been put into place during the regulated period. As we discuss below, employers and their organizations actively pushed for many of these changes, thereby tilting the terrain once again in their favor. Together, this new context served to undermine unions' positions and accounts for much of the union decline we witness during the dis-regulated period.

U.S. Labor Legislation and the Courts

The dis-regulated period saw little federal legislation, either for or against unions. Despite the major changes to the economy and the workforce, labor–management relations were mostly governed by the laws passed during the regulated period (NLRA and the Taft-Hartley Act). One important exception was the 1974 amendment to the NLRA to include private sector hospitals (with a strike prohibition unless unions gave the required notice).

Employment law, which focuses on the rights of individual workers, rose parallel to labor legislation. This class of legislation rests on the employment-at-will doctrine, which allows employees to be fired for any reason. In return, employees are free to quit at any time. This doctrine leaves workers in structurally powerless positions with regard to their employers. Employment law addresses this issue to some degree by adding restrictions to the employment-at-will doctrine through workplace safety, child labor, social security, protections in the workplace, employment standards, pay equity, employment discrimination, and the like. The Social Security Act (1935), the Fair Labor Standards Act (1938), the Equal Pay Act (1963), and the Civil Rights Act (1964, and its extension to cover age discrimination in 1967), discussed in Chapter 3, fit into this category. Three new laws adding to employment law during the dis-regulated period are the Americans with Disabilities Act (1990), the Family and Medical Leave Act (1993), which provided for twelve weeks of job-protected and unpaid family and medical leave for covered employees, and the Pension Protection Act (2006), which strengthened protections of workers' pensions. Employment law refers to workers' rights as individuals, and it is orthogonal to the concept of workers' collective rights under unionism (Budd 2008). As employment law expanded, workers acquired an alternative avenue to union-based collective action: they could file class-action law suits against employers for offenses such as racial discrimination and potentially win large compensation claims. The rise of rights consciousness most likely contributed to a decline of class solidarity and trade unionism (Lichtenstein 2002).

While organizing federal and state public workers began decades before, federal law governing these efforts began in 1962 with President Kennedy's Executive Order, which along with subsequent developments were codified into the 1978 Civil Service Reform Act. In the 1960s and 1970s, many states passed collective bargaining laws to structure employment relations (Dixon 2020; Goldfield 1989b).

While more restrictive, the Civil Service Reform Act essentially corresponds to the NLRA for most federal public sector workers, with the Federal Labor Relations Authority administering elections and unfair labor practices. The main differences include a strict prohibition against strikes for most occupations and sometimes the exclusion of wages and benefits from bargaining (Budd 2008, chapter 5).

Labor relations for other public (state and municipal) workers are governed by state laws and courts. State laws vary and changed considerably during the dis-regulated period. Some allowed for collective bargaining for all government occupations (these are called comprehensive laws, which were in place in twenty-five states in 2008); some allowed for collective bargaining for only some occupations (these narrow laws were in place in sixteen states in 2008); some had no laws (eight states had no laws in 2008); and some had laws prohibiting collective bargaining (only one state in 2008). Most state laws covering state and municipal workers prohibited strikes altogether (Budd 2008).

These state-level laws contributed to reshaping labor relations in the public sector. In the 1960s, only 2 percent of public workers worked within a legal framework of "duty to bargain." By the 2010s, that percent had soared to 62.8 percent. Zero percent had the right to strike or binding arbitration in the 1960s. By the 2010s, around 20 percent had obtained strike rights and 10 percent had binding arbitration (Keefe 2015). In terms of states, twenty-three states had no laws regarding public workers' strikes in 1969; by 2014, all states had some laws. The state trend regarding strikes was toward their prohibition: in 1969, seventeen states prohibited strikes in all five categories; in 2014, thirty-two did.[1]

Pro-Employer Legislation, Court Decisions, and Case Law

So-called right-to-work laws empower employers by prohibiting union and agency shop agreements. Their passage is associated with increased union free-riding (from 6 to 10 percent),[2] reductions in union organizing, and NLRB election success. Right-to-work laws were estimated to decrease unionization by an estimated 5–8 percent in the states where they are passed

---

[1] Figures are compiled from Valletta and Freeman (1988) and Sanes, Milla, and Schmitt (2014).

[2] Free-riding is when workers do not join the union but benefit from its representation of them in the workplace.

(Moore 1998). The struggle to pass right-to-work laws as well as those constraining public workers' rights was initiated by employer groups on a state-by-state basis, beginning in the 1940s, and ramped up in the union-strong states beginning in the 1950s. Dixon (2020) demonstrates that unions' success in union-strong states depended on their ability to attract influential allies and build broad coalitions, as well as employers' missteps in campaigns.

Right-to-work laws continued to expand during the dis-regulated period. Twelve states passed right-to-work laws affecting private sector workers in the 1940s; six additional states added laws in the 1950s; only one additional state added a law in each of the following three decades (1960s, 1970s, and 1980s). No additional states added laws until Oklahoma in 2001, and then five additional states in the 2010s. So right-to-work laws were in place in nineteen states before the 1980s, and between 1980 and 2017, five more states added such laws; importantly, these included the former union strongholds of Michigan, Wisconsin, and Indiana, bringing the total to twenty-five (half of all states). While this development was well underway during the second half of the regulated period, it gained substantial momentum during the dis-regulated period.

The accumulation of case law developed through NLRB and court decisions were also crucial over time. Of continuing importance in the dis-regulated period were the Mackay doctrine (allowed replacement workers), the Borg-Warner doctrine (distinguished among mandatory, permissive, and illegal bargaining issues), the Excelsior list (required employers to provide unions with a list of workers), and Weingarten rights (gave members' right to representation at a meeting with employers).[3] A Clinton-era decision extended the Weingarten right to non-union employees and a Bush-era decision (2004) retracted non-union workers coverage of the right (Budd 2008).

NLRB case law continued to develop in a way that benefited employers over the dis-regulated period. While the NLRB is not intended to be political, many of the most consequential decisions have been split along party lines. One crucial decision involved determining the balance between employers' property rights and workers' rights (Wright Line test, decided in 1980).[4] This decision outlined the distinction between employers' right to discipline and discharge workers and workers' right to union activities without discipline.

---

[3] See Chapter 3 for a full description of these decisions.

[4] Under this test, the NLRB General Counsel must demonstrate that the disciplined employee was engaging in protected activity, the employer knew this, and disciplined the employee due to this activity. The employer must demonstrate that the discipline was not due to the protected activity.

Another important decision during this period articulated workers' rights to refrain from joining a union by paying only partial dues, even if the union had secured a union shop clause (Beck rights, 1988). This decision put unions at a disadvantage vis-à-vis employers and made them susceptible to free-riders (because unions are required by the principle of exclusive representation in federal labor law to represent non-union workers in collective bargaining and in their grievances).[5]

Although we end our analysis in 2015, we note that the courts continued to erode workers' and unions' rights immediately afterward. In 2018, the Supreme Court further reduced union security by overruling a forty-year precedent in *Janus vs. State, County, and Municipal Employees*, which had required all non-union members at covered workplaces to pay their fair share of union costs. Now unions must bargain for and represent nonmembers without any compensation from them. And, in 2021, the Supreme Court fortified employers' property rights even further in its Cedar Point Nursery decision, which overturned union organizers' right to enter workplaces to recruit union members.

Strike Restrictions

Added restrictions to the right to strike over the years made it increasingly difficult for workers to strike legally. A full 80 percent of public sector workers lacked the right to strike by the 2010s (Keefe 2015). Private sector workers were subject to provisions that they agreed to in collective bargaining agreements (namely, the no-strike clause) as well as rules that governed the purpose of the strike, the timing of the strike, and strikers' conduct. The NLRB interpreted the rules, which had high stakes for workers (reinstatement and back pay on the positive side, dismissal on the negative side). When strikes were deemed lawful, they fell into two categories. The first was economic strikes, which concerned wages, hours, and working conditions. Workers involved in economic strikes continued as employees and were protected against discharge. But this protection was close to meaningless because workers could be permanently replaced by their employers during a strike; and upon its completion, they were not entitled to reinstatement, only to recall when openings occurred. The second type of legal strike concerned

[5] This section relies on Budd (2008).

unfair labor practices. Workers had a higher level of protection during these strikes in that they could be neither discharged nor permanently replaced (assuming that the strike involved no serious striker misconduct). Strikers of either type were entitled to back pay awards by the NLRB if they proved that they were unlawfully denied reinstatement, but any earnings they made in the meantime were deducted from awards (Budd 2008; U.S. NLRB website).

Strikes were deemed "illegal" under certain conditions: when they sought certain objects or purposes (e.g., forcing an employer to discontinue business with another employer), when their timing was not in sync with the requirements (e.g., breaking a no-strike clause or when they failed to satisfy specific strike notification conditions outlined in the NLRA when striking upon contract expiration), and when workers engaged in certain conduct (e.g., violence, threatening violence, or blocking business access). If any of these strikes concerned an unfair practice on the part of the employer, they were legal and classified as unfair labor practice strikes (NLRB website). Specific legislation or executive orders barred many public workers from legally striking.

Political Context

During the late twentieth and early twenty-first centuries, the Democratic and Republican Parties alternated occupying the White House. The House and Senate also alternated among divided, Democrat, and Republican control. In comparison to the earlier periods, presidents and governors intervened in labor disputes less often. With the collapse of unions' use of the strike, the use of the National Guard in labor disputes also dropped: only six incidents occurred (an average of one per year) between 1984 and 1990, the last period for which we have data (Adams 1995, 204).

Appointments to the five-person NLRB and their decisions became more partisan during the dis-regulated period (Flynn 2000). At the start of the dis-regulated period, Reagan appointed individuals with management backgrounds to lead the NLRB, and afterward, its rulings shifted toward employers (Dubofsky 1994, 228). Subsequently, appointments typically followed party politics.

Labor's political influence weakened during this period, both in terms of unions' ability to deliver workers' turnout in elections and the proportion voting Democratic (Form 1995). During the 1990s, the AFL-CIO reinvigorated its political efforts by creating a political training institute. In alliance with community organizations, unions made some progress (e.g., on living wage campaigns) and beat back certain regressive legislation, but they did not succeed in making a major difference. Even more so than in the regulated period, union contributions to Democratic campaigns were not reciprocated by Democratic office holders. Although several attempts were made to reverse anti-union legislation and case law, none made meaningful progress (Zieger and Gall 2002). The most important of these efforts was organized labor's sponsorship of the ultimately unsuccessful Employee Free Choice Act (EFCA), which sought to dramatically change three aspects of the NLRA: to substitute card check for secret ballot elections;[6] to increase employers' penalties for violating labor law and to increase workers' relief; and to institute mandatory interest arbitration after failed bargaining.

Employers also became more politically active beginning in the late 1970s and pursued a broad-reaching set of legislative and legal interpretation changes, including limiting workers' rights to organize and collectively bargain under the NLRA, enhancing the rights of replacement workers, dismantling social welfare, expanding right-to-work laws, pursuing privatization (schools, prisons, services), and initiating legislation that constrained public worker unions. Employers' efforts to elect Republicans to states offices and to the U.S. presidency had tangible effects on the reduction in union density in states and nationwide (Jacobs and Dixon 2010).

Deregulation, pursued by both Democratic and Republican office holders, was devastating for workers (and, in many cases, employers) in trucking, rail, airlines, and utilities. It seriously compromised transportation unions in trucking and airlines by sharply reducing the number of unionized firms in operation and significantly reducing non-union workers' wages (Henrickson and Wilson 2008).

The Economy

The dis-regulated period also saw growing levels of inequality. Top executives' pay soared. In 1978, CEO to average worker pay ratio was 31 to 1; in 1995, it was 188 to 1; and by 2019, it was 320 to 1 (Mishel and Kandra 2020). During

---

[6] "Card check" refers to situations in which employers agree to remain neutral and accept the union if a majority of workers sign cards indicating that they favor union representation.

this period, rises in productivity far surpassed increases in average wages, and the stagnant minimum wage was not adequate to cover basic living costs by the end of the period (Bivens and Mishel 2015). Scholars point to the decline of unions as one major contributor to these growing inequalities (Western and Rosenfeld 2011).

At the macro level, the period is characterized by relative economic stability, with several recessions, including the Great Recession of 2008. The temporary help industry, which is considered a leading indicator of employment cycles, reached an all-time high in 2015 (Ghanbari and McCall 2016). Unemployment vacillated, but declined overall, and inflation dramatically declined from its high in the regulated period (but began to reemerge in the late 1980s to a period of sustained and substantial inflation, 2.9 percent consumer price index [CPI] average annual increase; Reed 2014). Benefits became a larger portion of the compensation package, and as health insurance costs rose, unions and employers clashed over benefit costs. The workforce had become considerably more educated, had more immigrants, and had grown more diverse. Child labor had mostly ended. Along with these changes, technology advanced again with the widespread use of computer and communications developments.

In the dis-regulated period, the percent of the world's economic output involved in international trade greatly expanded. Whereas the United States had a positive trade balance before 1970, since 1976, it has had a yearly negative balance of payments in goods (Ghanbari and McCall 2016). Increased international production and competition put pressures on job security and social welfare benefits for U.S. workers. The North American Free Trade Agreement (NAFTA) (1994), backed by the Democratic Clinton administration as well as Republicans, created a trilateral trade block among the United States, Canada, and Mexico. The Economic Policy Institute estimates that 700,000 U.S. jobs were eventually lost, mostly in manufacturing, as production moved to Mexico, with only small upticks in newly created jobs from the deal (Faux 2013). NAFTA, and other trade agreements from this deregulated era, smoothed the flow of capital, while depowering workers. They provided workers with few protections and gave employers ample opportunity to seek capital flight from union strongholds.

In the postwar period, constraints on employers' ability to relocate in search of lower labor costs reduced (challenges in transportation, communication, technology, and logistics all declined) and the incentives (conglomerations, more favorable tax and tariff regulations, recessions, and

international competition) increased. The courts decided that firm relocation was outside the purview of collective bargaining.

Labor Force Shifts

Employment rose in most industries, with especially large increases in
health, trade, and public administration/education. Manufacturing, which
dominated employment during the regulated era, experienced persistent
decline, especially in apparel (which lost 86 percent of its employment
since 1990) (Ghanbari and McCall 2016). Mining fluctuated in response to
changing energy prices (Ghanbari and McCall 2016) and agriculture held
steady. Figure 4.2 shows that of the major industries we examine, public
administration/education and trade had the highest levels of employment
and mining the lowest by the end of the dis-regulated period, and that

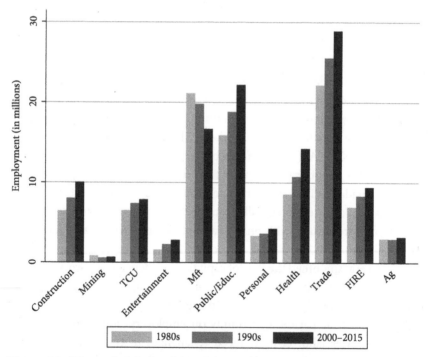

Figure 4.2 Dis-regulated period: Employment by industry, average by
subperiod.

manufacturing had experienced a major decline in employment during the period.

Craft workers continued to be mainly concentrated in construction, and to a lesser extent in TCU, mining, and manufacturing, industries traditionally dominated by white workers who were, for the most part, male. Technical and professional workers continued to concentrate in public administration/education, health services, and to a lesser extent, entertainment. Public administration/education and health, with large numbers of women workers and workers of color, began to constitute a considerable proportion of unionized workers during this period. Figure 4.3 shows the percent skilled and technical/professional workers by industry.

As the workforce expanded, the demographic composition of industries shifted considerably from the earlier twentieth century. Women's labor force participation increased dramatically during this period: from 51.5 percent in 1980 to its peak of 60 percent in 1999, then declined to 56.7 percent in 2015.

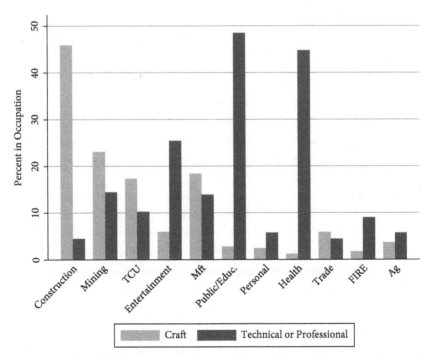

Figure 4.3 Dis-regulated period: Percent of the workforce characterized as craft or technical/professional occupations, average for period.

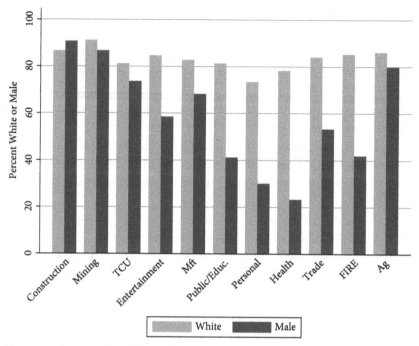

Figure 4.4 Dis-regulated period: Percent of the workforce characterized as white or male, average for period.

The Equal Pay Act (1963) required employers to pay women the same wages for the same work,[7] but women's wages as a percentage of men's did not begin to increase until the early 1980s. Full-time women's median weekly earnings as a percentage of men's moved considerably, from 64 percent in 1980 to 81 percent in 2015 (BLS 2017b).

Figure 4.4 reports industrial concentrations by race and gender averaged over the period. White men continued to make up the majority of the workforce, but declined as a percentage of workers in all industries except for personal service. Women had particularly high employment in public administration/education (59 percent women), personal service (70 percent), health (77 percent), and FIRE (58 percent), and were just under half in trade (47 percent) and entertainment (42 percent).

---

[7] The act did not address comparable worth, which refers to the practice of paying lower wages for traditionally "women's work."

Workers of color (Black, Native American, Hispanic, Asian and Pacific Islander) increased their proportion of the workforce in all industries. Personal services continued to have the highest percent of workers of color during this period (27 percent), followed by health (22 percent), TCU, and public administration and education (19 percent each). Full-time earnings inequality by race and ethnicity increased slightly during the dis-regulated period. In 1980, Black workers earned 79 percent and Latinx workers 78 percent of white workers' median weekly wages. In 2015, the comparable percentages were 77 percent and 72 percent, respectively (Boone 2015; Gifford 1990; U.S. BLS Reports 2017a).

Replacement Costs

The Green Light for Replacing Striking Workers

Throughout this period, it became increasingly easy for employers to replace workers who struck or threatened collective actions. This shift in power occurred in multiple ways, as we describe below. While it is rare that a single incident changes the direction of labor relations, one strike sent a dramatic message to employers that they could replace striking workers with more confidence. The August 1981 Professional Air Traffic Controllers Organization (PATCO) strike carried important implications; some even claim that it was "the most significant single event in accelerating the decline of organized labor in the United States in the late 20th century" (McCartin 2006b, 215).

Upon election, Ronald Reagan advanced neoliberal conservatism and economic restructuring, along with a new state-driven aggression against striking workers. His handling of the PATCO strike provided employers with a powerful symbolic message that the decades ahead belonged to them. Employers were eager to assume their new empowered role.

PATCO was a relatively new union in the public sector and, like all federal unions, its workers did not have the legal right to strike. It previously conducted "sick outs" to avoid this restriction, with only minor negative ramifications. But accumulated grievances around pay and the stress associated with an excessively long work week, along with a management that was non-responsive to workers' needs, led to the strike. The workers voted down

Reagan's offer, and Reagan, using troops, federal marshals, and judicial writs, acted swiftly to break the strike and the union.[8] Two days after the walkout, he fired all 11,350 striking controllers and replaced them with a combination of retired and active military personnel, new civilian recruits, and other strike breakers. Reagan's rhetoric, depicting strikers as disloyal citizens who unfairly leveraged their power over air traffic to bilk the American people, was reminiscent of that of earlier hostile Republican presidents (like Grover Cleveland during the Pullman strike and Warren Harding during the 1920s). Reagan's actions sent a clear message to employers that solidified the growing acceptance of employers' strike-breaking tactics: using state power, existing laws, and especially replacement workers, employers could have things go their way.

In addition, cumulative advantages accrued to employers as the rights of replacement workers continued to be secured during the dis-regulated period; these included permanent rights to their jobs, their right to vote in NLRB elections in the aftermath of strikes, and the withdrawal of replaced strikers' right to vote in those elections after twelve months. Employers continued to use union avoidance firms for advice and persistently committed unfair labor practices (which carried only small penalties) to gain the upper hand during strikes.

Employers Ramp Up the Use of Replacement Workers

In the early 1980s, employers began to use replacement workers (or the threat of replacing workers) more extensively compared to the regulated era (LeRoy 1995a). In 1994, the AFL-CIO collected the names of twenty thousand permanently displaced workers to present to the Senate during one of its discussions regarding changing the replacement worker law. With concerted employer counterefforts, the discussion went nowhere (LeRoy 1995b). Employers continued to send a strong signal that they were willing to pursue this strategy to prevent unions from forming in new workplaces and to bust existing unions. Workers took notice, and strikes dropped sharply, as we show later in this chapter.

---

[8] Reagan offered the union small gains during a time when most unions were accepting concessions. The proposed deal also "broke new ground by getting the FAA to bargain over compensation" (McCartin 2006a, 221).

What do we know about strike replacements? LeRoy (1995b) considered 292 NLRB-adjudicated decisions between 1938 and 1994 regarding strike replacements to document their frequency and variations in the types of violations over time. He found that some cases occurred every year since 1938, but their frequency increased sharply after 1982. NLRB rulings for six types of violations demonstrated the following patterns. First, employers violated the 1968 ruling that required economic strikers to be placed on re-instatement lists, in more than half of the cases in the first seven years after the ruling; but in later years (1982–1991), violations fell to 12.5 percent of cases. Fewer violations over time didn't help workers because reinstate-ment lists don't help during slack labor markets. Violations of the require-ment to recall strikers on reinstatement lists averaged around 30 percent throughout the entire period. Second, over this period, employers largely eliminated overt discrimination against discharged strikers (down from 17 percent in the early years to 4 percent in the later years). There are two developments of note here: legal advice employers received discouraged overt discrimination; and the courts decided that the alternative strategy of replacing *all* strikers is not a violation, giving employers another pow-erful option. Third, unlawful discharge remained steady around 34 percent, while court decisions may have made it easier to replace strikers. Fourth, preferential treatment for non-strikers declined from 34 percent (1935–1963) to 25 percent (1964–1991). Finally, denying reinstatement to unfair labor practice (ULP) strikers rose slightly, from 11.5 percent (1957–1981) to 14 percent (1982–1991). Overall, LeRoy (1995a, 23) concludes that since 1975–1980, "employers have attempted to expand their right to hire re-placement workers. They have hired permanent replacements more often, concentrated this strategy in settings where previously they had bargained successfully with unions, and violated the very limited rights of replaced strikers in roughly one-third of all cases, notwithstanding their consider-able advantage under Mackay Radio."

Our analysis of LeRoy's data, industry by decade, reveals that the lion's share of strike replacement cases occurred in manufacturing. Although TCU and trade also had a considerable number of cases, manufacturing had the largest number of cases in each decade between 1930 and 1990 and seven times the average of all other industries overall. We also see that the 1980s had approximately double the number of cases compared to the average of all other decades.

Traditional Replacement Costs

Skill Closure Through Apprenticeship Programs

Construction continued to stand out as the industry with the highest proportion of craft-based skilled workers, followed by continuing moderate proportions of craft workers in mining (which dropped sharply over this period), TCU, and manufacturing.

During the dis-regulated period, unions remained actively involved in jointly training most skilled workers in the unionized sector. But the non-unionized sectors favored training programs that were "more flexible, less formal, and use shorter-term methods" (Glover and Bilginsoy 2005, 2). Apprenticeship programs continued to be mainly jointly union-employer run, with Department of Labor and community/technical college participation. Overall, we see that employers became more prominent in apprenticeship training over time, with sole control in many programs (Glover and Bilginsoy 2005).

The Department of Labor (DOL), which oversees the regulation of apprenticeship programs through the National Apprenticeship Act (1937), listed registered (nonmilitary) apprenticeship programs. For 2001, the first year the DOL (2015) provided this data, it reported 35,000 registered apprenticeship training programs (for a partial count including only programs from states that reported). The number of programs declined to 20,910 in 2015 with almost half a million participants. The vast majority during 1996–2003 (75 percent) were in the construction industry, with 11 percent in public administration and 8 percent in manufacturing. Most programs (73 percent) were jointly sponsored and financed (through trust funds) by unions and employers (this estimate may be understated, but the North American Building Trades Unions [2015] similarly estimates 74 percent in joint programs in construction in 2014). This percent varied by trade (e.g., from 46 percent jointly sponsored among electrician programs to 85 percent of carpenters' and 98 percent of structural steel workers' programs).[9] The remaining 27 percent of programs were sponsored and financed solely by employers. The proportion of jointly sponsored programs greatly outweighs

---

[9] Figures are from Glover and Bilginsoy (2005), who analyzed the Department of Labor (DOL) database. It omits data from twenty states that do not fully report to the DOL. They estimate that their data include 65 percent of all programs and may be somewhat biased in favor of employer-run programs.

the percent unionized in the construction industry (25 percent during this period), demonstrating a continued reliance on union participation there. Many programs also coordinated with colleges or universities (including the Meany Center's National Labor College), giving enrollees the opportunity to earn college credits.

Although neither type of program succeeded in attracting large numbers of women, joint programs were slightly more successful, with 3.9 percent women apprentices versus 2.5 percent in employer-sponsored programs. Similarly, they attracted slightly more workers of color (33.2 percent versus 28.9 percent). Joint programs also fared better at graduating women and workers of color. Many pre-apprenticeship programs developed during this period aimed to open more apprenticeship opportunities for women (Hegewisch and Anderson 2018).

In addition, the North American Building Trades Unions (2022) boasted of 1,600 training centers in the United States. In partnership with nonprofit organizations, they promoted apprenticeship readiness programs and used Project Labor Agreements that specified the number of local residents that must be hired on specific projects, both with the aim of diversifying apprentices. Candidates for readiness programs were reviewed by referral committees made up of representatives from training directors, employers/ employer associations, unions, and participating community organizations for acceptance. Once they completed the readiness program, they were often recommended to apprenticeship programs by these same committees (North American Building Trades Unions 2022).

Reducing Workers' Leverage Through Deskilling

Deskilling continued to plague craft workers. Only 41 percent of the construction industry workers had craft skills in 2015—down from 69 percent in 1910. In addition to deskilling (especially craft work), there was also a proliferation of new technical (mostly white-collar) jobs that required similar amounts of training. However, after 1990, there was a shift away from middle-skilled jobs, from 58 percent in 1981 to 44 percent in 2011, primarily due to automation and capital flight (Scopelliti 2014). Mining (especially coal) was particularly hard-hit by changing technology and the industry's geographical movement to discover new natural resources as existing ones were depleted. With disintegrated unions in abandoned areas and inadequate union organizing in the new locations, density declined (Goldfield 2007).

Timing Continues To Be a Source of Workers' Power
The same industries that had timing advantages in the earlier periods continued to benefit from them during the dis-regulated period. Workers in
TCU (e.g., longshore and rail workers), as well as in health services (e.g.,
doctors and nurses), public administration/education (e.g., teachers and
mail carriers), and entertainment (e.g., professional athletes and actors) continued to have timing on their side. But the timing advantage is most effective
when put to test in strikes; as strikes declined, this advantage became less
impactful.

Spatial Issues: The Declining Importance of Isolation
In an increasingly interconnected world, employment isolation of the miners
enjoyed in the early twentieth century continued to become less important. The United Mine Workers (UMW) severely declined during the dis-
regulated period due to mechanization, severely fluctuating employment
levels, and mass layoffs. Still, miners dramatically continued to exercise their
right to strike often throughout the 1980s.

"New" Replacement Cost Factors

A host of "new" replacement costs became increasingly relevant during the
dis-regulated period. Many of these had roots in the early period, but they
were accelerated during this period due to new technologies, the organization of work, the political and economic context, and specific strategies
embraced by employers and unions.

Capital Flight and Worker Displacement
Capital flight continued to significantly reduce employment in the industries
where unions had the largest strongholds, especially manufacturing. In the
dis-regulated period, employers in some industries increasingly adopted
this strategy of capital flight—or what Silver (2003) calls the "spatial fix."
Employers had long considered a number of factors in deciding plant
locations, including the volatility of local labor relations. But as unionization
grew in the regulated period, employers sought to actively avoid areas where
unions, especially Congress of Industrial Organizations (CIO) unions, were
strong and militant. Collectively, employer decisions to relocate targeted
various sites where cheaper labor could be utilized, until union militancy

there raised its price. Silver (2003) documents the movement of production facilities and shortly thereafter, worker militancy, in auto production from North America to first northwestern and then southern Europe (1960s and 1970s), followed by destinations in newly industrializing nations (1980s and 1990s), including Argentina, South Africa, Brazil, and South Korea. The trade deals of the dis-regulated era, like NAFTA, helped to smooth the ability of employers to take advantage of capital flight.

Within the United States, employers relocated operations from the union-strong Frostbelt to the union-sparse Sunbelt, devastating communities along the way (Bluestone and Harrison 1982). Besides actual geographical moves, employers' threats to move also reduced unions' leverage. One estimate during the mid-1990s found that employers threatened to close plants in 50 percent of all union certification elections, and nearly 12 percent followed through with these threats and shut down part or all of the plant before the first contract was reached (Bronfenbrenner 1997).

The immediate result of capital flight was long-term displaced workers. Worker displacement soared in highly unionized industries, while the new jobs created were non-union (Bronfenbrenner and Luce 2004). The Bureau of Labor Statistics (BLS) collected information on workers experiencing long-term displacement and reported the reasons for displacement, including plant closings, insufficient work, and their position/shift was abolished (Helwig 2004). In the early 1980s, the displacement rate was by far the highest in mining (nearly 14 percent), followed by manufacturing and construction (close to 8 percent each). The last year of available data was for 2000, and rates had dropped somewhat for these industries, but still remained above average. By contrast, public administration/education had minimal displacement rates, under 1.5 percent, from 1982 to 2000. Trade, which became the largest employment group during the dis-regulated period, had about average displacement, from 3 to 5 percent from 1981 to 2000. Although we don't have industry breakdowns, in 1986 plant closings accounted for 55 percent, and in 1996 they accounted for 44 percent of displaced workers. Records of mass layoffs (a slightly different measure) in 1985 reveal that they were approximately equally likely to have occurred in union and non-union establishments.

Double-breasting is another locational strategy designed to undercut union work. Double-breasting is when unionized employers shift work to a non-union location, running both union and non-union operations, to avoid collective bargaining commitments or strikes. Originating in the construction industry, this gambit became more widespread in other industries beginning in the mid-1970s. Because the NLRA does not have the power to restrict the practice, employers have been free to apply it at will—to the determent of organized labor (Marsh 1999).[10]

Licensing and Credentialing

As in the regulated period, credentialing and licensing represented an alternative to closure through apprenticeships. With the proportions of high school graduates in the population increasing from 69 percent in 1980 to 87 percent in 2010 (Fisk 2003), vocational training was possible on a larger scale. Supported by the Chamber of Commerce and the American Council on Education, it was boosted by federal government funds starting in the 1960s and 1970s. Community colleges now provided skills training in many trades, leading to associate arts or science (AA/AS) degrees (e.g., in healthcare, business, engineering) as well as short-term (mostly in healthcare and computer science) and long-term certificates (mostly in healthcare, business, and mechanics). The rise of community college training meant that employers were now responsible only for on-the-job training. During the dis-regulated period, community college enrollment soared (Pincus 1980).

In this period, professional/technical skills continued to be most prevalent in public administration/education (average of 50 percent of the workforce) and health (45 percent), with moderate proportions in entertainment (27 percent) and mining and manufacturing (with about 15 percent each). Training for these skill categories continued to occur primarily in higher education (community colleges and universities). For example, nursing required either an associate's or bachelor's degree, and public sector teaching required a bachelor's degree; in addition, both required credentials or licenses. By the end of this period, the BLS reports that two-thirds of labor force members had at least some college education (Brundage 2017).

Similar to craft-based apprenticeship programs, licensing requirements (of classroom time, competency tests, and on-the-job training) created closure on behalf of workers. Unions and occupational licensing had similar effects on relative wages, causing a 10 to 15 percent increase. And just as unions confronted employers' anti-union sentiments, licensing requirements faced some (mostly unsuccessful) resistance from opponents who argued that licensing inhibits job growth. Since the vast majority of

---

[10] Unfortunately, we do not have industry-wide data on double-breasting.

licensing requirements were accomplished through state-level legislation, "de-licensing" required additional legislation. Occupational groups and their lobbying arms were able to stave off de-licensing attempts, at least through the dis-regulated period (Thornton and Timmins 2015).

In 2015 (the first year the BLS reported these data), 25 percent of employees had certificates (3.1 percent) or licenses (22.4 percent). They were most common among workers in education and health services (47 percent), government (39 percent of state and 47 percent of local, but only 25 percent of federal) workers, and financial activities (32 percent) (note that the industry classifications differ from ours) (U.S. BLS 2015a). Because licenses were normally required to perform the work involved in these jobs, they provided some closure for workers and unions who organized them, and therefore power vis-à-vis employers.

During the regulated period, professionals, who commanded high replacement costs, began to move into the union fold, and they continued to play an important role in boosting union density in industries where they worked during the dis-regulated period. But professional and licensed workers oftentimes had some supervisory responsibilities. While the NLRA allowed supervisors to join unions, the Taft-Hartley Act prohibited them from doing so. The distinction between worker and supervisor was hazy. It was unclear how much time a worker must spend supervising others before being considered a supervisor. During the dis-regulated period, NLRB rulings broadened the definition of supervisor to include more employees, rendering them ineligible for union membership. Employment increased dramatically during the dis-regulated period in the heavily professional and licensed healthcare industry (which experienced much anti-union aggression) and in the public sector (with less employer aggression), and union density only managed to remain relatively steady.

Financialization and Mega-Corporations

Financialization, or the increasing reliance of nonfinancial firms on finance, increased considerably during the 1980s and 1990s, especially in manufacturing. Since the late 1970s, U.S. corporations realized a higher proportion of their revenue from financial income. This shift decoupled firms' surplus generation from production, affording more power to employers and elite workers vis-à-vis other workers. This trend was likely associated with employers' eroding support for welfare state development (Krippner 2005), less investment in fixed capital, increasing earning inequality among workers, a decrease in labor's share of income, and, potentially, a decline in unionization (Lin and Tomaskovic-Devey 2013).

We do not analyze financialization by industry, but we do flag it as another potential way that employers, with deep pockets and profits that are not based on production or services, likely gain power. These sorts of profits help to ease the financial impact of strikes, allowing companies to withstand collective action, even when workers successfully stop production.

Along with financialization, the dis-regulated period also saw the rise of what some call "mega-corporations." These mega-corporations tended to have bundles of features that made them difficult to organize (Rajendra 2022). They typically employed large numbers of workers, which often included workers at multiple worksites (e.g., Walmart, which employed over 1 percent of the workforce by the close of the period), franchised arrangements (e.g., McDonalds), and complex layers of subcontracting (e.g., Amazon). They also often had multiple sources of revenue, including from financialization, and were able to withstand substantial financial pressures. And they tended to hold a significant place in our everyday lives (e.g., Facebook) and had strong lobbying arms. By the close of the dis-regulated period unions had not organized these mega-corporations.

Fissured Workplaces, Contingent Work, and Subcontracting

The dis-regulated period also saw the rise of new work arrangements that shifted the risk from firms to workers. "Fissuring" is a process that includes the use of subcontracting as well as the expansion of franchising, in which corporations, such as McDonald's, franchise out individual establishments. These arrangements placed the risk, as well as the responsibility of abiding by labor laws, on the franchisee. Consequently, franchised establishments had higher levels of labor law violations (Weil 2014).

Companies also transferred risk by embracing "alternative" work arrangements, which include part-time and on-call workers, temporary help (where the temporary agencies are the legal employers), workers employed through (sub) contracted companies (who supervise their workers to some extent), and independent contractors or freelancers. Some companies also embraced a business model of high turnover, which minimizes attachment to the firm (Leonhardt 2021). These arrangements externalized employment outside of the firm and minimized the number of workers eligible for the protections of internal labor markets.[11] These arrangements also reduced

[11] Internal labor markets refer to administrative systems (rules and procedures) within firms that specify routes for employees' upward mobility within the firm.

employers' costs by lowering administrative and training requirements and transferring fixed costs and risks to workers.

Subcontracting was one strategy corporations used to insulate themselves from potential labor disputes and to keep labor costs down. Subcontracted workers did not bargain—or strike—with the lead firm where they actually worked and who held the power. In many cases, lead firms dropped subcontractors during labor disputes and gave their business to non-union firms. Such a triangular employment relationship, whereby the legal employer was the subcontractor and vied for contracts with lead firms, made traditional union organizing difficult. For example, janitors and security guards moved from largely in-house to subcontracted work during the 1980s and 1990s (Dube and Kaplan 2010). Not surprisingly, many of these marginalized workers were women, workers of color, and immigrants. Several high-profile campaigns, including Justice for Janitors (begun in 1990) and the Coalition for Immokalee Workers (begun in 1993 with farmworkers in Florida), developed innovative ways to address these imbalances, including codes of conduct, striking for recognition, boycotts, reclassification, and forms of symbolic protest (Chun 2011). Some of these campaigns purposefully sought to circumvent the restraints of NLRB elections, allowing them to use tactics that are otherwise prohibited, like secondary boycotts. On balance, though, organizing subcontractors in the United States remained challenging and had limited success in the dis-regulated period.

In general, workers with these alternative employment arrangements faced a harder road to unionization. Part-time workers were often not eligible for full benefits and were generally less engaged in the firms for which they worked, including union organizing efforts. Independent contractors were excluded from labor protections enshrined in the NLRA. Some industries that used to be highly unionized moved to independent contractors, including truck driving (Viscelli 2016). Platform-based gig workers, such as Uber or InstaCart workers, were also independent contractors and not covered by standard labor laws—at least during the dis-regulated period. Thereafter, these issues have shown up on state ballot initiatives and in court cases. Temporary or contingent workers were employed by firms other than the lead firms for which they provided labor and were thereby not eligible to join the unions organized at their actual workplaces.

Until 1985, the National Association of Temporary Services prohibited its members from supplying strike replacements. But when the Federal Trade Commission under the Reagan presidency complained that the ban constituted an illegal restraint of trade, the association dropped it (Hatton 2014). An examination of all labor-management disputes involving temporary agency workers as reported in seventy NLRB decisions between 1984 and 2010 discovered four ways that employers used temporary workers to obstruct unions. First, during organizing campaigns, employers replaced union supporters with temporary workers and also used temporary workers to directly disrupt NLRB certification elections. Second, in unionized firms, employers replaced union members with temporary workers in attempts to weaken unions. Third, during contract negotiations, employers replaced or threatened to replace striking workers with temporary workers or locked out workers and replaced them with temporary workers to increase the economic pressure on unions. And, fourth, employers used temporary workers to harass workers, especially during strikes (Hatton 2014).

How much movement toward these alternative work arrangements occurred during the dis-regulated period? The most prevalent form of nonstandard work was part-time work, which typically offered lower wages and fewer fringe benefits. Part-time work was most heavily utilized in retail, education and health, and leisure and hospitality. It fluctuated with recessions, but it seemed to have slowly increased during the dis-regulated period. In 1980, estimates put part-time work at about 18 percent of total employment, compared to a little under 20 percent in 2011 (Valletta and Bengali 2013).

Temporary help agencies began offering their services in the 1920s, but they supplied an insignificant part of the workforce until the 1970s, when the annual growth rate of temporary workers grew to 11 percent (compared to a 2 percent growth rate for all non-farm employment). In 1972, temporary workers constituted less than .3 percent of the U.S. workforce; by 1998, it was 2.5 percent. In effect, temporary agencies began to provide a reserve army of labor (Kalleberg 2000), thereby reducing unions' leverage during tight labor markets and strikes. Katz and Krueger (2019) define alternative work as temporary help agency workers, on-call workers, contract workers, and independent contractors and freelancers. Using a supplemental survey of the Current Population Survey (CPS) conducted in 1995 and 2005, they estimate rates of alternative work in the 10 percent range during this period, with some indications that those numbers slightly increased by 2015 (rising 1–2 percentage points between 2005 and 2015). According to the president of the SEIU, "there are now five times more American workers who have no legal right to union representation than there are union members covered by contracts" (Rolf 2016, 1–2).

Even though alternative work arrangements only represented a relatively small percentage of workers in the dis-regulated period, they were important in two specific ways: their slowly growing size and the ways in which they were used by employers. Indeed, the "detachment of employees from their employers made it difficult for unions to organize, and the existence of multiple employers provides them with leverage against unions" (Kalleberg 2000, 358). In addition, the increased use of temporary workers to deliberately bust and defuse unions was an important new development in the dis-regulated period. Finally, as the workplace became more geographically dispersed and alternative employment arrangements more common, labor law remained stagnant. Combined, these factors made it increasingly difficult for unions to engage in the once successful multi-employer organizing strategies that were able to set industry-wide standards in the past (Rhinehart and McNicholas 2020).

To sum up, in the previous periods, we considered skill (and apprenticeship), timing, and spatial (workplace isolation) factors as major contributors to replacement costs. In the dis-regulated period, the main spatial factor at work was capital flight (measured through worker displacement). Our measure of traditional replacement cost therefore includes skill (and apprenticeship) and timing and it drops isolation. Our measure of new replacement cost factors include the ones described above for which we have industry-level data: worker displacement (to represent the role of capital flight), licensing/credentialing, and percent contingent workers (we do not have data to capture subcontracting or franchising patterns by industry). These replacement costs are a mix of structural features and the strategies that employers and unions developed and used.

Union and Employer Strategies: Making and Breaking Unions

Employers went on the offensive during the dis-regulated period. They became increasingly proactive in enhancing their positions vis-à-vis workers by continuing to apply new labor-saving technology to the work process, automate, move production away from union strongholds, revise NLRB case law to their benefit, and dis-organize unions. As we discuss in this section, employers were quite successful in their efforts. Workers were far less likely to strike during this period, and employers succeeded in driving back most gains unions made during the regulated period, except for in the public sector.

Employers' Associations Aim to Dis-organize Unions

The developments in the regulated period that led to the decline of union power in apprenticeship programs and the creation of the Business Roundtable expanded even further to serve employers' interests in the dis-regulated period. The Business Roundtable (made up of the CEOs of many of the largest U.S. firms) was central to dis-organizing unions in the building trades and beyond. With the aim of shrinking the union sector, it targeted building trade unions as the source of prohibitively high costs to industrial users by identifying several key issues that allowed unions to maintain power there. These included strikes in vital industries and services, restrictive work practices and resistance to automation and prefabrication, hiring halls, and wage determination. It boosted construction contractors' power through its legislative efforts (seeking to reverse or curb union empowering legislation like the Davis-Bacon Act), providing model collective bargaining clauses for use in their agreements, expanding the legality of double-breasting, and providing aid for strike breaking, decertification elections, and securing non-union workers to work on their projects (Goldfield 1987, 191–192).

Meanwhile, other employers' associations continued to fight for capital. The National Association of Manufacturers (NAM) and the Chamber of Commerce continued with their work. The National Restaurant Association (NRA) was instrumental in organizing employers to keep the minimum wage low and tipped workers at a subminimum wage. All were unified in their opposition to unions. These lobbying efforts saw substantial success at the state level, where they were able enact laws that eroded wages, benefits, job discrimination protections, and union rights (Lafer 2017).

Employers' associations also tended to support the mobility of capital. International trade expanded exponentially during the dis-regulated period, with the help of the 1974 Trade Act and its extensions. The Trade Act gave the executive branch more authority to fast track the reduction of trade disputes and offered relief to U.S. industries and their workers who were negatively affected by increased trade—although, in the end, relief was rarely provided. This act also initiated a set of advisory committees, rooted in trade associations and overwhelmingly staffed by individual members of the corporate community, including members of the Business Roundtable, the Chamber of Commerce, the National Association of Manufacturers, and others (Domhoff 2020). During the 1990s and over the objections of unions and environmental activists, the Business Roundtable played a major role in the further expansion of trade, as manifested in NAFTA and entry into the World Trade Organization (WTO).

Employers' Use of Union Avoidance Firms

As union density increased throughout the regulated period, union-ized employers had greater incentives to reduce the growing gaps between their firms and non-union firms' ability to control production and wages. Employers' efforts to avoid unions spurred the growth of an industry of ex-pensive consultants who refined anti-union tactics, increased their level of sophistication, and tailored them to specific industries. This union avoid-ance industry's four basic types of firms—consultants, law firms, industrial psychologists, and strike management firms—claimed over 90 percent vic-tory rates (Logan 2006). Together with the scope and prevalence of their use and the state's unwillingness to curb their excesses, this effort translated into serious trouble for unions.

While union avoidance has been around since the nineteenth century, a new wave of consultants arose during the 1970s and 1980s. The industry exploded, moving from approximately one hundred active firms during the 1960s to over one thousand active firms in the 1980s. With this growth came a new union-free mindset—the idea that employers were justified in calling for the permanent elimination of unions. To spread the word, the NAM published a collection of union-free statements that employers could insert into their employee handbooks to explain their anti-union position. One company even required workers' signature of acceptance to abide by the anti-union policies and procedures as a condition of employment (like the yellow-dog contract of old). The NLRB ruled the acceptance agreement to be a violation of the NLRA, but not the other anti-union policies and procedures listed in the handbooks (Lissy 1990).

Although unions sought to curb consultants' extreme activities, Reagan's election closed down those options and moved the needle in the opposite direction: under Reagan, the NLRB significantly expanded the possibilities for campaigns involving consultants (Logan 2006). By the early 2000s,

75 percent of employers facing NLRB elections in large workplaces (over fifty employees) employed union avoidance consultants (Bronfenbrenner 2009). Later estimates show that employers spent around $340 million a year for this guidance with the aim to become or remain union-free (McNicholas et al. 2019). Confident in their ability to deliver, consulting firms often based their fees on outcomes, with full payment or bonuses only upon successful completion (a petition withdrawn or an election lost by the union).

Union avoidance law firms, which were often staffed with former NLRB national and regional lawyers who ran seminars, also grew in number and importance during the 1970s and 1980s. They wrote handbooks outlining effective anti-union strategies and partnered with anti-union consultants on campaigns (Logan 2006). With this aid, employers used a range of tactics to thwart union efforts, including delaying elections, changing the bargaining unit after the petition, and discharging workers.

Industrial psychologists also have a long history of advising employers on industrial relations. Again, they grew in importance and sophistication in the 1960s and 1970s, and reached their peak importance in the 1980s. Their forte is screening out potential union supporters before they are hired, by using surveys, identifying and addressing possible union hotspots, ensuring that all firm leaders accept their duty to uphold the union-free climate, and, in general, maintaining non-union environments. These firms have been victims of their own success: by 2006, about half of human relations managers were unconcerned about the union threat and found less need to hire these firms (Logan 2006).

The unregulated period saw a streak of violent strike breaking and abuse at the hands of Pinkerton guards and internal labor relations personnel. In the regulated period, the La Follette Committee exposed these abuses, and the NLRA made them illegal. The strike breaking of the dis-regulated period was more sophisticated, using photography and video documentation and high-tech law enforcement equipment. Sophisticated surveillance methods had become more possible, from monitoring social media to what workers type on their computers (Garden 2018).

Strike management firms, boosted by both the real and symbolic permanent replacement of PATCO strikers in 1981, provided security personnel (mostly recruited from the ranks of former law enforcement officers and veterans) to ensure replacements' ability to work. Some firms also provided struck employers with replacement workers. Likewise, these strike management firms "helped transform economic strikes into a virtually suicidal tactic for U.S. unions, their business has suffered accordingly" (Logan 2006, 667).

Overall, the rise of the sophisticated union avoidance industry hampered and constrained the tactics available to unions, including the use of strikes and successful NLRB election campaigns. As we will see, the number of annual ULPs increased in the 1980s, and annual strikes dramatically declined, as did NLRB elections throughout the period. Unions responded by turning to sanctioned organizing tactics, such as card check recognition and neutrality agreements, or strategies outside of NLRB elections, all of which were less effective than tactics used under the 1930s NLRB rules. The unchecked anti-union consultant industry increased employers' power vis-à-vis workers and unions, and made it much more difficult for unions to maintain density.

The Union Response—Revitalization in the 1990s

Lane Kirkland, the AFL-CIO's new leader in 1979, emphasized the need to reverse Republican success and their anti-union agenda. Yet the resulting push was largely unsuccessful in reversing anti-union trends. By the 1990s, labor activists began working with allies to secure other progressive advances. But even when the Democrats won the White House, Democratic leaders took a cautious approach to reasserting labor rights. Labor made advances with the Family Medical Leave Act (1993); the repeal of the Hatch Act, which prohibited federal workers from partisan political activity; and executive orders concerning government contracting. But in some cases, Democratic presidents oversaw efforts that undermined union strength (as, for instance, with NAFTA or privatization efforts under the Clinton administration) (Zieger and Gall 2002).

Looking to reverse the downward slide of unions under the old AFL-CIO guard, John Sweeney was elected AFL-CIO president in 1995 under the New Voice slate. During his term, he oversaw a vastly expanded role for the federation in organizing (with thousands of new organizers), collective bargaining and strike support, help with pension investments, and innovative programs (like Union Summer, Senior Summer, and Union Cities), as well as internal AFL-CIO modifications to enhance the effectiveness of its political efforts, to diversify its leadership, and to give a long-overdue voice to women (with a new Working Women's Department). In 2000, with the increasing importance of women, workers of color, and immigrants in the workforce and the politics of the AFL-CIO, the federation abandoned its long-standing opposition to "illegal" immigration. Despite these moves, Sweeney fell short of ushering in a profoundly new social justice orientation (Fletcher and Gapasin 2008).

In 2005, a new challenge for further reform came from the New Unity Partnership, which sought to redirect political spending to union organizing, merge small unions, rethink and enforce union jurisdictions to eliminate destructive union raiding, and further reduce the number of AFL-CIO departments. The AFL-CIO response was inadequate in the eyes of the challengers, who created a new labor federation in 2005 called Change to Win. Shortly thereafter, seven unions, most of which were considered to have a social-movement orientation, joined (Teamsters, Laborers, Service Employees International Union [SEIU], Carpenters, Farm Workers, United Food and Commercial Workers [UFCW], and Union of Needletrades, Industrial, and Textile Employees/Hotel Employees and Restaurant Employees [UNITE HERE]). The AFL-CIO lost over five million, or 39 percent, of its members. The big plans for enhanced organizing largely failed to materialize. By 2015, only four unions remained in Change to Win (Teamsters, SEIU, Farm Workers, and Communication Workers), with four and a half million members.

During the dis-regulated period, unions increasingly experimented with a range of tactics to halt or even reverse their decline. In addition to the tactics discussed above, many unions also conducted corporate campaigns. Using this method, unions sought to damage firms' reputations and attract community support for workers' rights in order to pressure employers to bargain (Juravich and Bronfenbrenner 2000). Some also used salting, which involves supporting pro-union workers to apply for jobs at firms that unions seek to organize. In limited numbers, some unions brought back disruption, including striking to win recognition. Other renewed tactics, which we detail below, aimed to expand solidarity within and beyond the workplace, including through alliances, worker centers, campaigns to raise standards for all workers, and reclassification efforts.

Expansive Solidarity: Social Movement Unionism, Worker Centers, and (Re)newed Strategies

After years of decline while pursuing more bureaucratically minded strategies, some unions began in the 1980s to turn toward a social movement orientation reminiscent of the CIO and other earlier unions. In 1984, the SEIU formally affiliated with United Labor Unions (ULU, one such community-labor organization), and several years later, launched its successful Justice for Janitors campaign. HERE also successfully used more militant social movement tactics to organize a considerable number of low-wage workers. These campaigns had substantial top-down (by the national leadership) approaches (Voss and Sherman 2000), which created a dilemma with regard to accomplishing the other crucial component of social movement unionism: the mass mobilization of workers across unions and industries necessary for substantial change (Clawson 2003).

The weakness of organized labor during the dis-regulated period initiated new union thinking on alliance building. Students, clergy, and seniors were deliberately brought into some union organizing campaigns. In addition, unions forged more formal alliances with immigrant rights, environmental, peace, and anti-globalization groups. Yet even as the conditions for calling and winning strikes had become more difficult, union efforts to attract allies were not as frequent as one might expect (only about 25 percent of strikes enlisted allies), and they mostly formed alliances with traditional partners (other unions and politicians) (Dixon and Martin 2012). Still, some unions leaned into social movement alliances, including with the Occupy movement of the early 2010s, where activists used occupations and demonstrations to denounce the growing riches of the top 1 percent (Lewis and Luce 2012).

Worker centers began to appear in the late 1970s. They assumed a variety of structures and had different goals and strategies, but in general, worked outside the NLRA framework to support low-wage workers (most commonly those working in food service, construction, and agriculture) in their communities by organizing, advocating (against wage theft, for example), and providing services to them. They were place-based and tended to have strong racial or ethnic identification and sometimes have affiliations with unions. Worker centers, which the Chamber of Commerce considers "union front groups," grew from 5 in 1992 to 137 in 2006. They provided another way of filling the gap left by union decline (Fine 2006; Milkman and Ott 2014). Around 2006, the AFL-CIO began partnering with worker centers and their networks.

Worker centers demonstrated their importance for supporting workers who were ill-suited for, or excluded from, NLRB elections. They were successful at passing bills of rights (for domestic workers or for fair scheduling), enacting codes of conducts, agitating for improved material conditions, pushing for legislation and local ordinances to support workers, and drawing public attention to how exploitation is organized in the contemporary United States. For the most part, members of worker centers were not unionized. However, this era in labor relations is just beginning to unfold, and we suspect that these centers are still in their infancy, as the fledgling industrial organizations were in the unregulated era.

Other types of community-based organizations also stepped in to fill the void left by union decline. Perhaps the most successful of these was the Association of Community Organizations for Reform Now (ACORN), founded in the 1970s to address economic issues in poor communities. It grew during the 1980s and 1990s, and was a driving force in successful living wage campaigns between 1995 and 2008, but was ultimately destroyed by a scandal that led to its dissolution in 2009.

Other major campaigns that worked mainly outside of the NLRB process began to emerge toward the end of the dis-regulated period. Perhaps the most prominent was "The Fight for Fifteen and a Union" (begun in 2012 and backed by the SEIU), which sought to organize fast-food (and later other low-wage) workers in hundreds of cities with the aim of securing union recognition and raising their hourly wage to $15 per hour. Using a combination of one-day strikes (after which employers are required to allow workers to return to work), media campaigns, and social movement tactics (marches, rallies, and strong allies and coalitions) yielded "stunning successes . . . in changing city and state minimum wage laws" (Ashby 2017, 368). In this way, the campaign succeeded in raising the wage floor for large numbers of workers. However, these multi-employer campaigns have been costly (one estimate is that the SEIU spent $12 million in 2012 alone) and so far have been unsuccessful at bringing in new union members.

Reclassifying Workers to Obtain NLRB Coverage
Some jobs excluded from NLRB jurisdiction experienced tremendous growth during the dis-regulated period. Unions applied tactics (alliances, political brokering, and actions) to press for job reclassification so that they met NLRB jurisdiction rules. Home healthcare workers, for example, compensated by vendors who arranged for care using state funds, were not classified as workers under NLRB jurisdiction. Because they often aid sick or elderly relatives, they sometimes fail to see themselves as workers. The first step these mainly poor women of color took toward securing better conditions was recognizing themselves as workers, followed by a fight for

recognition as public workers using political brokering with the state to accept its co-employer status (Chun 2011; Klein 2020). This effort contributed to a growth in health sector unionization as density was falling in most other sectors. Employers and their allies fought back through the courts, eventually winning a reversal of the hard-fought home healthcare workers' status and have pushed even further toward de-unionization. And the fight goes on.

NLRB Elections and ULPs

Union Elections

Not surprisingly, the overall number of NLRB elections and the workers involved in elections declined drastically during the dis-regulated period. Elections fell from 8,198 in 1980 to 1,639 in 2009 (an 80 percent drop). The number of workers eligible to vote in NLRB elections (which represents the number of possible new union members) also dropped precipitously, from 521,602 in 1980 to 97,134 in 2009 (an 81 percent drop). We see these huge declines as a reflection of the changed terrain of labor struggles. Employers had the upper hand (through degraded laws, the use of anti-union consultants, employment organization that was ill-suited to the NLRB, and for some, the use of capital flight as a threat). In response to this climate, unions focused on elections that they believed they could win. While unions did not organize as ferociously as many labor supporters advocated for during the dis-regulated period, major obstacles created unfavorable conditions. While unions won some large workplaces through standard NLRB elections, many high-profile losses tempered union enthusiasm to run risky campaigns, which would further deplete resources and worker morale.

In part due to their selectivity, the elections that unions did run were relatively successful. Union success in these elections (the percent of voting workers in elections won by unions) improved from 46 percent in 1980 to 64 percent in 2009. Still, the absolute number of new wins declined dramatically from 3,744 in 1980 to only 1,047 in 2009—unions just were not running and winning nearly as many elections as they had in the regulated period. With the drastic decline in the use of the NLRB elections beginning in the 1950s, fewer and fewer new union members were added to union membership in each decade.

At the industry level, the lion's share of elections was in manufacturing, even as elections dramatically dropped in that industry. In 1980, manufacturing had close to 3,500 elections with nearly 300,000 workers eligible to vote. By 2009, there were only 233 elections, with just shy of 19,000 workers eligible to vote. This number represented about .3 percent of all manufacturing workers—down from yearly 4 percent that were eligible to vote in the mid-century. By 2009, more workers were eligible to vote in NLRB elections in TCU than in manufacturing. Manufacturing union election success rates dropped from the regulated period (from 48 percent in the 1970s to around 40 percent thereafter).

Trade also had a large number of elections per year in the 1980s (1,000), and its numbers also dropped precipitously to about 250 in the 2000s. Because employment in trade was higher, the percent participating was even lower than in manufacturing (.2 percent in the 1980s, .1 percent in the 1990s, and .05 percent in the 2000s). Union election success in trade moved slightly upward, from 38 percent in the 1980s to 45 percent in the 2000s (see Figure 4.5).

TCU had a moderate number of NLRB elections, averaging just above five hundred per year during the 1980s, with a decline after 2000, and between .4 and .5 percent of workers involved during the dis-regulated period. The success rate there was in the mid-to-low 40 percent range in the 1980s and 1990s, and jumped to just over 60 percent in the 2000s. Health and construction also had a moderate number of NLRB elections (about 450 and 300 average respectively per year); the percent involved was much higher in health (upward of 1 percent in the 1980s, and down to just under .4 thereafter, compared to around .1 in construction), and the success rates were high (between about 50 and 60 percent) and moved up over the dis-regulated period, especially after 2000.

Mining, entertainment, personal service, and FIRE all had low numbers of NLRB elections (and percentages of workers involved). But when unions attempted to organize in these industries, especially when using reinvigorated strategies, they often succeeded in winning. Success rates were relatively high in FIRE throughout the period (just under 60 percent) and entertainment neared those high rates during the 2000s. Mining win rates remained relatively low (around 40 percent), like those in manufacturing and trade.

Overall, the drastic drop of NLRB activity (especially in manufacturing) over the dis-regulated period is consistent with union density decline. With a climate increasingly favoring employers, unions held far fewer elections. When they engaged in NLRB union elections, they were more likely to face

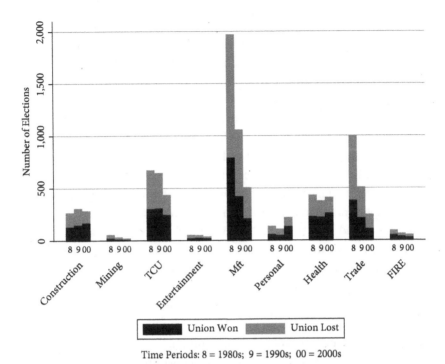

Figure 4.5 Dis-regulated period: Number of NLRB elections and win/loss outcome, average by decade.

Note: Public administration/education and agriculture are excluded because they are mostly not covered by the NLRB.

employers who were equipped with union avoidance consultants (75 percent in units with fifty or more workers). Employers were charged with violating the law in 41.5 percent of NLRB elections (and more often—54.4 percent—in large bargaining units) (McNicholas et al. 2019).

After an NLRB win, the union must secure the first contract. Contrary to common expectations, this outcome is far from automatic. Some unions win elections and never secure a contract. Employers who rely on advice from anti-union firms use a combination of legal and illegal tactics to intimidate workers and cause legal delays and economic retaliation to prevent the first contract from being signed (Lafer and Loustaunau 2020). Even when unions managed to win elections, their chances of negotiating a first contract declined in the dis-regulated period. Whereas in the 1950s, 86 percent of successful elections resulted in first contracts, in the 1970s that number was down to 70 percent, and by the 1990s to only 56 percent.

This context led some unions to pursue extra-NLRB organizing methods, such as card check or even striking for recognition (Mishel et. al. 2020). There is not systematic data on the extent to which workers used "voluntary" recognition as opposed to NLRB elections to establish unions and win contracts during this period. However, there is some evidence that extra-NLRB methods gained in popularity over the dis-regulated period (though they were still far less common than NLRB elections). The Federal Mediation and Conciliation Service (FMCS) had become concerned with the difficulty newly organized workers had in securing first contracts, which led them to place "special emphasis on mediation of initial contract negotiations between employers and newly certified or recognized bargaining units" (FMCS 2000, 33). To address this, the NLRB notified the FMCS of all new union certifications, and the FMCS then assigned a mediator. For a handful of years (1996–2004) the FMCS tracked data on how cases on new bargaining units arrived to the FMCS. In 1996, there were 1,333 new contract cases, of which 176 (13 percent) came from "voluntary" recognition rather than NLRB elections. In 2004, there were 1,053 new contract cases, of which 258 (24.5 percent) came from voluntary recognition.

Finally, unions still faced decertification efforts, though these campaigns waned over time. The peak for decertification elections was in the early 1980s, with close to 900 decertification elections covering around 40,000 union workers each year. Unions lost the majority of these elections. Roughly 75 percent of decertification elections voted the union out in the 1980s. The number of decertification elections, however, dropped over time and workers became slightly more likely to vote to stay unionized. In 2015, there were 178 decertification elections (an 80 percent decrease from 1980), of which unions lost 57 percent.

Unfair Labor Practices

The number of ULP claims filed by unions—a measure of employer aggression, as well as unions' efforts to defend themselves—continued to rise from the regulated to the dis-regulated period. Overall 1980s ULP filings went up from the 1970s and then declined in many industries in the 2020s.[12] We see the soaring ULPs filed during the 1980s as a reflection of the aggressive

---

[12] The count of ULPs does not reflect the number of workers impacted, so we are unable to standardize the measure to account for differences in employment.

employer offensive, and unions' attempts to fight back. Then, as many unions retreated in defeat, they filed fewer ULPs. As union organizing activity (which often prompts ULP employer actions) declined along with the number of NLRB elections and strikes, and as fewer and fewer workers were members of unions (and the number of unions in existence to file ULPs on behalf of workers declined), so, too, did the absolute number of union-filed ULPs.

Again, we see differences in industries. Several industries had large increases in ULPs in the 2000s, including personal services and health services, which were in the medium density category. Industries with an uptick in ULPs also had relatively more success with winning NLRB elections (though the absolute numbers of elections were still low compared to earlier decades). This winning may be partly due to strategies like filing for ULPs during elections, which sometimes curbs employer aggression or brings in state NLRB oversight. It also could be due to some actively organizing unions striking over unfair labor practices, thereby requiring them to file ULPs. Remember, ULP strikes prohibit employers from permanently replacing workers, whereas employers may permanently replace workers on strike for economic reasons. Figure 4.6 presents the number of ULPs filed in each industry, differentiating by worker- and employer-filed cases.

In 1980, illegal discharge was the most common ULP complaint (59 percent), followed by refusal to bargain (32 percent). However, by 2009 the majority of charges (52.7 percent) were for refusal to bargain, followed by illegal discharge (38.8 percent) (U.S. NLRB Reports 1980). Among employer-filed charges, illegal restraint and coercion of employees continued to be the most common (78.8 percent) in 2009 just as it was in 1980.

The NLRB offered remedies of reinstatement less often during the disregulated period, down from 10,033 in 1980 to 2,109 in 2015. Conversely, the amount of backpay increased fairly steadily from $32,136,000 in 1980 to $94,300,000 in 2015, slightly higher than the rate of inflation.[13] This rise indicates that after 1980 employers continued to consider violations of the NLRA to be a viable strategy to prevent unions from forming or continuing in their workplaces.

[13] 1980 inflation adjusted dollars of $32,136,000 are $92,436,630 in 2015.

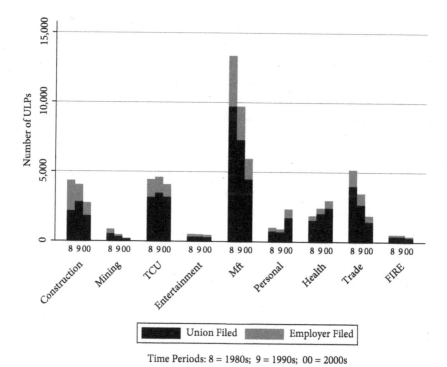

Figure 4.6 Dis-regulated period: Number of unfair labor practice cases filed by unions and employers by industry, average by decade.

Note: Public administration/education and agriculture are excluded because they are not covered by the NLRB.

Strikes

Workers in the dis-regulated period faced formidable obstacles to striking, and unsurprisingly, strikes declined in both absolute numbers and workers involved as a proportion of the workforce. The BLS ceased to report on all work stoppages in 1981, so in the dis-regulated period we use data from the FMCS, as other scholars do.

We argued in earlier chapters that successful striking was one necessary component to enhance union density, because without strikes, workers and unions exercised little leverage vis-à-vis employers. The 1980s was the only decade in the dis-regulated period when unions continued to use strikes as a major mechanism for forming unions and renegotiating contracts; after that, strikes nearly evaporated as a major union strategy (at least until the educators strike wave of 2018, which we discuss in the Conclusion). By 2000, strikes were as low in absolute numbers as they were in 1900–1910, with the lowest proportion of the workforce striking since 1900. Strike trends and union density were similar during this period: both declined drastically.

The number of work stoppages continued its downward trajectory and fluctuated considerably. In 1980, there were 3,885 work stoppages with nearly 1.4 million workers involved. By 1990, that total number had plummeted to 676 with under 300,000 workers involved. By 2014, there were only 68 stoppages with under 21,000 workers involved—nearly a 98 percent decrease from 1980 for both measures.

Large strikes tell a similar story of decline. The BLS tracked strikes with over 10,000 workers, which we coded as full or partially successful vs. lost. The decades from 1950s to 1970s saw around twenty of these large strikes per year (some years with more or less), and high win rates for workers (over 75 percent of these large strikes were won). These large strikes became less frequent beginning in the 1980s. Since the 2000s, most years have had just one or two massive strikes. The win rates of these large strikes fell, too, since the regulated period, with closer to half of large strikes won.

Some industries remained relatively more strike-prone than others—though all of these strike rates were far below their mid-century levels. Figure 4.7 shows the number of workers involved in strikes by industry, averaged for each decade of the dis-regulated period. As in earlier periods, manufacturing had the largest absolute number of workers on strike during the 1980s, 1990s, and 2000s (with the number dropping each decade). TCU, construction, public administration/education, and trade also had relatively high numbers of striking workers, as did mining, but only during the 1980s.

Standardized strike rates were a bit different. Mining had the most elevated standardized strike levels (as measured by mean percent of workers involved in strikes per year), with 6 percent in the 1980s; but the rate fell well below 1 percent in the 1990s and 2000s—compared to rates of 24 to 54 percent during the regulated period. The strike rates were also relatively high in construction and TCU, with close to a 1.5 percent rate in the 1980s, but well below .5 in the 1990s and 2000s. Manufacturing also dropped, with 1 percent in the 1980s, down to .2 percent afterward. Rates declined in every industry during the dis-regulated period, except for TCU, where they had a slight uptick in the 2000s (see Figure 4.8).

Again, all of the industries in our high-density category continued to have relatively higher strike rates compared to other lower-density industries,

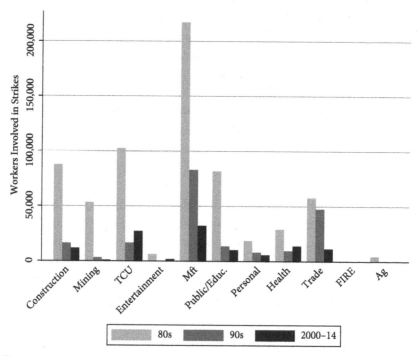

Figure 4.7 Dis-regulated period: Number of workers involved in strikes by industry, average by subperiod.

except for entertainment and public administration/education, which had more moderate strike levels (both of these industries had moderate strike levels in our earlier periods also). The entertainment industry unions, whose workers had high barriers to entry, continued to be anomalous with regard to their relative success without frequent strikes. The public administration/education industry was also able to maintain its union density while decreasing strike participation over time. Still, it is important to note the variation among unions. Some unions, especially those that were more successful at recruiting new members, were more likely to strike than others (Martin and Dixon 2010).

Industries in our medium union density category, personal services and health, both experienced relative moderate-to-low strike proneness. All three industries in our low-density category, trade, agriculture, and FIRE, had uniformly low strike proneness during the dis-regulated period, with under .5 percent of workers in each industry participating in strikes.

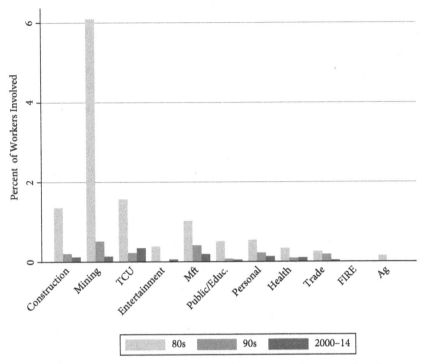

Figure 4.8 Dis-regulated period: Strike rate by industry (percent of workers involved in strikes), average by subperiod.

Similar to the ending decades of the regulated period, several factors continued to contribute to the decline of strikes in the dis-regulated period, including unfavorable labor laws and restrictive contracts (e.g., substituting arbitration for strikes, the proliferation of managerial prerogatives clauses and explicit or implicit "no-strike" clauses, and reporting requirements that made strikes more predictable). New weaknesses also impacted unions' abilities to strike and win. The new organization of work lowered replacement costs for many unions, with the increased threat of capital flight, new forms of contingent workers, financialization, and an increased employer offensive that Reagan spearheaded by giving the green light on replacing workers. As unions disbanded, shrank, and increasingly vanished from the workforce in most industries, their absence made resources like organizing committees, strike funds, and experienced leaders scarce to workers in disagreeable circumstances who may have favored union representation.

Eventually, strikes became less associated with workers' economic gains (Rosenfeld 2006). In this hostile context, it makes sense that even militant unionists hesitated to strike—winning matters, and the ability to win appeared to be eroding as the decades passed. The prevailing impression of the dis-regulated period is that the absence of strikes and their decreasing ability to secure improvements were central components of declining union fortunes.

Race and Gender

In some ways, divisions by race and gender worsened or stayed the same during this period; in other ways they improved. The failures of labor laws to cover workers in agriculture, who were disproportionately workers of color, for the most part extended into the dis-regulated period. Despite the 1966 decision to include some agricultural workers in the 1938 Fair Labor Standards Act and the passage of the Migrant and Seasonal Agricultural Protection Act in 1983, agricultural workers continued to have very little protection and low unionization rates. Labor laws also did not extend to other groups of workers, including independent contractors, who were also disproportionately workers of color.

During the 1970s and beyond, consent decrees[14] aimed to address systemic discrimination in the workplace but unfortunately made little impact in that respect (Zieger 2007). Meanwhile, employment in the traditionally strong union sectors declined. In the six years around the turn of the twenty-first century, more than three million jobs were lost in manufacturing; Black workers were disproportionately impacted. By contrast, the largely non-union service sectors (with higher proportions of women and workers of color) grew.

As mentioned in the previous chapter, the explicitly exclusionary policies of apprenticeship programs finally ended with the Civil Rights Act (1964), which forbade discrimination on the basis of race. Workers' complaints poured in, and by 1975, 125,000 cases were on backlog (Zieger 2007). The Reagan (1981–1989) and first Bush (1989–1993) administrations ushered in a retreat on affirmative action, but between 1992 and 2015, workers filed

---

[14] Consent decrees specify conditions (including ending discriminatory actions and making payment to victims) under which disputes are resolved, without attributing blame.

an annual average of over 89,000 harassment complaints with the national Equal Employment Opportunity Commission (EEOC; established by the Civil Rights Act). In 2015, monetary benefits topped $348 million (EEOC website). In 2019, approximately 60 percent of cases alleged disability, race, or sex, and 40 percent alleged age discrimination. Although large in scope, these were individual fillings on the part of workers rather than collective efforts to improve their workplaces.

Caucuses within the labor movement and new organizations fought to elevate the position of workers of color. The Coalition of Black Trade Unionists (CBTU), which was formed in 1972, worked to amplify Black workers' voices and to push organized labor to be more responsive and relevant to Black and poor workers. Worker centers began to emerge across the country. These organizations focused on supporting immigrant, low-wage workers, who had been left out of the halls of labor. Unions, too, began to (re)embrace the idea of organizing immigrants (Milkman 2006). The SEIU as well as several other unions began to orient their organizing drives to reach workers of color. The 1995 reform-minded leadership of the AFL-CIO expanded Black and women representation on its executive board. During the dis-regulated period, the labor movement began to increasingly recognize that interracial solidarity and cultural diversity were fundamental to its mission and success, although much work around racial justice had yet to be completed (Zieger 2007).

In the dis-regulated period, the majority of union members were white. But, compared to their rates in the labor force, Black workers had grown to have the highest rates of union membership. In 1985, 80 percent of all union members were white,[15] and by 2015, the percentage was 76 percent. With the overall downward movement in union membership, the proportion of union members in all racial/ethnic group declined. In 1980, 17.3 percent of white workers were union members; compared to only 10.8 percent in 2015. Black union membership declined from 24.3 percent to 13.2 percent, and Latinx from 18.9 percent to 9.2 percent, over these same years.[16] Overall, unions became more diverse, and they contributed to more egalitarian attitudes—namely, reduced racial resentment among white workers (Frymer and Grumbach 2021).

---

[15] Historical Statistics reports that 80 percent of union members were male in 1985.

[16] Percentages come from U.S. BLS Reports (2016), U.S. BLS News Releases Union Membership (Annual) (2015), and Gifford Directory of U.S. Labor Organizations (1990). Calculation methods differ slightly.

The unionization of women, driven by organizing in women-dominated professional sectors, especially education and health, made a big difference during this period. Whereas women represented 34 percent of all union members in 1985, by 2015 they constituted 46 percent. Just as in all categories of workers, the proportion of women workers represented by unions also fell, but it declined much less than men's representation did: from 13.2 percent in 1985 to 10.6 percent in 2015, compared to 22.1 percent to 11.5 percent for men. Even though the number of members and union density were much lower in this period, the union movement accomplished near gender parity in membership (Boone 2015; U.S. BLS Reports 2016b).

With the increase of women's representation in unions and collaboration with feminist organizations, unions integrated more women leaders at the top ranks of international unions and the major labor federations and adopted what were previously called "women's issues" as union issues (equal pay, work/family balance, elimination of violence against women in the workplace). Arguably, women became one new face of labor, bringing new vitality and militancy to the cause (Boris and Orleck 2011).

Analysis of Union Density

We continue to use trichotomous variables to indicate the presence of each factor. Codes of 1 are favorable for workers' power; 0 for employers' power; .5 in between. Codes for variables used in the previous chapters remain similar: union density, timing, skill (craft or technical/professional), apprenticeship programs, strike proneness, protective laws, NLRB election and ULP activity, and race and gender. However, we are unable to capture strike success rate. We also add new variables to replacement costs: prevalence of licensing/credentialing, contingent workers, and displaced workers in the industry (representing capital flight). These are trichotomized as above the mean, close to the mean, or below the mean for each industry (see Table 4.1 notes for exact measures).

Overall, how did each of these factors contribute to producing high (over 20), medium (5–20), and low (below 5) percent of workers organized in an industry? Similar to the previous periods, high-density industries continued to have high combined (traditional plus new) replacement costs—when workers were difficult to replace, they were better able to form and maintain

Table 4.1 Dis-regulated Period: Characteristics of Industries With High, Medium, and Low Union Densities

	Union Density	Replacement Costs—Traditional				Replacement Costs—"New"		Race Gender	Strikes	Laws	NLRB		
	1980s/2000s	Timing/Isolation	High Skill	Apprentice Programs	High Licensing or Credentialing	Low Contingent Workers	Low Displacement	White/Male	Strike Prone 1980s/2000s	Protective	Election Effort 1980s/2000s	Election Wins 1980s/2000s	ULP Increase 1970s vs. 1980s/2000s
High Density													
Construction	33/19	0	1	.5	.5	0	0	0	1/0	.5	0/0	0/.5	1/0
TCU	43/25	1	.5	0	.5	.5	.5	0	1/0	.5	0/0	0/1	1/1
Entertainment	31/18	1	.5	0	—	—	—	0	0/0	.5	0/0	0/.5	1/1
Manufacturing	34/21	.5	.5	0	0	1	0	0	1/0	.5	.5/0	0/0	1/0
Public Administration	34/33	1	1	0	1	1	1	0	.5/0	.5	—	—	—
Medium Density													
Mining	27/13	.5	.5	0	.5	.5	0	0	1/0	.5	0/0	0/0	1/0
Personal Serv.	15/11	0	0	0	—	—	—	0	.5/0	.5	0/0	.5/1	1/1
Health	8/8	1	1	0	1	.5	—	0	0/0	.5	1/0	.5/1	1/1
Low Density													
Trade	5/3	0	0	0	0	.5	.5	0	0/0	.5	0/0	0/0	1/0
FIRE	.7/.3	0	.5	0	1	.5	1	0	0/0	.5	0/0	.5/.5	1/1
Agriculture	1/6	1	.5	0	0	0	0	0	0/0	0	0/0	—	—

Density: High = >20 percent; Medium = <20 to 5 percent; Low = <5 percent.

Timing or Isolation: Following Kimeldorf (2013) and Chapter 3.

(continued)

Table 4.1 Continued

High Skill: Coded as 1 if census data indicate that the percent of craft or technical/professional workers is greater than 40 percent; .5 for between 10 and 40 percent; 0 for less than 10 percent skilled craft, technical or professional workers.

Apprenticeship Programs: Unions are mostly unable to enhance closure through apprenticeship programs during this period; they remain in some building trades (see text), which we code as .5.

High Licensing and Credentialing: Uses 2015 BLS data (U.S. BLS Labor Force Statistics Table 52 and 53) to capture the average percent of workers that are licensed or credentialed in each industry. On average, 25.5 percent of workers are licensed or credentialed. Above 30 percent licensed/credentialed = 1; between 20 and 30 percent =.5; under 20 percent = 0. Health and Education are combined, and these industries and related occupations have high licensing and credentials, and we code both as 1. Personal services and entertainment are not included.

Low Contingent Workers: We use CPS estimates by industry averaged for 1995 and 2005, as reported in Katz and Krueger Table 4 (2019). Contingent workers account for roughly 10 percent of the workforce during this period. We use three cut-offs to indicate above average, around average, or below average use of contingent workers. Over 13 percent contingent = 0; 7–13 percent = .5; under 7 percent = 1. These codes are estimates, as some of the industry categories did not directly align, and some data are missing. Katz and Krueger present a combined industry category of health and education, along with relevant health-related occupations, suggesting health should be coded as .5. They do not have a separate category for personal services or entertainment, though occupation data suggest that contingent work is likely high in these categories. It is possible that contingent workers might have increased in some industries after the 2005 period. Research by Katz and Krueger suggests that by 2017, contingent workers had risen substantially in retail trade, education and health services, and manufacturing.

Low Displacement Rate: The BLS tracks the number of long-tenured workers who were displaced from their jobs (Table 2, Helwig 2004). In 1999/2000, displacement was due to company closure or relocation (50 percent of displaced), abolished positions (30 percent), or insufficient work (20 percent). We use the first available years to measure displacement by industry, 1981–1982, as they set the context for the dis-regulated period. Displacement rates ebb and flow over the period, but the relative difference between industries is similar (e.g., manufacturing and mining have relatively high rates, the public sector has low rates, and trade is around average). On average, 3.9 percent of workers were displaced according to the 1981/1982 report. We code over 5 percent displaced = 0; 3–5 percent = .5; under 3 percent = 1 of the workforce was displaced. There are no data on health or personal services; however, a general "services" category has low displacement rates (2.3 percent).

Race and Gender: Coded as >90 percent white and >60 percent male = 1; all else = 0.

Strike Prone: This is based on strike rates, or the number of workers involved in work stoppages divided by employment. Industries are coded as 1 if the strike rate averages 1 percent or more of workers struck per year; .5–.99 percent = .5; <.5 percent workers struck per year = 0.

Protective Laws: This is a proxy to account for the relative erosion of labor laws from the regulated to the dis-regulated period. We compare to the laws during the regulated period, and we downgrade by .5.

NLRB Election Effort: This is the percent of workers involved in yearly elections. 1 percent or more = 1; .5–.99 percent = .5; <.5 percent = 0.

NLRB Election Success: This is the percent of NLRB elections won by unions. 80 percent or higher = 1; 65–79 percent = .5; <65 percent = 0.

ULPs: This measure is the change in the average annual union–filed ULPs from 1970s to the 1980s and the 2000s. 1 = increase since 1970s; 0 = decrease since 1970s. Most industries saw an increase of ULPs from the 1970s to the 1980s, reflecting the employer offensive and unions' attempts to defend themselves.

BLS, Bureau of Labor Statistics; CPS, U.S. Census Current Population Survey; TCU, Transportation, Communication, and Utilities; Public Admin, Public Administration and Education; Health, Health Services; Personal Serv, Personal Services; Trade, Wholesale and Retail Trade; FIRE, Finance, Insurance, and Real Estate; Agriculture, Agriculture, Forestry, and Fishing.

unions. The two industries that did not decline during the dis-regulated period (public administration/education and health) were those with the most factors increasing worker replacement costs. Among the industries that had high density, most saw replacement costs eroded as the dis-regulated period progressed. Outside of the high-density category, health and mining (medium union density) and FIRE (low union density) had relatively high combined replacement costs.

While workers in all industries with high union density (except entertainment) continued to strike at relatively high rates during the 1980s, none of them did so in the 2000s. Employers' growing ease with replacing workers during strikes made strikes less effective; workers' response was to drastically reduce the number of strikes. Without the threat of strikes or supportive labor laws, union density maintenance was the best outcome workers and unions could hope for.

We cannot present a direct rate for ULPs filed, as reports indicate the number of ULPs, rather than workers covered. However, we do see that for all industries, the number of union-filed ULPs increased in the 1980s compared to those filed in the 1970s. We use the difference in the number filed in each industry (comparing the 1970s to the 1980s and the 2000s) as a proxy to capture the degree to which unions defended themselves against employer aggression.

We also consider the role of the law. For the most part, the broad contours of the more protective laws of the regulated period remained but were weaker than their original intent and had more exceptions (e.g., right-to-work laws). To indicate as much, we downgrade our measure of protective laws from 1 to .5 for most industries. We note that this measure is comparative over time within the United States; what we deem as "protective" pales in comparison to laws in place in most other industrialized democracies of the era.

Race and gender factors changed considerably: in this period, no industry had a preponderance of white male workers—due, in large part, to the large-scale entry of women into the labor force (they increased in all industries except for manufacturing and FIRE) and higher percentages of non-white workers in all industries. All industries (in all density categories) shifted away from the heavily white male concentrations of earlier periods.

When we consider NLRB activity, we see a similar dropoff: only manufacturing (moderate) and health (high) maintained considerable election effort during the 1980s, and none did in the 2000s. Election success rates were more mixed, with moderately high rates in health, services, and FIRE during the 1980s. Of these, only health had high election activity as well. We expect that this information helps accounts for the maintenance of union density in health. But high win rates in personal services and FIRE combined with a low level of election effort there did not bring in many new workers. In the 2000s, we see the continuing pattern of low election effort with an uptick in election success rates. Again, with a large number of union jobs disappearing, higher win rates in fewer elections created a trickle of new union members—certainly not enough to prevent the decline of union density in most industries.

Features of High Union Density Industries

Five of the six industries with high union density (over 20 percent) in the regulated period lost density throughout the dis-regulated period: construction, mining, entertainment, TCU, and manufacturing. All but mining maintained an average of over 20 percent during this period, while two others (construction and entertainment) fell below 20 percent by the 2000s. Only one high-density industry maintained its density throughout the entire period: public administration/education.

Unions in TCU, entertainment, manufacturing, and public administration/education continued to benefit from their power based on higher traditional striker replacement costs, while construction suffered some decline in its ability to keep striker replacement costs high. High-density industries varied on the new replacement cost variables: TCU and public administration/education maintained more power than did construction and manufacturing (data are missing for entertainment). Added to these circumstances were increasing rights to replace workers in all industries, greatly disadvantaging unions across the board.

High-density industries used strikes during the 1980s, except for entertainment which continued its lower strike pattern from earlier periods. But this was the decade of concessionary bargaining and givebacks, after which strikes became increasingly rare, especially large strikes. By the 2000s, all industries largely gave up striking. Strikes became constrained, more predictable, and less effective. Overall, unions' ability to prevent strike replacements and to win declined significantly during the dis-regulated period.

Unions' use of NLRB elections also collapsed in all high-density industries, with only manufacturing unions posting moderate usage during the 1980s.

Election success rates declined in the 1980s and recovered in construction, entertainment, and especially in TCU in the 2000s (most public administration/education workers did not use the NLRB). Winning elections and striking for recogntion were the two main ways to organize new members in earlier decades—both approaches had shattered by the early twenty-first century.

Employer opposition to unions continued to grow, even in high-density industries. Unions in all industries had higher ULP filings in the 1980s than in the previous decade. While still constituting the largest number of union-filed ULPs, the manufacturing industry drastically reduced its ULP filings over the dis-regulated period, which we see as partly reflecting the decline in union density, strikes, and NLRB elections. A few high-density industries maintained or increased ULPs during this period (construction, TCU, entertainment), perhaps as one tactic to defend themselves and win new members.

Unions in manufacturing, which spurred the mid-century boom in overall union density, encountered new difficulties during the dis-regulated period. They faced a new sophisticated form of anti-union oppression, stimulated by the union-avoidance industry. Employers learned how to exploit every loophole in NLRB case law to their advantage and to break the laws with only small fines in return. And manufacturing unions faced credible threats of the ultimate replacement: plant closures. As the courts secured replacement workers' rights, and as new replacement cost factors (displacement and the growth of contingent work) devastated manufacturing unions, workers lacked the ability to successfully strike and win elections. With the departure of union manufacturing jobs and unions' inability to organize new workplaces, density declined to just above the 20 percent density threshold in the 2000s.

The maintenance of union density in the public administration/education industry was the only positive trend for high-density industry unions during the dis-regulated period. Teachers maintained union density by continuing to rely on their professional closure through credentialing and engaging in a moderate spurt of strike actions in the 1980s. This effort maintained the inflow of new union members needed to offset the relatively small loss of union jobs there. Workers in education and public administration also faced less aggressive anti-unionism from their employers, which helped them tremendously in this period.

As in earlier periods, high replacement costs alone were not sufficient to achieve high union density. Workers had to be able to strike and win and to run and win union elections, especially if they did not have much state support and faced powerful anti-union employers. Many unions were unable to do either in the dis-regulated period and density declined.

Features of Medium Union Density Industries

Unions maintained medium union density in three industries during the dis-regulated period—personal services, health, and mining, which slipped just below the cutoff for our high-density category. Personal services continued to have little leverage on worker replacement costs, a moderate strike rate in the 1980s and low rates in the 2000s, low rates of NLRB elections, and high ULP filings in the 1980s compared to earlier (union-filed ULPs in personal service increased dramatically in the 2000s). Election outcomes in personal service were moderate to very successful. The personal service industry had about 15 percent union density during the dis-regulated period, down from 18.5 percent at the end of the regulated period.

The health industry experienced quite different conditions; its union density was only slightly down from the regulated period. Health workers continued to utilize their professional skills, credentialing, and licensing to press for unions along with better wages and working conditions, but their strike proneness remained low during this period. They engaged in a high level of NLRB elections in the 1980s and dropped to a low level by the 2000s, but their success rates were moderate to high. Union-filed ULPs in health continued to increase dramatically through the 2000s. Although we do not have comparable data on contingent workers and independent contractors in health, these work arrangements seem to be fairly prevalent in this industry.

While the mining industry played an important role in the union movement during the unregulated and regulated periods, and it maintained its traditional militancy during the 1980s, throughout the dis-regulated period it faded in terms of its strike proneness, NLRB activity and success, and overall consequence. It ultimately slipped into the moderate-density category.

Features of Low Union Density Industries

The same three industries with low union density during the first two periods remained largely unorganized in the dis-regulated period: agriculture, FIRE, and trade. These industries continued to have some factors that increased workers' traditional replacement costs. Agriculture still had timing on its side but also faced high levels of subcontracting and turnover and continued to be excluded from labor laws at the federal level. FIRE experienced some enhanced replacement costs (FIRE enjoyed high licensing, low numbers of contingent workers, and low displacement). Workers in these industries did not strike often, and unions did not often use NLRB elections. However, when FIRE unions used NLRB elections, they were moderately successful and their level of union-filed ULPs, while low, remained constant through the 2000s.

Retail trade had become a major organizing target for the labor movement in the dis-regulated period. Trade had grown to be the largest employer—and remained almost union-free. The retail industry had a number of characteristics that made it difficult to organize. It was dominated by a handful of mega-corporations, like Wal-Mart and Amazon, which were virulently anti-union. Their units were typically small compared to manufacturing, meaning that multiple elections had to be won—and then first contracts accomplished—in order to make union progress. These work arrangements were not well-suited to NLRB election campaigns, and unions called relatively few elections, and of these, win rates were not particularly high. While union-filed ULPs increased from the 1970 to 1980s, they dropped dramatically in the 2000s.

Conclusion

The dis-regulated period experienced substantial decline in overall union density. The right to strike was severely eroded, and for many workers, the ability to win strikes became more challenging, as employers adopted new strategies to effectively replace striking workers or to prevent collective action in the first place. At the same time, NLRB election processes, which had been designed in the 1930s, had become increasing difficult for unions to use successfully. Employers changed the character of their opposition to unions, and pursued employment arrangements, such as subcontractors, franchises, and contingent work, that made winning elections and first contracts difficult. Union strategies were not successful in combatting this hostile and unequal environment. Although the majority of the U.S. public approved of unions (PEW Research), that support did not translate into strong unions.

Still, unions in a few industries were able to maintain their density, even as other industries saw large declines.

The overall economic climate, including financialization, global competition, and deregulation, gave employers a pretense to define unions as greedy, harmful to employers' ability to compete, and outdated or obsolete. These shifts also empowered employers to take bold actions. At the beginning of the dis-regulated period, President Reagan led the charge by making an example of the PATCO workers and reassuring employers that using strike replacements was a legitimate strategy, and a very effective one. Employers ramped up their political efforts to pass pro-employer legislation and to influence NLRB case law. The outcome was an increasing narrowing of workers' right to strike. They employed new economic strategies and restructuring that displaced thousands of union workers, and externalized employment to temporary agencies, subcontractors, and independent contractors, thereby shrinking the percent of workers suitable for traditional union membership. They hired union-avoidance firms, spending hundreds of millions of dollars annually to get targeted advice to avoid unions.

The union response was too little, too late. Unions barely weathered the tremendous onslaught against them during the 1980s with little adaptation to the new conditions. It was not until the mid-1990s that challengers came to the fore in the AFL-CIO and began to innovate a response. Some revitalization and another split in the main federation occurred, but the results were nothing like what happened with the CIO challenge to the AFL during the regulated period. Social movement orientations became more common, some unions made alliances with other workers' organizations and community groups, and unions added some innovative tactics to their repertoires. Importantly, community-based worker centers emerged, engaging with a population of workers who were outside of most union aims.

The domination of white men in all high-density industries ended, and the energetic actors in the dis-regulated period tended to be the relative newcomers to unions and union leadership: women and workers of color. But the erosion of state protection and continuing employer opposition were difficult to surmount. Unions' actions were not enough to stop the density decline, except for a very small increase in 2008–2009, followed by more decline through 2015.

While manufacturing unions had become the backbone of union density by the mid-twentieth century—the industry employed a huge number of workers and many of them became unionized—this wasn't to last. In all, the gutting of pro-labor laws, capital flight away from unionized workplaces, and workers' declining ability to win strikes set manufacturing unions on a downward trajectory. Because they represented a large (but in this period, shrinking) proportion of the workforce, their decline erased many of the mid-century union density gains. The inability of unions to organize workers in trade was also a drain on overall union density, given its increasing share of the workforce.

But workers in public administration/education, with power vis-à-vis employers in the form of timing and professional status (and licensing/ credentialing), worked within a different legal context with less aggressive employers. This industry was less affected by the new dangers of displacement and contingent work. Given their growth as a percentage of the workforce, once educators and public workers accomplished high density using strikes and the new laws allowing collective bargaining, they continued to add to overall union density.

Power differentials moved away from workers and toward employers during the dis-regulated period. Employers in industries originally organized by the AFL continued seeking to reduce skilled workers' replacement costs while unions actively worked to maintain or increase them. On balance, employers gained the upper hand even there. Employers in manufacturing led the anti-union drive that characterized the dis-regulated period. The uncontested status of the AFL-CIO as the leader of union interests led to complacency and eventually resignation to the new reality. Only in the 1990s did some within the labor movement awaken to the coming disaster. But the proposed solutions were not enough to turn the tides during the dis-regulated period.

What is most telling of the dis-regulated period is sophisticated employer aggression, the successful strategies of employers to lower replacement costs, and the disappearance of strikes—all while the state did little to even the playing field. Neither unions nor employers sat idly by during this period. But unions tended to be less successful in their strategies to tilt the playing field in their favor. By contrast, employers were very active, backing legal changes, reducing workers' ability to successfully strike, restructuring their workplaces to their benefit, and equipping themselves with expert advice. Those actions account for their success.

5

Conclusion

It's not news that distinct period-related patterns characterize U.S. union density over the last 115 years (1900–2015): a slow start at the turn of the last century, a mid-century boom, followed by a bust in all but a few industries in our current time. Our contribution here is to demonstrate industry-level variations and the clues that they provide for understanding the drivers of the booms and busts.

The biggest booms for unions came when the conditions were favorable (workers had some leverage over employers) and they were inclined and able to act on this leverage through strikes, elections, and other forms of action. They had leverage in part because of the macro conditions of their industries—but also because they had successful strategies to increase their leverage (e.g., through solidarity, apprenticeship programs, sit-down strikes, and so forth). Unions were able to build industry-level density when they had high replacement costs and successful strikes in the early period. Aggregate union density increased in the 1930s and 1940s, when unions successfully adapted their strategies to the emerging conditions in the largest industry (manufacturing). New National Labor Relations Board (NLRB) procedures helped, along with increased wartime demand for production. In the 1960s and beyond, unions made substantial gains in the public sector, where changing laws, less employer opposition, work resistant to capital flight, and more worker militancy made the difference and helped to counteract union density decline in the private sector.

However, union surges were often followed by counter-mobilization from employers, who sought to undo their gains. We see that throughout the century employers were actively and often successfully engaged in dis-organizing unions, minimizing replacement costs, pushing for favorable laws, and moving toward new employment arrangements. Employers, with their vast resources, were able to out-maneuver unions for most of the past century, but as we demonstrated, not without some surges in unionization that generated crises for employers and the state. In each period, strategies by

Union Booms and Busts. Judith Stepan-Norris and Jasmine Kerrissey, Oxford University Press.
© Oxford University Press 2023. DOI: 10.1093/oso/9780197539859.003.0005

unions and employers, along with the macro state and economic conditions, set the stage for subsequent labor relations.

The pattern of all or nothing, fits and starts, and radical innovation followed by containment reflects the social movement character of the U.S. labor movement. We explore the broad contours that characterize each period and how they relate to the fortunes of the labor movement, with a focus on what happened in each of the eleven basic industries. We consider both structural factors governing labor's fortunes in each period (legal, political, and economic) as well as the actions of both workers/unions and employers/employer organizations, as they created new structures and conditions that constrained and enabled actions in future periods.

Our strategy has been to interrogate industry variations using comparative-historical methods in search of discovering larger patterns. In the broadest scope, we see that the timing for mass unionization has differed by industry and organizing logic. Among the first industries that saw booms were craft-oriented industries (along with industries characterized by other forms of high replacement costs). By the late 1930s, manufacturing unions boomed with a new industrial organizing logic. Both the early unionizers as well as manufacturing industries saw large increases mid-century, followed by major busts. Workers employed by the state began their major boom about thirty years later and have not (yet) experienced a major bust (we say "yet" because we see employers pushing for changes that could make public workers' unionism more difficult in the future). Unions in some industries have not yet seen a boom because they haven't experienced the combination of favorable conditions and appropriate union strategies. Most prominent among these is retail and wholesale trade, which has now become the largest employer.

Over 115 years, the state and economy changed considerably. Our three main periods, the unregulated period (1900–1934), the regulated period (1935–1979), and the dis-regulated period (1980–2015), reflect these large-scale shifts. Our comparative analysis considers four sets of factors that pave the way for union density in each period: the state and macro context, replacement costs, employer and union strategies and actions, and race and gender. The beginning of each chapter discusses the broad legal, political, and economic conditions that shaped union/employer relations during that period. Then we discuss industry-specific replacement costs and unions' and employers' activities to make or break unions. The race and gender section examines how women and workers of color came into play, how they fared in the workplace and in unions, and traces their increasing inclusion over the century. Table 5.1 summarizes the major characterizations of these mechanisms for each period.

Table 5.1 Summary of Mechanisms by Period

Period	State and Macro Context	Replacement Costs	Strategies: Making and Breaking Unions	Race and Gender
Unregulated				
Workers/Unions	Few protective laws Hostile courts Hostile or agnostic politicians Boost with World War I Bust after World War I	Skill/apprenticeship Timing Isolation	Boycotts Union label Moderate strike rate AFL craft organizing Increasingly apolitical AFL Radical rivals IWW/TUUL	Exclusionary AFL Inclusionary IWW Faced employment segregation Cultural barriers
Employers	Used injunctions Used violence/repression Used employer-friendly courts	Deskilling/Scientific management Professional identification	NAM, CC activity Used detectives/spies Politically active employers Allied with employer-friendly Republicans	Exclusionary Paternalistic Used race to divide
Regulated				
Workers/Unions	Helpful New Deal legislation—NLRB, but it eroded Depression → solidarity World War II → tripartite authority Executive Order for federal workers Laws for state & municipal workers	Skill/apprenticeship begins decline Professional solidarity Timing Isolation Expanded right to strike Several union strategies increase costs, esp. un/semi-skilled solidarity, sit-down strikes	CIO & industrial organizing Sit-down strikes High strike rate NLRB elections Solidarity among unskilled AFL and CIO merge Public workers organize More union political activity	Inclusionary CIO Mixed AFL Operation Dixie Fails Laws force inclusion Civil rights/women's movements

Employers	New controls on their power La Follette Committee Control regained Taft-Hartley Arbitration begins to replace strikes	Deskilling/automation Several employer strategies decrease replacement costs: capital flight and contracts	NAM, CC activity Taft-Hartley Act More political activity Contracts increase management rights Capital flight	Mostly exclusionary Laws force inclusion
Dis-Regulated Workers/Unions	NLRB is gutted Strike protections gutted Courts side with employers Democrats less responsive More favorable laws for state and municipal workers	Skill/apprenticeship declined Professional status Licensing/credentialing Timing	AFL-CIO sluggish response Revitalization- organizing Change to Win NLRB elections decline Strikes decline drastically Public sector less opposition Rise of worker centers Alliances Social movement vs. business unionism	More inclusion Workers of color, immigrants, women on the move
Employers	Control solidified through courts and NLRB Friendly politicians Globalization Financialization Trade deals Right-to-work laws More replacement worker rights	Deskilling/automation Changing apprenticeship Several employer strategies decrease replacement costs esp. capital flight, contingent work	NAM, CC activity Sophisticated union avoidance Capital flight Privatization Double-breasting Contingent work More replacements hired	More inclusion Employment law alternative

The Unregulated Period

The unregulated period had a mainly conservative political context. Neither political party considered labor concerns to be central, presidents more frequently deployed the National Guard on employers' behalf to end strikes, and the courts were more than willing to uphold employers' private property rights through injunctions. Many state and local laws made organizing more difficult, including laws on criminal syndicalism. The Sherman Anti-Trust Act, although not passed to control unions, was regularly used against them. Public sector workers had even more constraints, including restrictions on their rights to strike and collectively bargain, and on federal workers' lobbying. The nation had yet to develop a national unified labor policy, and free from legal constraints, employers used their resources to (often violently) suppress workers' collective actions.

Besides the usual business cycles (to which unions were more sensitive in their formative years), the major economic features of this period were World War I, which helped create a boom in union density followed by a bust, and the Great Depression, which produced unprecedented unemployment. World War I gave the government an opportunity to repress and essentially destroy radical (Industrial Workers of the World [IWW]) unions using the Palmer Raids. But worker and unemployed radicalism and unrest returned in response to the Great Depression and was a major impetus to industrial union growth and to New Deal legislation toward the end of this period.

Labor unions' main strategy was characterized by the American Federation of Labor (AFL)'s craft unionism, which dominated during the unregulated period. Most unions moved away from politics and became fairly apolitical, consistent with the AFL's policy of "reward your friends, punish your enemies." Nevertheless, they managed some political gains: the AFL gained a seat at the table during World War I with the first War Labor Board (the IWW decidedly did not). The AFL's challengers, the IWW and Trade Union Unity League (TUUL), both promoted industrial organizing, but neither made substantial progress in organizing the mass of industrial workers.

Employment was largest in agriculture, followed by two industries that showed substantial growth during this period: manufacturing and trade. White men dominated the work force and were especially concentrated in industries with high union density. Traditional skilled (craft) workers dominated the construction industry and were numerous in transportation, communications, and utilities (TCU), and manufacturing. Professional and technical workers were mostly located in health, public administration/education, and entertainment. Employers and unions were often exclusionary. Employers relegated women to lower status jobs in personal service, health, and public administration and education. Workers of color were concentrated in the low-paying personal service and agricultural industries.

Unions used the boycott and union label, but the strike was their main weapon in workplace battles. Employers and unions both acted to enhance their advantage during strikes by adjusting striker replacement costs to their favor. Major struggles revolved around skill and skill closure, which were the main drivers of high replacement costs. AFL unions used apprenticeship programs to control access to training, thereby keeping replacement costs high. Some programs allowed skilled workers to reserve apprenticeship training spots for relatives and acquaintances, and some systematically excluded women and workers of color. Together with employers' preferences, this made the workforce and AFL unions largely white and male organizations.

Two other features of work contributed to workers' power during strikes: timing and isolation. When work was necessarily provided at specific times and when workers labored in geographically isolated areas, it was more difficult for employers to obtain replacement workers during strikes. This, in turn, increased workers' power during strikes.

Overall, strike rates were moderate. Workers in mining were by far the most strike prone and faced the most strike violence. Other strike-prone industries included construction, manufacturing, and to a lesser extent TCU, entertainment, and public administration/education. According to AFL records, strikes were over 60 percent successful in the industries with high to moderate strike levels, with the exception of manufacturing, where workers were less successful.

Employers organized and actively pursued union disorganization with a combination of paternalistic, repressive, or even violent means. They used tactics in the welfare capitalism vein, including developing company unions, industrial relations counselors, and benefits that unions regularly offered (e.g., recreational programs, pensions, insurance). They also pursued repressive means to prevent new union formation and to disorganize existing unions. These included hiring spies and private police, establishing blacklists, engaging in violence, and using injunctions and replacement workers to end strikes. They formed employer organizations to coordinate and amplify their resistance.

In their attempts to reduce skilled worker power, many employers implemented the new principles of scientific management in their workplaces and sought to mechanize and deskill the work. And while employers were not directly involved in promoting professional associations, they benefited when employees chose professional identification over unions.

Workers in some industries fared better than others in forming unions during the unregulated period. Despite employers' unchecked power and their ability to use injunctions to thwart strikes, unions in some industries had the power to win strikes and succeeded in growing union density to above 20 percent—construction, mining, TCU, and entertainment. They did this by keeping worker replacement costs high and using unions' most powerful weapon: the strike. Workers in industries with more limited access to conditions and strategies that enhanced worker replacement costs tended to be less strike prone and less successful when they did strike. And where workers had little to no access to these conditions and strategies, they rarely even tried to strike and were unable to establish a foothold to build union density.

All of the industries that achieved high union density during this period were dominated by white, male workers. Women and workers of color were clustered in industries with lower replacement costs, and they faced additional challenges, including gendered preconceptions about women workers and racialized state and white vigilante violence against workers of color. We see moderate union density in the public administration/education industry during the unregulated period, driven primarily by the organization of mainly white male workers who organized successfully in pockets of public work (e.g., postal workers). Teachers, on the other hand, who were mostly women, were split between pursuing professional and union identities and had minimal unionization during this period. Workers in personal services; health; agriculture; finance, insurance, and real estate (FIRE); and trade were only able to achieve very low union density.

The Regulated Period

At the beginning of the regulated period, pent-up frustration among workers—greatly exacerbated by the Great Depression and massive unemployment—led to major upheavals in many large cities. A considerable contingent of AFL union leaders who saw the benefit of organizing semi-skilled and unskilled workers offered solidaristic leadership and funding, brought in seasoned leftists who had been working outside the AFL for many years, and launched a major union organizing effort to ensure that the workers longing for power found new union homes. Their strategy was based on industrial organizing, which included all workers throughout workplaces—not only skilled craft workers. In this industrial spirit, workers launched innovative, dramatic, and successful strikes, especially in large workplaces. This internally controversial and ultimately federation-splitting strategy ended up attracting new members not only to manufacturing unions but also to unions across all industries and skill levels.

The Congress of Industrial Organizations (CIO) was born, with a resulting boon to the entire labor movement. Worker disruption and growing union power gave union leaders more influence in forming government policies and legislation. The New Deal labor law transformations followed, solidifying workers' right to strike and to join unions as the state reined in employers' previously unconstrained power through the La Follette Committee and through providing unions the option to file unfair labor practice cases.

The National Labor Relations Act (NLRA) offered most (not all) workers a new avenue to unionization, one that did not rely solely on replacement costs. Workers now had clearly defined rights, and employers were prohibited from engaging in certain practices that they had long been using. Unions could now file unfair labor practice cases if they thought employers were violating their rights. The NLRB also offered secret ballot elections to determine the outcomes of organizing drives. Manufacturing workers used this new state machinery at the highest rates. Millions of manufacturing workers formed unions through NLRB elections and their demonstrated ability to strike and win.

Unions won strikes and elections at high rates during the early regulated period. This is demonstrated by the last year that the Bureau of Labor Statistics (BLS) collected data on strike outcomes, in 1936. Of 2,156 strikes that year, unions fully won 46 percent and partially won another 24 percent, for about a 70 percent win rate combined. From 1937 to 1947, unions conducted thousands of elections and won the vast majority (with annual win rate of between 75 and 90 percent). Using strikes and elections, millions of workers formed unions during these first ten years, ushering in a new era of labor relations.

In 1947, the employer-sponsored Taft-Hartley Act passed, swinging the balance of power back to employers. It gave employers the right to file unfair labor practices cases against unions, restricted many solidaristic actions by workers, barred Communists from union leadership, made strikes more predictable, elevated the role of arbitration, and created the Federal Mediation and Conciliation Service to help settle disputes without strikes. As union power waned, the courts followed the new momentum in employers' direction by bolstering the rights of replacement workers, solidifying the role of arbitration as the alternative for strikes, and eroding employers' duty to bargain.

Both the AFL and CIO were active in politics, but the results of their efforts that accrued during the Roosevelt presidency evaporated under subsequent Democratic and Republican administrations.

The two big features of the regulated period's economy were the ongoing effects of the Great Depression and World War II. The Great Depression was a stimulus to worker action and union formation, especially in manufacturing. The war effort necessitated continuous production and created a shortage of labor, opening space for women and workers of color. The World War II War Labor Board provided an opportunity for unions to secure their place at the table and to consolidate their gains, but it also institutionalized certain collective bargaining practices that continued after the war, including a moderate form of union security, called maintenance of membership, and importantly, arbitration, which began to replace strikes as the main method of adjudicating grievances.

Employment shifted across industries, away from agriculture and mining and toward trade, health services, government, construction, manufacturing, TCU, entertainment, and FIRE. Race and gender demographics by industry did not change much from the unregulated period.

Employers acted on the regulated context by continuing to deskill work and increasing their organizational activity, the latter with great success. After they suffered a major loss with the NLRA, it didn't take them long to regroup and reclaim their dominance in the workplace. The effective employers' organization, the National Association of Manufacturers (NAM), successfully originated and pushed for the passage of the Taft-Hartley Act, which set the groundwork for reasserting their exclusive workplace rights. Employers began taking advantage of their new rights immediately, by filing unfair labor practice cases against unions (especially in construction) and beginning their drive to pass "right-to-work" laws in states.

The CIO upsurge, which allowed large numbers of women, workers of color, and previously ignored white men to join unions' ranks, was labor's major accomplishment. The AFL followed along, adding new members at an even higher rate than the CIO, but integrating women and workers of color into their unions at a much slower pace. The CIO and especially its left-leaning unions were more deliberate and effective at including them in leadership positions, though most unions continued to be dominated by white men. Later, civil rights legislation (pushed by demonstrations) further opened employment doors for women and workers of color, including in unionized industries that had been dominated by white men.

The CIO more enthusiastically used NLRB elections than the AFL, but as the AFL ramped up its NLRB participation, it brought in more un- and semi-skilled workers. With the shift of teachers and nurses from professional to AFL union identity and the CIO challenge, the AFL moved away from its traditional reliance on its craft worker base.

As it turned out, the CIO's vitality and more left-leaning orientation was only a relatively short blip in the century-long saga. The McCarthy-period hysteria reached unions and was institutionalized in the Taft-Hartley Act with a prohibition against union leadership by Communist Party members. Concurrently, Communist union leaders broke from the larger CIO by advocating support for the third-party presidential candidate (Henry Wallace), making their expulsion more likely. The purge of the so-called Communist-dominated unions from the CIO destroyed many of the most effective, equity-oriented, and democratic unions.

The 1955 merger of the AFL and CIO favored the numerically larger AFL, granting it dominance over strategy and operations. The AFL-CIO's more conservative leaders tended to focus on union member financial interests in a bureaucratic way as opposed to energizing workers to act on their own behalf and strategizing about the overall fate of the labor movement. As workers' power vis-à-vis employers declined and strikes became less successful, the labor movement's main federation surrendered to relative complacency for the next four decades.

Unions' leverage during strikes was relatively high, especially during the first two decades of the regulated period. But a primary mechanism for strike leverage (craft skill closure) began to shift. As apprenticeship programs moved toward publicly supported efforts to recruit potential apprentices and as community colleges began delivering vocational education to large numbers of students, closure became more pronounced in professional/technical occupations requiring training in higher education programs. Timing as a source of strike leverage remained fairly constant, but isolation faded in importance as a different spatial factor, capital flight, began to give some employers new strike leverage. Consistent with the shift in leverage from unions to employers throughout the regulated period, the incidence of strikes also experienced a boom (mid-1940s through mid-1950s) followed by a bust (mid-1950s through the mid-1960s) and then another smaller increase in the late 1960s followed by a decline beginning in the mid-1970s. Similar to the unregulated period, strike rates were highest in mining, followed by construction, TCU, and manufacturing. Public administration and education also had high rates, but not until the late 1960s. With Taft-Hartley's restrictions and the expulsion of left-wing CIO union leaders, union collective bargaining contracts began to include more employer-friendly clauses, namely, no-strike and managerial prerogatives clauses. These clauses further restricted workers' strike leverage, even in industries that had enjoyed high replacement costs. Thereafter, court decisions moved unions further toward a focus on bread-and-butter issues.

The industries that prospered during the unregulated period continued to prosper and grow union density while adding the use of NLRB elections and unfair labor practice cases to their traditional repertoires. Two new industries also moved to the high-density fold: manufacturing and later, public administration/education. The CIO upheaval fueled the tremendous surge of union density in manufacturing, and these workers used both NLRB elections and strikes to secure their unions. Teachers' eventual choice to adopt union—as opposed to professional—identity and to strike boosted the public administration/education industry. These industries reached or maintained high union density in the regulated period: construction, mining, TCU, entertainment, manufacturing, and public administration/education. Except for public administration/education, these high-density industries began to experience union decline toward the end of the regulated period.

The Dis-Regulated Period

Workers' rights to organize and to strike were dismantled at an accelerated pace during the dis-regulated period, through court decisions, right-to-work laws, and President Reagan's green light to permanently replace striking workers. As a more sophisticated version of employer repression took hold, and new factors contributed to the power of employers in labor struggles, unions lost strike leverage vis-à-vis employers. Winning strikes became increasingly difficult, and unions faced demands for concessionary bargaining. Unions in all industries drastically reduced their strike activity and suffered great losses in union density except for public administration/ education and health services, where they managed to hold relatively steady.

Unions' political influence weakened and employers' influence solidified during the dis-regulated period. Unions' ability to deliver workers' votes to Democratic presidential candidates began to diminish toward the end of the regulated period, making the anti-union Nixon and Reagan administrations possible. But even when Democrats were in the White House, advantages didn't accrue to unions. The political context, shaped by employers and their organizations, favored Republicans, and the period saw deregulation in transportation, the passage of additional right-to-work laws, and the negotia- tion of trade deals that undermined replacement costs of many U.S. workers.

The Reagan administration solidified a new aggressive anti-union gov- ernment stance with its firing of striking PATCO workers in 1981 and its employer-oriented appointments to the NLRB. This gambit opened the floodgates for employers seeking to disarm workers' ability to successfully strike. They coupled this effort with their use of sophisticated and expen- sive union avoidance firms to further render strikes ineffective as well as by committing unfair labor practices and hiring workers with alternative relationships to the firms, which took them out of unions' reach. These em- ployer actions led to a significant decline in the number of union members as well as in overall union density.

Replacement costs in the dis-regulated period were also altered in new ways. The new context of global competition legitimized employers' calls for belt tightening. Unions' traditional leverage though skill closure declined even further with continuing changes to apprenticeship programs. Meanwhile, the cumulative rise of employment law gave workers an indi- vidualistic alternative to collective action through unions. Unions were still able to win strikes on occasion, and they did gain new leverage through professional and licensed/credentialed workers, who were now trained in colleges and universities as opposed to the previous employer-sponsored training programs. Workers' timing-related advantages continued in some industries as in earlier periods, while spatial factors, especially capital flight, accumulated employers' power. Other replacement cost factors also fa- vored employers, including the rise of alternative work arrangements, finan- cialization, and legal restrictions on strikes. Almost exclusively, these new arrangements benefited employers.

As employers gained more power, strikes continued to decline, which both contributed to employer power and was also a reaction to it. Strikes hit historical lows, especially after the 1980s, with progressive declines in all industries except TCU and health, which experienced small increases in the 2000s.

Concurrently, unions were less likely to use NLRB elections to organize new workers, due to accumulating difficulties in doing so. NLRB elections drastically declined in this period (except in construction, personal services, and health). Thus, the paths to unionizing that had been successful in the earlier periods—a mix of strikes, apprenticeship programs, industrial organizing, and later NLRB elections—were no longer effectively in play during the dis-regulated period. Workers did show some remarkable instances of solidarity, but this did not prove to be sufficient to overcome other challenges. Unions continued to shrink and even dissolve in large numbers before the situation registered as requiring serious attention.

Finally, in the mid-1990s, a resurgence took hold within the AFL-CIO, calling for revitalization, more social movement–like unions, and greatly increased attention to union organizing. In addition to pouring resources into organizing, there was a flurry of new (or renewed) tactics, including attempts to reclassify workers previously outside the scope of the NLRB to obtain coverage and using card check to win union recognition. Other sorts of campaigns emerged to pressure employers and to raise awareness, including living wage campaigns and the Occupy Wall Street movement. Importantly, the period also saw the emergence of worker centers, which often sought to build power among low-wage workers who were not formally unionized. Many of the campaigns during this period, including Justice for Janitors, home health campaigns, and many worker center efforts, embraced workers of color and immigrant workers, bringing in new members and energy into the labor movement. But these efforts did not reverse the downward trajectory of unions, given the accumulated strength of employers.

Public sector workers faced a different set of circumstances. In the 1980s and 1990s, state employers were not as aggressively anti-union as their private sector counterparts. Public workers also benefited from being place-based—capital flight was less of an option (though privatization surely was). These workers were successful in maintaining their density through the close of our analysis in 2015.

The dis-regulated period also saw changes to employment and demographics. Employment continued to shift away from agriculture and mining and began to shift away from manufacturing. It continued to grow in trade, public administration/education, construction, TCU, entertainment, health services, and FIRE. Women and workers of color had increased representation in employment, and white men declined as a percentage of workers in all industries except for personal services. Women and workers of color also continued to gain membership in unions, with Black workers being the most likely to be unionized of all. Women, by the close of the dis-regulated period, had nearly the same union membership numbers as men, due in part to the surge of unionized teachers. In some unions, women and workers of color had risen to the highest ranks of leadership—a far leap from the predominantly white and male unions of one hundred years prior. While substantial work on race and gender equity remained, union initiatives during this period helped to address systemic issues, including equal pay initiatives.

Although they were weaker than in the regulated period, unions in several industries managed to hold the line on high union density (over 20 percent averaged over the entire period): construction, TCU, entertainment, manufacturing, and public administration/education. However, even among high-density industries, the trajectory during this period was downward for all but public administration/education.

What's Next?

While the future of the U.S. labor movement is uncertain, we can draw lessons from our comparative and historical analysis to suggest where it might be going. Our answer is that it depends. As we have emphasized, both structural conditions as well as actions on the part of workers and union leaders, on the one hand, and employers and their organizations, on the other, will be crucial in determining the outcomes going forward.

Lessons: The State and Macro Context

One major lesson is that state actions—including laws, court decisions, national guard deployments, NLRB appointments, and regulation of employment—deeply shape whether and how unions form. It is a mistake to think of labor relations as a free market process involving unions and employers, and based only on the desires of individual workers. Rather, state actions are a key factor in understanding unionization—and a major arena where both employers and unions struggle for influence.

Recognizing this, employers and unions have poured energy into influencing the political and legal terrains. Some changes to the legal context occurred within big, defining moments. Workers' disruptions often preceded major changes, especially the NLRA. But employers were organized to ensure that other big moments worked in their favor—like the Taft-Hartley Act and the expansion of right-to-work laws. In other words, we see that big actions by workers—strike waves—can help the state to "evolve" its labor policies in their favor. But history also reminds us that employers never sat idly by to let this happen—they pushed back. They sometimes were even able to use strike disruption to legitimize that push back (as in the World War II postwar period and PATCO).

The erosion of union protections happened slowly, beginning in the middle of the regulated period and accelerating during the dis-regulated period. With Republican presidents, Democratic politicians who were unwilling or unable to prioritize workers' rights, a conservative voting coalition in Congress, and a conservative-leaning Supreme Court, workers' rights were gradually chipped away through legislation and case law. Unions' attempts to reverse anti-labor legislation mostly failed. Importantly, the guarantee of the right to strike was decimated, thereby undermining unions' main source of power. This erosion of strike protections occurred through both changing laws and restricting workers' options to strike while covered by collective bargaining contracts.

While laws regulating strikes, organizing, and collective bargaining had major implications for labor relations, other sorts of state interventions to rein in employers and support workers' rights also mattered. The La Follette Committee investigated employer excess during the 1930s, which helped to restrain them through the negative publicity they received. It seems likely that a similar effort could be useful at the present time to expose employers' current more sophisticated illegal activities and to make the consequences of breaking laws greater. Likewise, empowering and resourcing federal and state agencies charged with labor protections to identify employers who break laws and to enforce meaningful penalties is key. And state action could earnestly address worker misclassification, preventing employers from transitioning workers to independent contractor status, which renders them ineligible for unions. The state could invest in the relationship between worker centers, vocational training, and rights enforcement. Or it could break up monopolistic mega-corporations, where workers face major power inequities. The list goes on, including publicly supporting strike efforts, addressing the impacts of capital flight, incentivizing Community Benefit Agreement (contracts between developers and community organizations, often including labor groups), and much more. Such state actions would likely depend on political allies ready to prioritize workers as well as pressure and direct action on the part of workers and their communities.

Importantly, other aspects of the macro context shape whether and how unions form. Economic and other external shocks, like depressions, wars, or pandemics, create new opportunities and constraints. While tight labor supplies were sometimes beneficial to union efforts, for example, during wars, the Great Depression provides a counterexample in which thousands of unemployed people and frustrated employed workers agitated for a fairer system, ushering in the surge of 1930s organizing. The devolution of formally good jobs, wage stagnation, and workers' frustrated expectations may play a role in the future, as wage cuts have tended to promote collective action.

Lessons: Replacement Costs

Replacement costs are partially determined by structural factors, namely the nature of the work and the legal context. However, as we have demonstrated throughout the book, both unions and employers have acted to influence replacement costs.

By the end of the dis-regulated period, employers had the upper hand in terms of their ability to replace workers, due in part to new replacement workers' rights but also to the changing political economy and employer strategies addressing them. It had become increasingly easy for employers to crush labor disputes, or avoid them altogether. In the dis-regulated period, employers had multiple avenues to accomplish this end. They could permanently replace striking workers. They could do a "spatial fix" and flee to an area with more seemingly docile workers. They could employ contingent workers, who lack union rights or who have high turnover and therefore are less likely to invest in union campaigns. They could subcontract work out or transition workers to independent contractor status, shifting all of the burdens and none of the protections to them. They could withstand strikes because of highly diversified, financialized portfolios. They could de-skill or automate. If faced with a union election, they could hire anti-union consultants. They could count on surprisingly small penalties if they broke the law. They could fight tooth and nail to refuse workers a decent contract, knowing that workers may not be willing to strike under unfavorable circumstances.

Unions have used three primary strategies to maintain the high cost of replacement workers. First unions have increased replacement costs through skill closure. Unions have used apprenticeship programs to influence skilled training so that there are few skilled non-union workers available to replace their work. They've also used hiring halls, where employers are required to hire workers from the union-run hall. These strategies require strong unions. And these strategies can be further augmented when unions take advantage of certain work characteristics, such as time-sensitive production or essential services. Today, substantial numbers of workers still have hard-to-replace skills (despite deskilling and automation), especially those with licensing or credentialing requirements. Hard-to-replace skills combined with work that is resistant to capital flight provides unions with leverage. For example, healthcare and education workers are often credentialed, in high demand, perform time-sensitive work, and are in place-based workplaces that are resistant to capital flight. These features helped them to maintain unions, even in the dis-regulated period.

A second strategy in the union toolbox has been to advocate for state interventions that increase replacement costs. This could be through actions such as restricting employers' abilities to legally replace striking workers, supporting sectoral bargaining where all workers are covered (and hence there is less incentive to replace workers, as their replacements are also covered by union contracts), or facilitating more connections between vocational and higher education training programs and unions.

A third strategy that unions use to increase replacement costs is based on solidarity. Some workers are not well positioned to use the first approach (building replacement costs through skill closure), and the second approach (state action) may not be feasible in the short term. But, even in these challenging circumstances, workers still have the potential to build solidarity to increase replacement costs. We saw this strategy with the CIO, which organized wall-to-wall and used sit-down strikes, which made replacing striking workers much more difficult. Unions also pursued boycotts (which now have more restrictions) and the union label (early on), which required community and labor solidarity. Unions have also built solidarity by supporting each other's strikes, including by not crossing picket lines and by sharing resources. At times, unions have also had deep community support, which limits who might be willing to serve as a replacement worker.

It's also important to note that while increasing replacement costs is helpful for unions, we find that workers must regularly exercise their power through a union orientation, solidarity, and strikes in order to make progress toward increasing union density.

Lessons: Employer Strategies—Breaking Unions

The strategies that employers and unions use to build their power are key to understanding union density. An important observation is that employers have *always* fought to minimize, prevent, or eradicate unions. Contemporary scholars stress that the employer offensive is largely responsible for the decline in unionization in the dis-regulated period. We agree. However, our analyses also show that employers never readily accepted unions. Even in the moments where unions were growing in strength, employers were working to reduce their influence over the long term. With different strategies and in different contexts, we see employer offensives against union solidarity in the unregulated, regulated, and dis-regulated periods.

Over the course of 115 years, employers strategized to regain control whenever workers were able to gain power. Employers found that business friendly courts, politicians, and laws made their efforts to disorganize unions easier. Through employer associations, such as the National Association of Manufacturers, the Chamber of Commerce, and other groups, they strategized to influence the state and economy. For the better parts of the unregulated and dis-regulated periods, employers saw substantial success is securing a capital-friendly climate. The major exceptions to this reign was the passage of the NLRA (and later public sector labor laws). Even then, employers were on the move to draft and pass the anti-union Taft-Hartley Act.

But influencing the legal and political climate was only one strategy in the century-long employer push to dis-organize unions. They also hired operatives to prevent unionization or disorganize existing unions. In the dis-regulated period these operatives were mostly company spies and Pinkerton guards, and violent suppression of workers was not uncommon. A century later, the tactics had become more sophisticated, with union-avoidance consultants, industrial psychologists, and lawyers.

They also sought to ensure that workers failed in their strikes. Early on, they used injunctions to halt strikes and later in the century they insisted on and won no-strike clauses in contracts. They replaced striking workers whenever they could, especially in the unregulated and dis-regulated periods. Throughout the century they aimed to reduce workers' replacement costs through strategies such as deskilling, scientific management, automation, and stockpiling. And they used hiring and strike-breaking techniques to create divisions by race, gender, and nationality. They also relocated to areas with less worker organization (capital flight) or reorganized their firms to be more resistant to collective action, including using subcontractors, franchises, or part-time, contingent, or high turnover workers.

With employer offensives as a feature of U.S. labor relations, an important question is: What makes them more or less successful? We see them as less successful when pro-worker state regulations and laws are passed, macro contexts empowering workers develop (labor shortages or sharp increases in demands for essential goods), and workers successfully strike. The latter occurred when workers and unions developed crises for employers through strategies that matched the context, creating credible strike threats, maintaining high replacement costs, and the possibility of drawing in state and community support to resolve crises.

Lessons: Worker Strategies—Making Unions

Over the 115 that we study, workers tried, over and over again, to form unions and improve their situations. In some industries and periods, they were successful. We draw out a few themes across the three periods: maintaining high replacement costs, striking, building worker and community solidarity, building effective leadership, matching union strategy to existing structures, and pushing for pro-worker laws and institutions.

For most of the twentieth century, strikes or credible strike threats and other forms of disruption were crucial to the labor movement. In the early 1900s, strikes were regular features of union life, and a key mechanism to forming, and then defending, unions. Without legal protections or the ability to conduct NLRB elections, strikes were a major way to force employers to recognize and negotiate with unions. Even after the NLRA protections were put in place, workers continued to strike. Strikes were especially important for organizing new industries. We see a large strike wave at the onset of the manufacturing union upsurge in the 1930s and 1940s as well as in the public sector in the 1960s and 1970s. These strike waves were not only important for winning union recognition and improved conditions; they also helped push politicians to act.

Only in recent decades have strikes ebbed to such low levels. As union density and protective laws eroded, strikes declined, and these dynamics reinforced each other. Strikes are difficult to win when the balance of power heavily favors employers. Workers are more likely to strike when they believe that they have a chance of winning; and labor leaders have stepped back from agitating for strikes, probably for a variety of reasons. At the same time, it is important to recognize that the revival of the labor movement may depend on workers' renewed willingness to take strike action.

Another lesson from our analyses is about solidarity. In hostile terrain, expansive solidarity is important to workers' leverage. Community members, former (or future) employees of the same company, and workers across multiple workplaces are all important to building the labor movement. We saw forms of expansive solidarity in the move from craft to industrial organizing, in campaigns that combined workers' struggles with those fighting for immigrant rights, civil rights, and women's rights, and with worker centers that organize at the community level rather than only in specific workplaces. Throughout the century, we saw that within-workplace solidarity is absolutely necessary—workers themselves must lead efforts in their workplaces. However, strong workplace solidarity alone is not always sufficient. Especially in the absence of state support and the presence of aggressively anti-union employers, solidarity must be expansive, including a broad range of workers and supporters, with backing from the community and among unions.

Unions have also been more successful when their strategy matches the structure of their work. Building high replacement costs through apprenticeship programs and skill closure was a viable strategy for craft workers in the early 1900s. This approach was inappropriate for the less-skilled manufacturing workers. Manufacturing workers eventually embraced industrial organizing and sit-down strikes. Public sector workers, by contrast, faced different opportunities and constraints, including employers who were less aggressively anti-union. They combined the advantage of their circumstances with strikes to win substantial gains.

By the end of the dis-regulated period, the political economy of work had changed substantially from the mid-twentieth century, including the existence of more mega-corporations (most of which were anti-union), subcontracted arrangements, contingent work, and weakened labor laws. These new circumstances will require approaches that build workers' power appropriate for these circumstances, along with the use of older techniques when useful.

Finally, union leadership matters, though short-term success is most forthcoming when the conditions are right (e.g., when worker replacement costs are high, the state effectively holds employers' abuses in check, labor markets are tight, and workers' grievances are high). A plethora of new ideas, orientations, debates, and new possibilities drive workers' excitement and sense of the possibilities through collective action. Collective action is inherently risky; leaders may alleviate workers' concerns with plans that inspire and invigorate them. The U.S. labor movement was invigorated by the IWW, the TUUL (especially once it disbanded and sent its organizers to work for the CIO), and especially with the most successful of the three, the CIO because the conditions were favorable and the CIO's strategies of industrial organizing and sit-down strikes were well-suited to the context and effective. Each entity infused new ideological orientations and convictions, gave ignored workers a voice, and broadened the horizon of possibility. To effectively revitalize, workers need to leverage conditions as best they can and win strikes. With new political insights, orientations, and organizing strategies adapted to the current situations and times, unions could make advances. Efforts must provide for the democratic inclusion of any and all workers who want to participate. Workers' hearts and minds are the focus; they must have a role in shaping their own destinies. Debating and participating is how they learn from each other and how to take charge.

Lessons: Race and Gender

Although most accounts of national-level union density don't assess race and gender dynamics, an industry-level analysis reveals how intimately tied race and gender have been to unionization in the United States. When our story began in 1900, gender norms, discrimination, and the physical demands of childbearing relegated women to specific, often lower-paying industries. White women were expected to cease work upon marriage. Discrimination against people of color and ethnic groups by employers and unions as well as by laws and political developments (e.g., Jim Crow laws and sharecropping arrangements, Chinese Exclusion Act, the internment of Japanese Americans during World War II, the Bracero Program) severely limited the types of work people of color could pursue and their skill acquisition opportunities. While many immigrants acquired skills in their countries of origin, white men, especially those with network connections to other skilled workers, commonly acquired access to apprenticeship programs to develop valuable skills. Unions oftentimes explicitly excluded women and workers of color from acquiring such training and from joining their unions. But even when unions did not explicitly bar women and workers of color, these workers were channeled into industries with lower replacement costs and outside of the traditional focus of AFL unions. When these workers tried to organize themselves, especially Black workers, they often faced state violence and hostility from white workers.

We saw that over the century, employers have had a long history of using race and gender to divide workers. Sometimes this was overt, such as using replacement workers to stoke animosity. But hiring and promotion patterns also divided workers by race and gender within workplaces.

Union leaders have had mixed stances on race and gender equity, with exclusionary, radically inclusive, and orientations in between. The early AFL focused on organizing skilled workers—who were also disproportionately white and male—due to practices of both unions and employers. Other labor organizations aimed to galvanize all workers, particularly the IWW and the TUUL. However, these organizations experienced more repression and accomplished far less durable unionization than the AFL. The result of AFL dominance was that the industries where we find the highest union density during the unregulated period were those with predominantly white male workforces: construction, mining, TCU, and entertainment. Especially in the unregulated period, women were both less present in the workforce and less likely to acquire skills. While there are examples of predominantly women unions within the AFL (e.g., International Ladies Garment Workers Union) and important women union leaders (e.g., the IWW's Elizabeth Gurley Flynn), unionism was mainly led by and represented white, skilled men.

This exclusive union character receded with the rise of industrial organizing, heralded by the CIO, which opened the doors for workers of all skills, but in practice was strongest in manufacturing. By mid-century, helped along by World War II, women and workers of color entered the labor force in greater numbers. The CIO responded to their presence by declaring itself to be "a people's movement, for security, for jobs, for civil rights and freedom. It speaks for all the working men and women of America, Negro and white . . . [and] fights to bring the benefits of industrial organization to all working people in the only way it can be done—by organizing all the workers, excluding none, discriminating against none" (CIO, qtd. in Stepan-Norris and Zeitlin 2003, 3). That is, just as the AFL opted for a craft-based model based on exclusion, the CIO chose an industrial orientation based on inclusion and maximizing solidarity, though sometimes its efforts fell short.

Still, the industries most populated by women and workers of color were not the key organizing targets of unions, even the CIO. The seminal NLRA excluded key groups of workers from protection, including agricultural, domestic workers, tipped workers, and public sector workers—all groups that were disproportionately women or workers of color and some disproportionately resided in the South. As unions leaned into NLRB organizing, these unprotected workers were left out.

Just as union's fortunes began to wane during the dis-regulated period, women, workers of color, and immigrants increasingly became the face of the labor movement. Caucus organizations inside the union movement pushed for their further inclusion and equality. And women's and race-based activity within and outside unions, along with civil rights laws in the 1960s and on, provided women and people of color opportunities to obtain better employment and began to diversify occupational hierarchies. Some of the largest growing industries of the time—health services, public administration, and education—had large numbers of women and workers of color. Around this time, some of the professional organizations for teachers and nurses (mainly women workers who had licensing or credentialing) ended their quest for advancement through professional status and instead pivoted toward the mainstream labor movement. This brought hundreds of thousands of women and workers of color into the labor fold, many of whom benefited from skill closure (licensing and credentialing) and industries that were resistant to capital flight. And dynamic organizing initiatives (like Justice for Janitors) also brought in workers of color and immigrants into the labor movement. Unions also played important roles in pay equity, which helped to invigorate a more diverse movement. In the dis-regulated period, unions launched major campaigns to promote "comparable worth" and to bargain over issues like paid family leave.

By the dis-regulated period, women and workers of color had become among the most dedicated members of the labor movement. Still, many of these workers worked in industries or jobs that were not unionized. Worker centers, especially, focused on organizing workers who have had less access to unions, including immigrant workers and low-wage workers in service, construction, and agriculture.

Divisions based on race and gender have plagued the labor movement. A strong, revitalized movement requires an anti-racist, feminist approach to union building.

Lessons: The Importance of Large Industries

National-level union density depends on organizing the industries with the largest employment. Today, trade is the largest employer, and almost completely union-free. It is hard to imagine a resurgence in unions without organizing trade, especially retail trade.

This situation is similar to that of manufacturing in the 1930s, which had grown to be the largest industry. Both the growth in manufacturing employment and the fate of manufacturing unions mattered greatly for the boom in overall union density during the regulated period. The CIO focused on manufacturing, using strikes and NLRB elections to bring tremendous numbers of workers into the union fold and to spur similar organizing by the AFL unions. These efforts built union density in manufacturing as well as in the overall economy. Conversely, as manufacturing employment declined and as unions in that industry shrank during the end of the regulated and throughout the dis-regulated period, the bust in overall union density was hastened.

Organizing trade in the contemporary era will likely require different tactics than those used in manufacturing during the regulated period. The path remains to be seen, but we suspect it will involve direct action, expansive solidarity that connects workers to the broader community, greater government regulation of the sector, and probably an eclectic set of tactics, from alliances to NLRB elections. In the past, new industries have not organized by slowly augmenting their numbers (Clawson 2003). Rather, upsurges are characterized by widespread organizing, as happened in manufacturing and public administration/education. We expect that if workers organize in trade, it will be with an upsurge.

Although trade has the largest employment, public administration/education, and health services also have substantial employment numbers. They also have relatively high replacement costs: they are place-based and have significant numbers of skilled, credentialed, or licensed workers. They provide critical services and are located in every county across the United States. Density in these industries has remained relatively steady, even against the tide of decline in almost all private industries. These workers, particularly educators, have flexed their strike muscles in recent years. The actions of these workers have pushed back against declining union density, given their large and growing numbers of employees.

Postscript: After 2015

We end our analyses in 2015 with an almost all-time low in union density and strikes. In some ways, this labor climate is similar to that of one hundred years ago, strongly favoring employers, despite the efforts of unions and workers.

However, even in this hostile climate, some workers have organized or won strikes to improve conditions. The 2018 mass walkouts by educators provide a good example of relatively successful strikes in an unfavorable political climate. Educators have replacement costs: they are credentialed and in demand, their work is time-sensitive, and their workplaces are relatively place-based. The strikes began in West Virginia, where public sector strikes are illegal. Strikes quickly spread to multiple states, involving more than 375,000 education workers in 2018. Many of these strikes resulted in at least partial victories and contributed to union strength. From 2018 to 2019, the American Federation of Teachers grew by 100,000 members. The states that saw union victories had the largest membership growth. For example, Arizona educators won a 20 percent raise and this victory spurred the local affiliate to grow by 10.3 percent. Oklahoma educators saw far less success and subsequently saw a drop in membership by 1.7 percent (Blanc 2020). It's also useful to note that educators have increasingly organized around "bargaining for the common good," which expands union efforts beyond bread-and-butter issues to those of the broader community, including class size, debt, and racial justice. This broadening of scope is a contemporary example of "expansive solidarity." The teachers strike wave of 2018 reminds us that workers—even in red states with low union strength—sometimes strike if they see similarly situated workers winning elsewhere.

Flight attendants, too, have high replacement costs, similar to other transportation workers. They also have a union president who has a bold vision of the power of strikes and disruption. When the U.S. government shut down in

2019, Sara Nelson, President of the Association of Flight Attendants, agitated for action, including calls for a general strike—a rare stance for a national labor leader in the twenty-first century. The situation culminated in some workers not reporting to work, some planes not taking off, and substantial media and political attention. Later that day, President Trump announced a plan to reopen the government. Some speculate that the pressure by the flight attendants pushed this capitulation, with Senator Bernie Sanders remarking to union President Nelson, "Between you and me, that's what ended the shutdown . . . when planes looked like they weren't taking off" (as qtd. in the *New York Times*; Kitroeff 2019).

Similarly, fast food workers sought to improve their conditions in the 2010s. But, compared to educators, these workers had lower replacement costs, especially in terms of scarce skills, and they faced highly franchised employers, along with some of the most powerful mega-corporations in the country with a powerful employer organization, the National Restaurant Association. Mostly subject to near minimum wages, unstable schedules, and other issues, workers called for "$15 and a Union." Structurally, traditional NLRB elections do not map well onto these work arrangements. Their small, dispersed workplaces would require thousands of individual elections, against some of the most deep-pocketed mega-corporations in the country. The 2010s saw fast food workers using coordinated, mostly one-day strike events to create pressure. These strikes did not result in widespread walkouts or shutdowns; nor did they result in unionization. However, they did bring the problems of low-wage work to the public eye, new activists into the labor movement, and perhaps led to a renewed energy to increase the minimum wage.

The COVID-19 pandemic uniquely altered work. The pandemic led to labor shortages, which contributed to higher replacement costs. It also contributed to a new set of experiences and grievances, including safety concerns at work, soaring inflation (meaning that wages do not have the same purchasing power), and high profits for many companies. Combined, these factors have led already unionized workers to push for better conditions and to consider strikes as a way to achieve this. Fall 2021 into 2022 saw a surge in strikes, and several large unions were prepared to strike but were able to negotiate agreements in the eleventh hour. These averted strikes spanned many industries and subindustries, including theater, health, and education.

Labor activity also surged among non-union workers. Given the odds stacked against them, some workers have strategized to act like a union, even without a NLRB election or winning exclusive representation. Reminiscent of the unregulated era, these workers use solidarity (sometimes called a "militant minority") to agitate for improved conditions and to reassert their voice in their workplaces. For example, the Alphabet Workers (workers at technology companies like Google, including its subcontractors) and Amazonians United (workers at Amazon) didn't win NLRB elections nor do they have union recognition from their employers. However, they are groups of workers who press for change within their workplaces through collective action. NLRB elections, however, still have a role to play.

As this book goes to press, NLRB elections have seen a sharp increase from previous years. Some workers are winning unions through these elections, including first-ever organizing wins at Starbucks, Amazon, Apple, Trader Joes, and REI. Not surprisingly, employers have fiercely fought these efforts. Starbucks workers have turned to strikes, among other strategies, to win first contracts. Nevertheless, the upturn in elections and strikes is a sign that workers and unions may be on the move once more.

Our research suggests that large-scale shifts in power toward unions will probably follow favorable conditions combined with the use of broad-based and expansive solidarity, bold democratic leadership, renewed tactics to increase replacement costs, and the courage of workers to take what may be big risks, including striking. It will also require state action to rein in employers' excessive power and to increase replacement costs for workers.

Conclusion

The fate of working people rests on the ability of unions to reinvent themselves to both adapt to and to shape the current economic, political, and legal context. Building the power to do so is a herculean task. Our century-plus account details the many obstacles that workers have faced, including powerful anti-union employers and a government with an inconsistent record of supporting workers' rights. And yet history tells us that working people have sometimes been able to form and defend unions. These unions were not perfect—race and gender inequities could be extreme and corruption sometimes crept in. And, as in all organizations, sometimes leaders failed. But at the same time, strong unions have been critical to creating decent workplaces and a more equitable society.

Rebuilding unions will require more favorable conditions for workers and unions, and the de-powering of employers. This, in turn, requires more serious enforcement of existing laws and the passage of new laws to reduce the great power differential between employers and unions. It's up to elected union leaders to provide vision and commitment, and it is up to workers to elect the forward-thinking leaders that they need and to be proactive with calculated collective action.

The many booms and busts, upsurges, strikes, and organizing innovations that characterize most of the twentieth century suggest that future workers will once again take actions to overcome obstacles and build unions.

APPENDIX A

A Brief History of Major Modern Union Federations

The population of labor unions exists within a hierarchy of organizations that changes over the century. At the highest level are federated and non-federated unions. The former are protected by their federations, while the latter are mostly independent.[1] Unions that belong to federations have extensive interactions with other unions inside their own federations (at federation conventions, within federation departments, in regional bodies, and during jurisdictional and other disputes) and sometimes with those outside of their federations.

Following is a short history of each of the major U.S. labor federations active during the last hundred (plus) years.

Knights of Labor

Although the Knights of Labor (KoL) ceased to be an effective labor federation by 1900, we briefly discuss it here due to its relevance to the structure and character of the AFL. The KoL was founded in Philadelphia in 1869, on the heels of the dissolution of the Garment Cutters' Association. It rejected the wage labor system in favor of the principles of coop-eration and education and maintained a policy of strict secrecy (until 1882). Importantly, it rejected the notion of craft unionism in favor of organizing workers of all crafts and skills. While it was very effective in its implementation of boycotts, it was less successful at strikes. Its heterogeneous locals were disadvantaged in strikes vis-à-vis employers due to a lack of coordination (Greenfield 1977, 22), and because its leaders opposed (but didn't or couldn't contain) strikes. Its proposals "ranged from the establishment of bureaus of labor statistics and the abolition of child labor, through a dozen other desiderata, to the call for cooperatives, both productive and distributive, and the 'substitution of arbitration for strikes, whenever and wherever employers and employes [sic] are willing to meet on eq-uitable grounds'" (Neufeld 1956, 374). The KoL became a national organization in 1878. It experienced a dramatic membership boom that peaked in 1886, which was immediately followed by a series of defeats. The added pressure of AFL rivalry hastened its quick de-cline. "By the end of the century, the KoL ceased to be an effective trade union organiza-tion" (Fink 1977, 165–167).

---

[1] Later in the century, several independent unions formed groups to pursue more coordinated po-litical influence and protection against raiding from AFL-CIO unions. These include the National Federation of Independent Unions and the National Independent Union Council.

American Federation of Labor

The American Federation of Labor (AFL) was formed as skilled craftsmen began to reject the form of organization offered by the then-dominant KoL. In November 1881, several KoL trade assemblies (mainly those of molders, cigar makers, printers, iron and steel workers, and lake seamen) organized a convention to found the Federation of Trades and Labor Unions. In 1882, while still loosely formed (and without a constitution), they called themselves the Federation of Organized Trades and Labor Unions of the United States of America and Canada. By its sixth annual convention in 1886, it was comprised of twenty-five national unions, which resolved themselves into the first convention of the American Federation of Labor and elected Samuel Gompers as the first president. The AFL's first constitution was adopted the following year in Baltimore, Maryland.

It advocated, in direct opposition to the then much larger and more successful KoL, that labor's interests were best advanced by an organization of autonomous trade unions. Within four years, the AFL overshadowed the KoL, marking a "change in the tactics and ultimate objectives of the labor movement, an abandonment of the idea that all workers had the same economic interests and a departure from the old 'producing classes' point of view" (Millis and Montgomery 1945, 75).

AFL unions mainly accepted only skilled workers and required considerable initiation fees and dues. Their view was that they could best advance the interests of members by using skill scarcity to pressure employers. They sought to control the labor supply, using apprenticeship programs to monitor and, if necessary, reduce the number of skilled workers. Thus, they were formed on the premise of high replacement costs, with little attention to less skilled workers. This excluded most women and workers of color. And many AFL unions had specific requirements that prevented workers of color or women from joining their ranks.

During its first two decades, the AFL admitted, chartered as affiliated bodies, and granted autonomy to every craft organization that applied for affiliation. The open-door policy created a situation where more than one affiliated union represented workers in a single industry or craft. The AFL recognized this as a problem, and in 1907 it developed departments to encompass all of the unions in the largest industries: building trades, metal trades, railway employees, and union label trades. It also developed the "one craft, one union" policy, which required unions working in the same or similar trades to merge. The implications of this new policy included conflicts among some unions over orders to merge and rejection of the proposed terms of mergers, and a reduction in the total number of affiliates through successful mergers. Unions that refused to merge were expelled from the AFL (BLS 1926). The AFL, which was initially funded by a small per-capita tax, "mediated jurisdictional differences among member unions; brought dispersed locals together into national unions; made the organizing talents of older unions available to new ones; aided its member unions in employer negotiations; heard complaints from individual union members; established new locals for its international unions; encouraged joint organizing campaigns with full-time AFL organizers (after 1900); and made loans and donations to member unions" (Reed 1977, 11).

In its early years, Gompers and other AFL leaders held a "position of tolerance and even of limited support for certain socialist doctrines," but they later moved toward "profound mistrust" (Laslett 1984, 119). And early on, socialists had "considerable strength in the organization." In fact, in 1894 the AFL narrowly missed adopting a political program that included a plank advocating collective ownership of all means of production and distribution (1984, 119). By the end of World War I, the AFL's principle of "pure and simple" or "job conscious" unionism set in, and it maintained distance from organized political advocacy thereafter.

Two principles characterized the AFL: "(1) the principle of autonomy ... and (2) the principle of exclusive jurisdiction, that there can be only one legitimate union in one recognized field of jurisdiction" (Slichter 1947). The principle of trade union autonomy ensured national unions' dominance over the various federations. In this early period, the AFL was itself not the center of power in the labor movement; rather, it was "primarily a collection of sovereign, independent trade organizations, with Gompers and his colleagues serving mainly as a broker between them" (Laslett 1984, 122).

For the AFL to assert control over local federations, it had to first "destroy the city centrals' ability to compete with the nationals for control over the local unions and to confine them largely to the sphere of political activity; [and] second, to require them to render active support in the campaigns to bring all of the locals in each trade jurisdiction under the authority of the appropriate national union" (Ulman 1955, 381). National union dominance over the national federation was accomplished by relegating power over "affiliation of the individual, standards of admission, standards of discipline, standards of government, control over strikes, and collective bargaining" (Ulman 1955, 387) to each national union rather than to the AFL. This was in contrast to the model of centralized (federation-level) control in the KoL.

Similarly, the principle of exclusive jurisdiction was established to avoid various challenges. One was a problem faced by national unions within the KoL, which admitted previously expelled workers and locals who occasionally undermined the standards of employment upheld by the national unions. A second challenge came from the KoL's local federations, which threatened the national unions' economic control over trade areas. And finally, it allowed for settlement in cases where two national unions claimed the same jurisdictions by limiting the federation's grant of charters to those areas not specifically claimed by another affiliate. This principle was amended in 1901 by the "Scranton Declaration," which authorized the United Mine Workers to organize all craftsmen working in and around the coalmines, at the expense of other national unions claiming those specific jurisdictions. This declaration was seen as addressing peculiar circumstances, yet many more of the same were to come along (Ulman 1955, 404–406, 413–414).

The political character of the AFL ebbed and flowed over the years with changing political and economic conditions. During its first two decades, it adhered to the ideology of voluntarism focusing on the pursuit of its "narrow organizational self-interest" coupled with a "hostility to the capitalist system that had at least vague overtones of socialist rhetoric" (Greenstone 1977, 26). During this period, though Gompers suggested rewarding organized labor's friends and punishing its enemies, the AFL mainly supported Democratic candidates and causes, given the Republican Party's anti-union character. In the early teens, its sizeable socialist minority urged the federation toward more progressive causes and alliances with farmers and the liberal middle class. But the launch of the American Plan and its harsh anti-union climate resulted in the AFL's conservative turn during the 1920s. The New Deal period and its more favorable conditions brought the federation to a position of closer Democratic partnership (Greenstone 1977).

AFL Federal Labor Unions and Directly Affiliated Local Trade Unions

Federal labor unions and directly affiliated local trade unions, which existed during the AFL period, were composed of groups of workers in unclassified occupations and/or located in areas where national or local unions didn't exist, including locals comprised of women or Black workers. Rather than their own national union, these locals directly affiliated with the AFL. They were not entitled to the rights and privileges accorded national affiliates.

As these locals accumulated within various trade areas, they were encouraged to form the beginnings of new national unions or join with the appropriate affiliates. This, in fact, was the founding route for many international unions that existed during the 1920s and many others merged into existing national affiliates.

Another category of directly affiliated local trade unions in the early part of the century was local unions of Black workers in jurisdictions belonging to international unions that disallowed African American admission into the union. The outstanding example of this practice comes from the Steamship Clerks, Freight Handlers, Express and Station Employees. And finally, some directly affiliated local unions existed where jurisdictions were unsettled or international unions were unstable or collapsed (BLS 1926, 4).

Departments of the AFL/AFL-CIO

Departments within the AFL were formed in response to the criticism that craft unions alone could not "meet the challenge of industrial society" (Neufeld 1956, 382). They conducted all business within the major trades, which included Building Trades (formed in 1908, called Building and Construction Trades starting in 1943), metal trades (formed in 1908), Railway Employees (formed in 1908), Union Label Trades (formed in 1909), Government Employees Council (formed in 1945), and Maritime Trades (formed in 1948). After the AFL-CIO merger, the following departments were added: Industrial Union (formed in 1955), Scientific, Professional, and Cultural Employees Council (formed in 1967), Department for Professional Employees (formed in 1977), and Transportation Trades Department (formed in 1990). Each relatively independent department managed and financed its own affairs and held its own conventions. The larger departments also had local councils. The AFL aimed to have all AFL internationals affiliate with the relevant department, but in practice, most, not all, unions required their locals to join. As of 2017, Building and Construction, Maritime, Metal, Professional Employees, Transportation, and Union Label departments remained as constitutionally mandated departments.

Systems of Jurisdiction

Unions' authority to represent groups of workers in particular occupations, industries, or geographic areas constitutes their jurisdiction. The AFL granted member unions nonoverlapping charters that specified their jurisdictions and thereby created jurisdictional systems that map organizing rights covering much of, if not the entire, economy. Rival federations (including the IWW, TUUL, and CIO) had distinct jurisdictional systems that created conflicting claims of authority over certain groups of workers. Because independent unions are not subject to any jurisdictional claims other than their own, their jurisdictions may overlap with those of federated unions.

Despite nonoverlapping charters, jurisdictional conflicts oftentimes occur within federations due to raiding of unions against each other and to uncertainties in jurisdictions following changes in work processes and industries. The AFL heard complaints regarding jurisdictional disputes and made recommendations during earlier years, and more formal decisions later. After the passage of the National Labor Relations Act, the questions of how mass production workers would be organized and the complexities of jurisdictions became issues that led to "open warfare" in the AFL, leading to the formation of the Committee, then Congress of Industrial Organizations (CIO). Despite their many differences, the CIO maintained the principles of international union autonomy and dispute resolution and its structure closely mirrored that of the AFL (Vaughn 1990, 16–17).

Inter-federation jurisdictional disputes, brought about through uncertainty over which union had claim to a particular set of workers (due to different logics of organizing [e.g., craft vs. industrial], political considerations, and/or technological change) and often resulting in unions raiding each other's members, had a long history within the AFL. Once the CIO was formed, it found that it wasn't immune from internal disputes either. Early in its history, the AFL had sought to avoid interference in inter-union disputes. The CIO sought to actively intervene by initiating its own internal Organizational Disputes Agreement in 1951. But the rise of the CIO also initiated a set of inter-federation industrial jurisdiction conflicts, given that their unions claimed jurisdictions that were orthogonal to and overlapped with craft union jurisdictions. In 1953, the AFL and CIO co-drafted and ratified a no-raiding agreement, which was signed by some, but not all, affiliated unions. When the AFL-CIO merger occurred, the idea of overlapping jurisdictions was inevitable. On the eve of the AFL-CIO merger in 1955, the AFL created the AFL Internal Disputes Plan with an impartial umpire. In addition, the AFL and CIO entered into a series of no-raiding agreements. In 1962, the merged federation activated the AFL-CIO Internal Disputes Plan through Article XX of its constitution to settle disputes of affiliated unions with binding decisions outside of the orbit of the NLRB (Vaughn 1990).

A wave a union mergers was another outcome of the AFL-CIO federation merger. Between 1955 and 1960, sixteen unions merged (amalgamated or were absorbed) (Chaison 1980). Union mergers continued after the AFL and CIO merger, becoming one strategy to consolidate resources, members, and power in the dis-regulated period.

Industrial Workers of the World

The Industrial Workers of the World (IWW), or the "Wobblies," as they were called, was founded in 1905 largely in reaction to the "pure and simple trade unionism" of Gompers' AFL (Buhle 1999, 66). Among the founders were only one substantial union, the Western Federation of Miners (WFM), and representatives from the Socialist Labor Party and the Socialist Party of America. The Wobblies, who emphasized the inevitability of class conflict, organized all workers along industrial lines, especially the most marginal (immigrants, seasonal laborers, the unskilled), and required no more than nominal dues from their members (Rothenbuhler 1988). They refused to sign collective bargaining agreements and prevented the creation of fixed organizational hierarchies by rotating their officials (Fantasia and Stepan-Norris 2004). A split developed at the IWW's second national convention, and in 1911 the WFM returned to the AFL. Another internal dispute in 1908 ended with the expulsion of the SPL leader (Daniel DeLeon), who initiated a rival (but largely ineffective) "Detroit IWW." The main IWW led a series of free-speech fights, followed by a series of spectacular and innovative strikes and organizing campaigns (Fink 1977, 151–154). The federal government targeted the IWW in 1917 due to its opposition to World War I and "it largely ceased to be an active organization after the government purges" (Fink 1977, 153). The context of a bureaucratic and conservative AFL unionism spurred the Wobblies' anarcho-syndicalist "anti-organization," and the fierce state repression during World War I all but destroyed it.

Trade Union Educational League

The Trade Union Educational League (TUEL) was formed in 1922 by communists as an educational organization to prepare members to "bore from within" AFL unions. This meant rallying AFL union members around everyday grievances, working to replace reactionary AFL leaders, and moving the AFL toward industrial unionism. In industries where no AFL union existed, TUEL activists worked to organize new unions. The TUEL unions were subject to government and police raids, and its members were routinely expelled from AFL unions. In 1929, the TUEL transitioned into the Trade Union Unity League (TUUL), which was a rival federation to the AFL.

Trade Union Unity League

The TUEL was reorganized into the TUUL in 1929 on the instructions of the Fourth Congress of the Red International of Labor Unions. It operated with low initiation fees and dues and its officers were to receive no more than the average wage in the industry in which the union organized. The TUUL's objectives included "organizing the unorganized, developing class-conscious unions, developing a new leadership in the 'reformist unions,' defending the Soviet Union, working for equal treatment of Negroes, abolishing the 'speed-up,' establishing a seven-hour day, and supporting the Communist program in America" (Fink 1977, 394). The TUUL was disbanded in 1935 in favor of the popular front strategy, and its members were instructed to rejoin their relevant AFL unions.

Committee for Industrial Organizations and Congress of Industrial Organizations

With the onset of the Great Depression, and after a decade of intense labor repression and union decline, another attempt to broaden the base of organized labor into the mass production industries was launched from within the AFL. Initially constituted as the Committee for Industrial Organizations, eight AFL unions pushed for organizing in steel, auto, rubber, radio, and other mass production industries. The AFL was skeptical and then hostile to the endeavor. But the successful CIO union campaigns took on a life of their own, and their leaders refused to halt them. The AFL responded by suspending ten unions involved in the effort, whereby the CIO affiliates officially formed the Congress of Industrial Organizations, a rival federation. The CIO leadership was composed of right (Democratic Party types, with a few [very rare] Republicans), center (mixed/wavering or Socialist), and left (Communists and their allies) elements, which made the CIO much more politically progressive overall than the AFL.

Due to its leadership composition and its focus on organizing the entire working class (skilled, semi-skilled, and unskilled), the CIO represented a more socially inclusive type of unionism. It focused on organized the growing numbers of semi-skilled and unskilled industrial workers by industries, rather than by craft. It was inclusive of all workers, regardless of sex, race, religion, and national origin, to accomplish complete representation of all workers within worksites. The industrial strike strategy was to enlist participation by every worker and to prevent replacement workers from continuing production through persuasion and picket lines. This strategy contrasted to the AFL strategy of representing only skilled workers with high replacement costs, who had the capacity to win a strike alone.

The CIO's political stance was decidedly progressive. Many of its leaders had experience in the various Socialist and Communist parties and movements of the Great Depression. CIO supported legislation that improved the lot of all working people. During the late 1930s, it initiated organizing drives in several industries and also brought into the union fold waves of militant workers who spontaneously struck in mass production industries.

The CIO was founded following a crucial opening in the political opportunity structure: greatly improved labor conditions, considerable political discontent, worker and unemployed unrest, and participation by left-wing and radical organizers (through the Unemployed Councils and other organizations). Massive demonstrations and growing union power put pressure on the government to pass legislation (see Goldfield 1987). Democrats passed the National Labor Relations Act, which tilted the balance of power away from employers and toward unions, thereby increasing the success of union organizing campaigns. This facilitated the success of the CIO's strategy of industrial organization.

With the explosion of union organizing activity, experienced union organizers were difficult to find. CIO President John L. Lewis found it necessary to look beyond the normal pool of organizers in order to accommodate the demand. Although Communists were normally prohibited from leading/organizing (and sometimes even joining) AFL unions, the CIO unions abandoned all such restrictions. Communists with recent union experience in the TUEL and TUUL, along with Socialists, Trotskyists, and other radicals with labor experience, signed up to help in the massive CIO organizing drives.

Whereas the CIO was already predisposed toward social movement unionism, this opening unintentionally set it in that direction. It was unintentional because Lewis was convinced he could prevent the radicals from gaining leadership within the new CIO unions by monitoring their actions and moving them between organizing sites, and thereby preventing them from gaining a base in any one union or local. But there were too many organizing campaigns to staff all at once, and the radicals proved to be dedicated and effective organizers. In short order, the Communists and their sympathizers rose to the leadership of roughly half of all CIO unions and led factions in several others (Stepan-Norris and Zeitlin 2003).

Communist leadership shaped the policies and priorities of many CIO unions. Regarding collective bargaining, Stepan-Norris and Zeitlin (2003) show that in contrast to right or center unions, left-wing unions were more likely to win enhanced worker control on the shop floor. They were more likely to reserve workers' right to strike, to refuse to cede management prerogatives, and to establish effective and timely grievance procedures. The left-wing CIO unions were also more likely to be internally democratic and to support women's and minority workers' rights both inside and outside the workplace. Because they constituted an organized oppositional voice against the more mainstream CIO leadership, their presence significantly enhanced the overall level of CIO democracy.

Growing union power and a huge postwar strike wave led to a backlash that culminated in the passage of the Taft-Hartley Act, which weakened union security clauses, severely restricted strikes, and required all union leaders to sign non-Communist affidavits in order to use NLRB machinery. Pressures from the McCarthy era, as well as Communist unions' split from the CIO in their 1948 presidential endorsement, led the CIO to request that its leaders sign the non-Communist affidavits. The CIO investigated and expelled eleven "Communist-dominated" unions in 1949 and 1950. In doing so, it eliminated its core of progressive and energetic voices. The effect was to shift the CIO from social movement unionism toward bureaucratic unionism. This enabled its merger with the AFL (Fantasia and Stepan-Norris 2004).

American Federation of Labor-Congress of Industrial Organizations

After 1952, with the deaths of bitter rivals William Green (president of the AFL) and Philip Murray (president of the CIO) and with the new political alignment after the CIO purge of left-wing unions, a merger became feasible. The largest remaining barriers were union raiding and how to handle jurisdictional differences. In 1954, the two organizations pressured their affiliates to voluntarily sign a non-raiding agreement (prohibiting organizing drives where an AFL or CIO union already had bargaining rights), and the jurisdictional issue was handled through suggested union mergers among unions that shared jurisdictions. The 1955 AFL and CIO conventions accepted the merger agreement, and the first AFL-CIO convention was held on December 5, 1955. Most unions moved toward mixed craft and industrial membership profiles. AFL state and local federations and corresponding CIO industrial union councils were given two years to merge. The AFL department structure remained intact, with the addition of the industrial union department. After the merger, the AFL-CIO largely supported the Democratic Party and racial justice/civil rights measures, although some individual unions defied this direction.

Immediately following the merger, the issue of corrupt union practices and both internal and external investigations into them absorbed much of the new organizations time and effort. The outcomes of these practices included AFL-CIO required reforms of some former AFL unions and expulsion of others. Congress responded with the passage of the largely anti-labor Labor Management Reporting and Disclosure Act of 1959, which imposed government reporting on unions.

With AFL-CIO stagnation in organizing new workers in 1968, the UAW, the largest affiliated union, withdrew from the merged federation and a year later joined with the Teamsters to form the Alliance for Labor Action. With little progress and UAW President Walter Reuther's death in 1970, the alliance dissolved in 1972 (Fink 1977, 15–19).

Independent Unions

Wolman (1936, 136–139) reports that almost 40 percent of all union membership was affiliated with independent unions as of 1897. But with the AFL's active absorption of many independent unions, that percent declined to 28 percent by 1900 and to 16 percent by 1934. Wolman describes two types of independent unions: "the traditionally separatist railroad unions which, though independent, are on friendly terms with Federation unions, and organizations that challenge the jurisdiction of affiliated unions and become therefore involved in conflict with them and with the Federation." Some of the latter have been intentionally rival organizations, formed from factions within AFL unions, and engaged in long-standing jurisdictional disputes with their parent unions.

The 1929 BLS Handbook identified over forty "unaffiliated" (not affiliated to the AFL) "bona fide labor organizations functioning nationally" (1929, 1–3). Many of the independent unions listed there had never been identified with the AFL and a few had withdrawn or had been expelled from the AFL. Most of the independent unions existing in 1929 were in railroad and postal service. There were thirteen independent railroad unions, some covering unique jurisdictions and others "dual" unions. Some of these unions predated the AFL. Nine of thirteen postal service unions were independent in 1929. A few of the railroad and postal unions and the purely craft or industrial organizations outside the AFL, mainly found in clothing, textile, and the shoe industries, were for the most part, formed through secessions from AFL unions.

The circumstances surrounding the large presence of the most well-known of the independent unions, the railroad brotherhoods, is unique. Historically, unions have been more strongly established in the railroad industry than in other industries. Within the railroad industry, the train-service employees were the most thoroughly organized. The onset of World War I aided the organization of other classes of railroad workers, but the postwar period saw the replacement of many of these unions by company-controlled unions. When the Railway Labor Act (passed in 1926 and amended in 1934 and 1966) forbade company contributions to labor unions, many of these company unions became independent unions.

The other main origin of independent unions has been larger-scale efforts to form a national alternative to the middle-of-the-road AFL. These include the Socialist Trade and Labor Alliance, the Industrial Workers of the World, and the Trade Union Unity League. In addition, the expulsion of corrupt unions from the AFL and left-wing unions from the CIO left most of these as independent unions.

The 1936 Bureau of Labor Statistics Handbook refined its definition of a national union as "having national scope and significance, with locals or branches in more than one State, and having recognized headquarters and general officers representing and governing the entire membership (1936, 3). It reported 156 unions: 110 affiliated with the AFL (with a total [US and Canadian] membership of almost four million) and 46 unaffiliated unions (with a total membership of almost 700,000). Most of the 25 new unaffiliated unions organized since 1929 came after the NIRA. Seventeen of these were independent: 5 organized along industrial and 12 along craft lines.

Local independent unions have been more prevalent than national independent unions. The Office of Independent Unions, Wage Stabilization Board's 1952 directory of independent unions lists approximately 2,500 independent unions. This report does not define the criteria for inclusion in its listing. The vast majority of these unions did not meet the standard of a "national" union, including having a collective bargaining contract in more than one state.

Change to Win (CTW)

In 2005, seven large unions affiliated with the AFL-CIO split off to create a new federation, called Change to Win. These unions disagreed with several organizing principles of the AFL-CIO. Most prominently, they sought to redirect political spending to union organizing, force the merger of small unions and to rethink and enforce union jurisdictions to eliminate destructive union raiding, and further reduce the number of AFL-CIO departments. The core unions of CTW included the Teamsters, Laborers, SEIU, Carpenters, Farm Workers, UFCW, and UNITE HERE. With their departure, the AFL-CIO lost over five million, or 39 percent of its members. Among these unions, several were considered to be unions with more of a social-movement orientation. The big plans for enhanced organizing largely failed to materialize. Their efforts did not result in increases in union density. By 2015, only four unions remained (Teamsters, SEIU, Farm Workers, and Communication Workers) with four and a half million members.

Methodological Appendix

Gathering data on 115 years of labor relations has its challenges. Our goal has been to get a bird's-eye view of union density over this long arc of time. To do so, we collected data from multiple government publications, union reports, and secondary sources. We had to make a number of informed decisions about how to treat missing data or what to do when sources differ. We recognize that some may disagree with some of our data or periodization decisions. When possible, we lay out the major alternatives that we could have used. We also encountered situations where different sources reported (usually slightly) different information. In those cases, we selected the information from the source we most trusted. We are confident that while alternative sources may have resulted in slightly different numbers, the overall trends within industries remain the same. In this appendix we describe the major decisions that we made and why.

We also had to consider the ebbs and flows, the booms and busts that characterize U.S. labor relations. The careful reader will notice that sometimes memberships, elections, strikes, or labor force numbers fall or rise dramatically. We checked for accuracy in these cases to ensure that such shifts happened due to special circumstances.

For these reasons, our estimates of membership, density, strikes, and accompanying data are inevitably approximate. We present averages over decade periods to indicate broad trends, rather than yearly changes.

Union Membership

We compile yearly data on union memberships, from 1900 to 2015. Following Bureau of Labor Statistics (BLS) reports, we use the requirement of collective bargaining in more than one state as our definition of a national or international union, and we exclude unions that exist for less than five years. We collect union membership data from BLS reports, compilations from other scholars, and union reports. We exclude memberships from outside of the United States. We then aggregate union memberships to the industry level, using industry data from union reports to categorize unions by industry, detailed below.

The major advantage to this approach is that it allows us to assemble a comprehensive, uninterrupted data set of union membership for well over a century. A popular alternative approach to estimate union membership is to use survey data. The main survey used to track union membership is the Current Population Survey (CPS), which is a monthly household survey that asks respondents about their union status in their primary job. The CPS surveys households, asking the "reference" person of the household questions about the work, pay, and union status for the primary jobs of all household members over fifteen years of age. Aggregated data begin in 1973; estimates by state, detailed industry, and occupation begin in 1983. CPS-generated data are commonly used by scholars studying the most recent decades; see Hirsch and MacPherson (2003). For this study, the major limitation of CPS data is that they only document the dis-regulated era.

Union-reported memberships provide the best approach to examining a long arc of U.S. labor dynamics. Early labor scholar Leo Wolman (1936) explains that union membership size is our best estimate of organized labor's strength and the most reliable and continuous source of its measurement. These membership numbers paint a broad picture of the ebbs and flows of unionization. However, they are just that—broad. They do not capture precise changes in union membership year by year. Several points should be taken into consideration when using this approach. Most importantly, although most unions have collected and reported their membership numbers, they vary in their policy and practice of arriving at them. We aim to use sources that report per capita, dues-paying members. When reports are based on union leaders' statements, they may be unreliable. Over the century, unions have generally developed more bureaucratic structures that help to run their financial affairs and since the Landrum-Griffin Act of 1959, they are not only subject to periodic audits but also to government reporting. But especially in the early periods and for small unions, membership figures may not exist. Another issue is that we sometimes find large fluctuations in year-to-year membership, which may indicate an error or may truly reflect reality. An example of a factual large yearly membership change is when a substantial strike effort inspires large numbers of workers to sign union membership applications, hence driving up union membership numbers. Upon completion of the strike, especially if it failed to accomplish the desired goals, many of those workers may not pay the deferred initiation fees and union dues, thereby driving the union membership numbers back down. Some unions report little variation in membership and round their numbers when they report members (e.g., reporting 50,000 members for four years in a row). This suggests that membership numbers are estimates, rather than precisely calculated. Further, reports based on union dues payment reflect fluctuations in employment, unemployment, and strikes, as workers who have been laid off, who are underemployed, or who are on strike usually don't pay dues.

Despite these challenges, relying on figures reported by the major union federations, which, during some periods, account for the vast majority of all union members, overcomes some of these difficulties. Their reports, based on per capita tax paid by affiliated unions, provide "conservative and comparable" (Wolman 1936, 9) membership estimates.

It's important to note that membership numbers do not capture the full strength of the labor movement. Unions may yield political and economic power and accomplish goals that are not captured by merely reporting membership size. Still, for early years, "the data of membership appear in the long run most faithfully to represent the state of unionism" (Wolman 1936, 4).

There may be disagreement about which estimates most accurately represent union memberships. However, because our strategy requires consistency over the 115 years we study, the best option for this study is per capita membership reports by unions.

Below we list the sources that we consulted to generate yearly union data. In some cases, sources conflicted. Our strategy was to consistently use the same source over multiple years, only drawing on other sources when information was missing or if there was major disagreement between sources. We prioritize sources that use dues-paying members.

Leo Wolman (1936): Our Main Source for 1900–1934

The main source we use for the unregulated period is *Ebb and Flow in Trade Unionism* by Leo Wolman (1936), who compiled union-level membership data from 1900 to 1934. Wolman does not specifically articulate his definition of a union. Data are drawn from annual reports of the Executive Council of the AFL, with supplements from individual unions (1936, 14). We compare Wolman's numbers to those of other sources, which typically cover only a handful of years from that period, including BLS reports starting in 1926.

Troy and Sheflin (1985) and Troy (1965): Our Main Source for 1935–1947

Leo Troy (1965) collected union-level data for 1935–1962. Troy defines membership as dues-paying members and draws on financial reports to federations. When unavailable, he supplemented with other sources, such as letters from unions, reports from union conventions, BLS directories, and monographs of particular unions.

Troy and Sheflin expand and improve on Troy 1965, but they provide less information on small unions. In *Union Sourcebook* they provide membership based on average annual dues-paying, full-time equivalent membership for every known national and not small union between 1897 and 1983. They derive their membership numbers mainly from financial information on unions derived under the Labor Management Reporting and Disclosure Act of 1959, the Civil Service Reform Act, and annual reports to the Department of Labor's Office of Labor-Management Standards Enforcement. When necessary, they supplemented missing information with union-supplied information (8 percent of the total) or extrapolation (6 percent of the total). For the former, the annual per capita revenues from local unions is divided by the union's per capita rate to arrive at the annual membership.

We use Troy and Sheflin (1985) and, if not available, Troy (1965) for membership between 1935 and 1947 (after Wolman [1936] ends and before the BLS begins biannual reporting). Because this is an update on Troy (1965), we use this as our first option; we use Troy (1965) only when information is missing. We also use Troy/Troy and Sheflin to fill in missing data from Wolman or when the BLS does not record a specific union. We also use it for reference and to provide a check on our own figures.

Bureau of Labor Statistics Reports: Our Main Source for 1948–1979

The BLS reported union membership beginning in 1926, and biannually since 1948. From 1948 to 1980 these BLS reports are our main source for membership.

The earliest reports went by the name *Handbook of American Trade-Unions* (1926, 1929, 1936). The 1926 edition was an effort to list all of the existing labor organizations of the United States having national entity and significance. The 1929 edition "deals only with bona fide labor organizations functioning nationally in June 1929, and disregards entirely unions which are purely local in character, works councils, and those organizations which are or may be fairly regarded as company unions" (1). The 1936 edition uses membership reported to the BLS. Note that these definitions include Trade Union Unity League unions, which Wolman reports separately. We use these early BLS reports for reference, comparing them to Wolman, Troy, and Troy and Sheflin.

Beginning in 1943, the BLS generated a bi-yearly report of union memberships called the *Directory of U.S. Labor Organizations*. Earlier years list unions and headquarters, but not membership. Beginning in 1948, the BLS compiled union membership for all unions affiliated with the AFL, CIO, AFL-CIO, and independent unions that had negotiated contracts in more than one state. They state that "All national and international unions known to the Bureau of Labor Statistics are included."

There are some variations in how the BLS collected this data over time. From 1948 to 1954, unions were asked to report their annual average dues-paying membership or membership in good standing. If the union organization did not report membership, it was left blank. However, for nonreporting AFL, CIO, and AFL-CIO affiliates, paid per capita membership was used (noted by asterisks in source).

From 1955 to 1979, the series included all unions affiliated with the AFL-CIO and independent unions that had negotiated collective bargaining contracts with different employers in more than one state or, for federal government unions, those that had exclusive bargaining rights under Executive Order 11491. During these years, the BLS created a special questionnaire for union reporting of membership that attempted to standardize, as much as possible, union reports of membership numbers. The questionnaire requested the average number of dues-paying members during the first six months of the year (U.S. Government. Department of Labor 1950, 2). Later years asked unions to report average annual dues-paying membership for the two previous years (U.S. Government. Department of Labor 1979, 20). For nonreporting AFL-CIO affiliated unions, paid per capita membership as reported in the AFL-CIO convention proceedings was used.

Bureau of National Affairs Directories, Courtney Gifford, Ed.: Our Main Source for 1982–2015

From 1982 to 2015 the BLS's *Directory of U.S. Labor Organizations* series continued under a private publisher, Bloomberg's *Bureau of National Affairs* with Courtney Gifford as editor. The first edition states that the long form list was "prepared by the Bureau of Labor Statistics' Division of Industrial Relations, with updates by the editor to reflect subsequent mergers. The basic BLS requirement for inclusion in the list is affiliation with the AFL-CIO or, for unaffiliated unions, the existence of collective bargaining agreements with different employers in more than one state." Gifford includes professional and state associations that engaged in collective bargaining (or representational activities) and claimed membership in more than one state. Gifford also includes organizations operating in more than one city of a state. We, however, exclude unions operating in only one state. Many of the editions include extensive notes regarding reporting, which we take into account.

Other Sources

Some small unions have missing membership information for some years. When our main sources did not provide membership information, we consulted other secondary sources, including Craft and Peck (1998), Spomer (1992), Fink (1977), and Hannan (1988). We also consulted union convention proceedings, websites, or other internal publications to estimate membership.

On Missing Data

Using the sources described above, we were able to compile membership data for all but a handful of small unions. Some small unions continued to have missing data for a series of years, typically at their founding or at the time of merger or death. When this was the case, we estimated membership numbers on a case-by-case basis, given what we know. Typically, we assume that total membership is smaller at the founding date and subsequently grows. Likewise, we assume that their membership declines as unions approach organizational death. A handful of small, usually short-lived unions have no available data. We assign them a small membership of 5,000 workers. These adjustments are our best estimates of likely memberships. Because they only pertain to a handful of small unions (large unions have better recordings), these adjustments do not influence the broad patterns that we report.

Accounting for Non-U.S. members

Because we are interested in U.S. union density, we exclude international members from union membership. Some unions had sizeable numbers of Canadian members, and occasionally members in other countries or territories. Most unions, however, were almost exclusively populated by members working in the United States. We use a series of sources that report both total members and U.S. members: Wolman (1920), BLS (1954), BLS (1966), BLS (1978), Gifford (1992), and Gifford (2002). When we lack information on U.S. membership for unions with international membership, we calculate the percent U.S. members for the dates for which we have information, and then interpolate the nearest known percent between data points.

We do not have international membership estimates prior to 1920 for individual unions. However, Troy (1965) estimates that the total percent of union members that were Canadian in 1900 and 1910 as 1.8 percent. That percent rises to 3.4 percent in 1920. To estimate memberships in years prior to 1920, we take the percent of international members for each union in 1920 and reduce it by the aggregate percentage decline that Troy estimated. This is a rough approximation, given union variation in the percentage of non-U.S. members.

The last data point we have for international union membership is in 2002. We identified unions that were large (over 50,000 members) and had at least 10 percent Canadian members in 2002. For each, we consulted union websites in 2019 to gather the percent of members outside of the United States. We could not find information on a handful of unions, most notably the Amalgamated Transit Union, the Boilermakers, and the Bakery, Confectionary, Tobacco Workers and Grain Millers International Union. If data were missing, we used the last known percentage of international members, which we then subtracted from the total membership. Finally, if no sources indicated non-U.S. members for a union, we coded it as all U.S. workers.

Industry

We focus on eleven broad industries. Our long time period prevents us from disaggregating industries further because long-term data sources change how they define subindustries. Our broad industry categories allow us to be relatively consistent over time. We do not present data on all industries, as some have little relevance to our analyses. For example, we do not present information on business service, other professional service, or industry unknown. We combine some industries if that was the standard practice for the major reports that we use from the BLS. The industries are as follows:

1. Agriculture, forestry, and fisheries. We call this category "agriculture."
2. Mining. This includes metal, coal, and nonmetallic mining, and crude petroleum and natural gas extraction.
3. Construction. Also called building trades.
4. Manufacturing. We combine durable and nondurable manufacturing for this category.
5. Transportation, communication, and utilities. We abbreviate this to "TCU." We combine these three categories because they are frequently combined on BLS reports. Transportation captures multiple categories, including rail, air, buses, and trucking. Communication and utilities include categories such as telephone, sanitary services, water supply, and electric and gas. TCU also includes information and warehousing.
6. Trade. The trade category combines wholesale and retail trade. This category includes everything from food stores to the sale of motor vehicles.
7. FIRE. This is finance, insurance, and real estate, and includes banking.
8. Personal service. This includes categories such as hotels and lodging places, laundering, cleaning, barber and beauty shops, funeral services, dressmaking, shoe repair, and private households. This category was regularly used during the mid-twentieth century, including the 1950 and 1990 census industry classification. However, as the service sector expanded, some agencies began to report their statistics for smaller or larger subsets of this industry. We try to be as consistent as possible, but note that this category became more fluid during the dis-regulated period.
9. Entertainment. The subsectors of this category includes entertainment, arts, sports, museums, and recreation, which we refer to generally as "entertainment."
10. Health services. This includes hospitals, nursing and residential care facilities, other health services, and social assistance.
11. Public administration and education. We combined public administration and education because other data sources did not always disaggregate these categories. Almost all workers in these categories are in the public sector. However, other industries may also include public sector workers (e.g., public hospitals). Public administration includes federal, state, and local administration as well as postal service. Education includes elementary and secondary schools, colleges and universities, and vocational schools.

We aggregate individual union membership to the industry level. Some unions have substantial memberships in multiple industries, especially after the AFL-CIO merger in 1955 and into the dis-regulated period as unions looked for alternative strategies to defend or expand membership. To account for this, we develop a coding scheme to estimate the percent of members in each industry. We use the best data available; however, the calculations are not exact.

Our baseline data on industries are from the Hannan (1988) data set. This publicly available data set provides information on the main industry that a union represented at the time of the union's founding. For unions that were founded after the Hannan data set, we code industries based on the main membership of the union.

We then identify unions that have grown to have substantial numbers of members in multiple industries. Little systematic data exists on this topic, so we aim to estimate union memberships by industries for large unions, and those with substantial memberships in at least two industries. We focus on the period after the AFL-CIO merger in 1955, when unions increasingly begin to organize in multiple industries. We use the AFL-CIO reports which list union memberships by industry in the 1960s and 1970s, and we are able to compare to BLS industry estimates. We access secondary sources for unions unaffiliated with the AFL-CIO and for later years. We also check qualitative descriptions provided by Peterson (1945) and Craft and Peck (1998). Many unions fall primarily in one industry category, though it is common for large unions to have members across multiple industries. See Appendix A for a description of how unions managed jurisdictions over the century.

We identify the following unions as large and having substantial numbers of members in multiple industries: Service Employees International Union (SEIU), Teamsters (IBT), American Federation of State, County, and Municipal Employees (AFSCME), United Auto Workers (UAW), International Association of Machinists (IAM), Communication Workers of America (CWA), International Brotherhood of Electrical Workers, United Brotherhood of Carpenters, United Food and Commercial Workers (UFCW), UNITE HERE, and the Laborers International Union of North America (LIUNA).

For these unions, we aim to code for membership in each industry. This type of information is not well documented. We are able to code for three time points: 1962 or 1969; 1979; and around 2015. Data for 1969 (occasionally 1962) and 1979 have similar formats and are found in "Union Membership and Employment 1969–1979" prepared by the AFL-CIO Department of Research February (1980). These reports list union membership in each industry for unions affiliated with the AFL-CIO. We code the first and last year available: 1969 and 1979.

We supplement this with BLS data on union membership by industry, available yearly from 1962 to 1978. The strengths of the BLS data are that they cover some independent unions and have an earlier beginning time point. However, because there are large amounts of missing data, we do not use it as our main source. When they report information on the same unions, the AFL-CIO and BLS publications report similar statistics.

Five AFL-CIO affiliates had substantial membership in multiple industries in the earliest time period for which we have AFL-CIO estimates (either 1962 or 1969): SEIU, Machinists, Laborers, IBEW, and Carpenters. To determine membership by industry prior to this period, we do the following. In 1955, we assign each union to 100 percent of the industry indicated by Hannan (1988) as the union's main industry. Then from the earliest data point (1962 or 1969) on secondary (and other) industries, we extrapolate down to 1955. The AFL and CIO merged in 1955, and this marks a time of many mergers between international unions.

Because they were independent at the time, the Teamsters and the UAW are not included in the AFL-CIO report by industry. To address this, we assign 100 percent of UAW members to manufacturing until the mid-1990s, which is when UAW began to expand to other industries, such as education. We take the proportion of UAW members in each industry in 2015 (as reported on their website) and extrapolate down to 0 in 1995 for all industries, except for manufacturing, which we designate 100 percent of UAW members up until 1995.

The Teamsters has a long history of organizing in multiple industries. They provide little systematic data to the public. However, the Teamsters' website accessed in 2017 breaks down membership by industry. At that point, over 50 percent were in transportation/communication, roughly 25 percent were in manufacturing, and the rest were scattered across various industries. We extend these percentages back to 1969. Because there is no systematic data on the Teamsters, we use secondary sources to roughly estimate industry memberships back to the early 1900s.

Beyond the earlier AFL-CIO reports on industry breakdowns, there is no systematic information on union membership by industry in the 2000s. Therefore, in 2017 we examined union websites and/or directly corresponded with the unions to obtain this information. These numbers reflect membership in the previous one or two years (2016 or 2015). There is likely little difference between 2015 and 2016. We assign these estimates to 2015, which is our last year of data for the project. We were unable to obtain estimates of membership by industry for several unions: the Carpenters, UFCW, and Laborers. To address this, we took the same percentage breakdown by industry that the union listed in 1979 for those three unions.

The merger between UNITE and HERE in 2004 requires additional attention. At the time of merger in 2004, HERE had 239,041 and UNITE had 203,411 members. The 2017 website reports UNITE-HERE membership at 270,000, but members of the divisions have members totaling 465,000 (100,000 in each of the following: Hotels, Food Service, and Gaming; 45,000 in Airports; 20,000 in Transportation, but the last number is from when the union constituting this division previously merged with HERE). UNITE affiliates did not report membership. Using the fact that UNITE and HERE represented approximately the same number of members at the merger date, we attribute 100,000 to Textile. Using the total of the reported members in the industries (465,000) as the base, we estimate the proportions as follows: Hotels, 21.5 percent; Airports, 9.7 percent; Food Service, 21.5 percent; Gaming, 21.5 percent; Textile, Manufacturing, and Distribution, 21.5 percent; Transportation, 4.3 percent.

Finally, the AFL-CIO data from 1969 and 1979 only list "services" generally. We are interested in more detailed measures of service, including trade, health services, education, personal services, and entertainment. However, Unions that list their membership by industry on their websites tend to distinguish the type of service work. We extend 2015 estimates of various service types to the earlier time points. Again, we do not have website information for the Carpenters, UFCW, and Laborers. Of these, only the UFCW has substantial service sector members, which we designate as wholesale/retail trade services.

Census Data: Employment, Race, Gender, and Occupation

Employment data are drawn from the Integrated Public Use Microdata Series (IPUMS) (Ruggles and Sobek 1997), which is composed of census samples. The census provides the most consistent source of quantitative data on employment, with industry information beginning in 1910. The census also has information by industry on other key variables, including occupation, race, and gender.

One challenge to using employment data over a long time period is that the questions and sampling design of the U.S. Census changed over time. We follow the methodology established by Sobek (2001), who worked with the census to construct a method to create consistent employment data over time by industry. Sobek does the following. Employment numbers are limited to employed non-institutionalized civilians age sixteen or older in the labor force (1940–2015) or with an occupation (1910–1920). Industry classifications were introduced to the census in 1910. The IPUMS infers industries from occupations prior to 1910, and therefore industries are not comparable prior to 1910. All of our industry data, therefore, start in 1910. Industries are based on the 1950 industrial classification system. Likewise, occupations are based on the 1950 occupational classifications. It is not possible to determine employment status prior to 1940 and therefore we include only the employed. From 1940 and on, occupation statistics are limited to currently employed people, which matches the criteria set by the modern BLS. Sobek also details the participation of females. Due to the wording of the census, scholars agree that the estimated female participation rate is artificially low prior to 1940. However, scholars disagree over the magnitude of the effect. Sobek does not modify numbers of females in the labor force prior to 1940. It is also possible that the 1910 census overcounted women. Sobek presents 1910 data but cautions users of potential issues.

We opt to use the decennial census because it covers the longest period of time with key indicators on race, gender, occupation, and industry. While we lose some yearly precision with this approach, we gain consistency in measurement over time.

Three main alternative measures provide employment by industry. Each has limitations, and none cover the full century. We compare our census-based method to these alternatives. There are differences in employment numbers between all of these measures, which the Bureau of Economic Analyses (BEA) describes.[1] However, these data sets are similar in their general employment trends.

First, the Bureau of Economic Analyses provides yearly employment by industry beginning in 1929. The early decades do not include key industries for our analyses, including education, health, entertainment, and personal services. It also does not provide demographic data by industry. It does, however, include information on wages, corporate profits, hours worked, and other industry-level information. The BEA makes adjustments to account for employment not fully covered by the state unemployment insurance programs. Still, its employment counts differ from others.

Second, the Current Employment Statistics (CES) is an office of the BLS. It includes employment data for non-farm industries. Broad, aggregate measures begin in 1939; more detailed data are available toward the end of the twentieth century. The CES Program is a federal-state cooperative program. They write "The CES survey is based on approximately 149,000 businesses and government agencies representing approximately 651,000 worksites throughout the United States." One downside is that the CES industry groupings are aggregated in early decades (e.g., education and health are lumped together) and agriculture is excluded. It also does not include demographic information on workers by industry. The CEW is commonly used by economists and policymakers to track shifts in

---

[1] See Frequently Asked Questions section of the BEA, "What Is the Difference between BEA Employment and Wages and BLS and Census Employment and Wages," https://www.bea.gov/help/faq/104.

employment. Its employment figures are sometimes higher or lower than estimates from the census or the Current Population Survey (CPS).

Third, the CPS is a monthly survey of households conducted by the Bureau of Census for the BLS, with industry-specific questions beginning in 1983. CPS data are the most common way that scholars calculate union density (using both its union and employment information to calculate density). The CPS uses wage and salary workers as its base and therefore does not include independent contractors. Because the CPS only began in 1983, it not suitable for this project. We do use it as a check by comparing CPS union density and employment numbers to our estimates.

Union Density by Decade

Union density is the ratio of union membership to employment. We are interested in broad patterns of density over time. Because we use census data for employment, we typically have employment on the decennial, or every ten years. Therefore, we report estimates of industry union density by decade. This approach is also consistent with the nature of our membership estimates, which paint a broad picture of ebbs and flows of unionization rather than a precise accounting by year. We average membership for each decade, which we then divide by average employment. Because our analysis does not end on an even decade, we average 2000–2015 for our last time point.

We compare our estimates to other research which presents industry-level union density, including Wolman (1936) and through our own estimates of CPS data starting in 1983. There are some differences, which stem from the different numerators (the union membership data source) and the denominator (the employment source).

Union-reported memberships differ from CPS survey estimates of union membership. Union reported memberships (based on per capita dues) tend to be higher than CPS survey indicators (based on household reporting of the union status for household members' primary jobs). For example, using the CPS survey method, Hirsch and Macpherson report around 14.8 million union members and 16.4 million workers covered by union contracts in 2015. Using our methods (collecting membership numbers for all unions and then summing them for an aggregate number), we find around 18.8 million members. This number is smaller than what the major federations report themselves on their websites: the AFL-CIO reports around 12.5 million members, CTW around 4.5 million, and the National Education Association (NEA), a large independent union, reports close to 3 million members—for a total of around 20 million union workers.

These differences in union density estimates are most apparent in industry-level density variation by source. The time trends within industry are similar across sources. For example, in the dis-regulated era, our approach (membership reports divided by census employment) produces higher-density numbers for the manufacturing industry than the CPS approach (household surveys). These differences could stem from a number of factors, including how unions reported their membership by industry (which is how we constructed union member by industry), and how CPS respondents reported their family members' union status and industry. However, both approaches show similar trends within manufacturing: union density declines within manufacturing during the dis-regulated period.

Strike/Work Stoppage Data

There is no data set on strikes that covers a long period of time. We draw on multiple sources, with varying definitions, methods, and periods covered.

Florence Peterson (1937), "Strikes in the United States, 1880–1936," Bureau of Labor Statistics, Bulletin No. 651

The federal government began collecting data on strikes in conjunction with the 1880 census. This report contains major statistical data on strikes and lockouts from the earliest recorded date (1880) through 1936. Between 1881 and 1905, it conducted "periodic surveys" of strikes, but it collected less data from 1906 to 1913. In 1914, the BLS began its regular reporting of the number of strikes. In 1927, it made another major advance, by including "man-days" idle, detailed industry descriptions, and more information on strike outcomes. As of 1938, the Bureau's information on strikes and lockouts came from "700 daily, weekly and monthly papers and journals" and reports from government labor boards (Peterson 1937, 170). BLS staff members followed up on these newspaper reports with questionnaires to firms and unions engaged in the disputes in order to gather more systematic information. In her 1938 publication, the BLS's Florence Peterson stated that "it is believed that few, if any, strikes escape the Bureau's attention."

Prior to 1922, the BLS tracked strikes and lockouts separately. After, the BLS did not distinguish between the two, stating that the "industrial causes and effects are practically the same" and that the number of lockouts was relatively insignificant, comprising only 1–2 percent of all disputes (p. 4). All labor disputes were referred to with the generic term "strike" beginning in 1935. The BLS reports information on strikes that involve at least six workers and that lasted at least one day. Strikes statistics include number of strikes and number of workers involved. There is some information on a range of issues, including cause, outcome, sex of workers, establishment size, and state. Industry-level information is sparse from 1900 to 1926. Beginning in 1927, data collection was improved, including more systematic data by industry.

American Federation of Labor, Reports of Conventions Proceedings, Yearly 1900–1921

The AFL convention reports from 1900 to 1921 contain details on member unions, including number of charters, membership, and number of strikes won, compromised, and lost. We use the strike information to estimate AFL strikes by industry and their success.

IWW History Project: Industrial Workers of the World, 1905–1935, University of Washington

Co-directed by Professor James Gregory and Labor Archivist Conor Casey from the University of Washington, this project explores the history of the IWW. It includes a yearbook of IWW strikes and other events. Specifically, it identifies nearly four hundred strikes that took place between 1905 and 1920 which involved IWW presence, but not systematically by industry or number of workers involved. Some of these strikes may be "double counted" with the AFL strikes numbers, since some of these strikes also involved members affiliated with the AFL.

Bureau of Labor Statistics, Analysis of Strikes and Lockouts (Various Name Changes), Yearly 1934–1980 (Excludes 1935)

These yearly reports compile data on all work stoppages, and data are reported by industry, not by union. All of these reports combine strikes and lockouts, and depending on the year they use the terms "work stoppages," "strikes and lockouts," or "strikes" (all of which refer to the same phenomena—we use the term "strikes"). Strikes are defined as involving at least six workers and lasting at least one day. Smaller or shorter strikes are not counted. The BLS collects information on strikes principally through the news, union publications, and trade journals. For some years when the BLS received notice of a strike, the BLS sent report forms to representatives of employers and unions to receive more detailed information. It is possible that some strikes escaped attention, especially small, short strikes or those with no union representation.

The reports include both aggregate data on national trends and data by industry. Strike statistics include the number of strikes, number of workers involved, and days idle. Some years also contain more detailed information, including reason for the stoppage and contract status (e.g., was the strike issue over a first contract, etc.). These reports do not systematically report strike outcomes for most strikes. However, they do include additional information on very large strikes, those involving over 10,000 workers. For these very large strikes, the reports include information on the major terms of settlement, which we code to determine general outcome (predominantly a win, compromise, or loss).

The BLS delivered its historical files to the National Archives, which now holds several electronic historical work stoppages files: 1953–1977, with information on number of workers involved, state, *SIC*, major issue, contract status, beginning and ending dates, and days idle. The 1978–1981 file adds several fields, including union and employer involved, violence, mediation, and settlement. The yearly strike reports have been digitized and are now available online.

Bureau of Labor Statistics, Major Work Stoppage Data

The BLS ceased publishing work stoppage reports in 1981. However, it did continue to publish information on "major" work stoppages, which it defines as involving over 1,000 workers and lasting at least one full shift. The BLS obtains information on strikes from major media sources, reports from the Federal Mediation and Conciliation Service (FMCS), state labor market information offices, and BLS Strike Reports from the Office of Employment and Unemployment Statistics. We use FMCS data for our main strike analysis since it includes smaller strikes.

The BLS also reported information on large strikes, or those involving over 10,000 workers. The BLS only describes the major terms of settlement up until 1980. Since the outcome was not reported in later years, we code the outcome for strikes involving 10,000 workers. After 1980, we construct the list of very large strikes (10,000 or more) from the BLS publication (U.S. BLS 1993) on major work stoppages. We consult news reports and union publications to code for whether these strikes resulted predominantly in a win, compromise, or loss.

Federal Mediation and Conciliation Service, Work Stoppage Data, Yearly 1984–2014

The FMCS collected data on nearly every authorized strike beginning in 1984, which is the data we primarily use to analyze strikes in the dis-regulated period.

The FMCS reports strikes by bargaining unit and includes industry information, size, and union affiliation, which we then aggregate to the industry level. The FMCS does not include strikes associated with new organizing efforts. Although strikes for recognition were common in earlier decades, they had become relatively rare during the dis-regulated period (Martin 2008), suggesting that their omission from the FMCS would not substantially change our analyses. The FMCS identifies strikes by bargaining unit, rather than firm or union, meaning that strikes by two unions at the same firm are counted twice. Even with this potential for overcounting, the strike rate is substantially lower in the dis-regulated period. Similar to other sources, the FMCS does not differentiate between strikes and lockouts, but evidence suggests that, like in the earlier periods, the rate of lockouts is small (Martin and Dixon 2010, fn 9).

National Labor Relations Board Data

The National Labor Relations Board (NLRB) published detailed yearly reports from 1936 to 2010. These reports have several types of information relevant to this project. These detailed annual reports were discontinued in 2011; however, aggregate measures on elections and decertifications are still available through the NLRB website.

The NLRB reports include the number of unfair labor practices cases filed by employers and unions. Only unions filed ULPs initially; employers began in 1948. We do not present ULP trends for industries that are largely uncovered by the NLRB, including public administration and education and agriculture, forestry, and fisheries. In 1964, the NLRB changed several aspects of its yearly reports, including adding several industries (entertainment, personal services, and health services).

The NLRB reports also include aggregate and industry-specific data on NLRB elections, including the number of elections and their outcome, as well as the number of workers eligible to vote and their outcome. The reports also include information on decertifications starting in 1948. Beginning in 2009, the reports use fiscal, rather than calendar, year.

Each yearly NLRB report has a table that breaks down elections by industry, which is the main table we use for this project. This table reports on the numbers of cases closed in any given year (rather than petitions filed) and outcome. The NLRB holds several different types of elections and their reporting methods change over time, especially on how they report on decertification elections. Until 1963, the industry table on elections excluded decertification elections. Beginning in 1964, the industry table reported on all elections combined, including decertifications, RC elections, and RM elections. As elections over new bargaining units, RC elections are filed by employees or unions and RM elections are filed by employers. RC cases make up the vast majority of all elections.

Decertification elections were a small fraction of overall elections. For example, in 1964 of the 7,529 elections held, 220 were decertification elections. In 2015, of the 1,687 elections held, 21 were decertifications. The industry-level tables do not indicate the type of elections; however, because decertifications comprise only a small number of overall elections, most of the trends can be attributed to new organizing (RC cases).

References

Aaron, Benjamin. 1962. "The Labor Injunction Reappraised." *UCLA Law Review* 10 (1962–63): 292–346.

Acker, Joan. 1989. *Doing Comparable Worth*. Philadelphia: Temple University Press.

Adams, David. 1995. "Internal Military Intervention in the United States." *Journal of Peace Research* 32 (2): 197–211.

American Federation of Labor. 1900–1921. *Report of Proceedings of the Annual Convention of the American Federation of Labor*. Washington, DC: The Law Reporter Printing Company.

American Federation of Labor—Congress of Industrial Organizations. 1980. *Union Membership and Employment 1969–1979*. Department of Research.

Apesoa-Varano, Ester C., and Charles S. Varano. 2004. "Nurses and Labor Activism in the United States: The Role of Class, Gender, and Ideology." *Social Justice* 31 (3): 77–104.

Aronson, Robert. 1985. "Unionism among Professional Employees in the Private Sector." *Industrial and Labor Relations Review* 38 (3): 352–364.

Ashby, Steven. 2017. "Assessing the Fight for Fifteen Movement from Chicago." *Labor Studies Journal* 42 (4): 366–386.

Ashenfelter, Orley, and John H. Pencavel. 1969. "American Trade Union Growth: 1900–1960." *The Quarterly Journal of Economics* 83 (3): 434–448.

Attwell, Paul. 1987. "The Deskilling Controversy." *Work and Occupations* 14 (3): 323–346.

Auerbach, Jerold. 1964. "The La Follette Committee." *The Journal of American History* 51 (3): 435–459.

Bernstein, Irving. 1954. "The Growth of American Unions." *The American Economic Review* 44 (3): 301–318.

Bernstein, Irving. 1969. *The Turbulent Years: A History of the American Worker, 1933–41*. Boston: Houghton-Mifflin.

Bernstein, Irving. 1972. *The Lean Years: A History of the American Worker, 1920–1933*. Boston: Houghton-Mifflin.

Bivens, Josh, and Lawrence Mishel. 2015. *Understanding the Historical Divergence Between Productivity and a Typical Worker's Pay*. Washington, DC: Economic Policy Institute. Briefing Paper.

Blackwelder, Julia K. 1997. *Now Hiring: The Feminization of Work in the United States, 1900–1995*. College Station: Texas A&M University Press.

Blanc, Eric. 2020. "The Red for Ed Movement, Two Years in." *New Labor Forum* 29 (3): 66–73.

Bluestone, Barry, and Bennett Harrison. 1982. *The Deindustrialization of America*. New York: Basic Books.

Bonacich, Edna. 1972. "A Theory of Ethnic Antagonism: The Split Labor Market." *American Sociological Review* 37 (5): 547–559.

Bonacich, Edna. 1976. "Advanced Capitalism and Black/White Race Relations in the United States: A Split Labor Market Interpretation." *American Sociological Review* 41 (1): 34–51.

Bonnett, Clarence E. 1922. *Employers' Associations in the United States: A Study of Typical Associations*. New York: Macmillan Press.

Boone, Daniel W. 2010. "Steelworkers Trilogy." In *Arbitration 2010: The Steelworkers Trilogy at 50*, edited by Paul Studohr and Mark Lurie, 100–141. Proceedings of the 63rd Annual Meeting of Arbitrators, Philadelphia, PA.

Boone, Graham. 2015. "Labor Law Highlights, 1915–2015." *Monthly Labor Review* 138 (October), https://doi.org/10.21916/mlr.2015.38.

Boris, Eileen, and Jennifer Klein. 2015. *Caring for America: Home Health Workers in the Shadow of the Welfare State*. Oxford: Oxford University Press.

Boris, Eileen, and Annelise Orleck. 2011. "Feminism in the Labor Movement: A Century of Collaboration and Conflict." *New Labor Forum* 20 (1): 33–41.

Bowles, Samuel, and Herbert Gintis. 1976. *Schooling in Capitalist America*. New York: Basic Books.

Boyle, Kevin. 1995. "'There Are No Union Sorrows That the Union Can't Heal': The Struggle for Racial Equality in the United Automobile Workers, 1940–1960." *Labor History* 36: 5–23.

Boyle, Kevin. 1998. *The UAW and the Heyday of American Liberalism, 1945–1968*. Ithaca, NY: Cornell University Press.

Branch, Enobong. 2011. *Opportunity Denied: Limiting Black Women to Devalued Work*. New Brunswick, NJ: Rutgers University Press.

Braverman, Harry. 1974. *Labor and Monopoly Capital*. New York: Monthly Review.

Brody, David. 2004. "Labor vs. the Law: How the Wagner Act Became a Management Tool." *New Labor Forum* 13 (1): 8–16.

Bronfenbrenner, Kate. 1997. "We'll Close! Plant Closings, Plant-Closing Threats, Union Organizing and NAFTA." Special Report. https://ecommons.cornell.edu/bitstream/handle/1813/73168/We_ll_Close_Plant_closings_.pdf?sequence=1&isAllowed=y.

Bronfenbrenner, Kate. 2000. *Uneasy Terrain: The impact of Capital Mobility on Workers, Wages, and Union Organizing*. New York State School of Industrial and Labor Relations, Cornell University.

Bronfenbrenner, Kate. 2009. *No Holds Barred: The Intensification of Employer Opposition to Organizing*. Washington, DC: Economic Policy Institute Briefing Paper.

Bronfenbrenner, Kate, and Tom Juravich. 1994. "The Impact of Employer Opposition on Union Certification Win Rates: A Private/Public Sector Comparison." *Economic Policy Institute*. Working Paper 113.

Bronfenbrenner, Kate, and Stephanie Luce. 2004. "The Changing Nature of Corporate Global Restructuring: The Impact of Production Shifts on Jobs in the US, China, and Around the Globe." Research paper submitted to US-China Economic and Security Review Commission. https://ecommons.cornell.edu/bitstream/handle/1813/73140/cornell_u_mass_report.pdf?sequence=1.

Brundage, Vernon Jr. 2017. "Profile of the Labor Force by Educational Attainment." *Spotlight on Statistics: U.S. Bureau of Labor Statistics*. https://www.bls.gov/spotlight/2017/educational-attainment-of-the-labor-force/pdf/educational-attainment-of-the-labor-force.pdf

Budd, John. 2008. *Labor Relations: Striking a Balance*. New York: McGraw-Hill/Irwin.

Buhle, Paul. 1999. *Taking Care of Business*. New York: Monthly Review.

Burns, Joe. 2012. "Labor's Economic Weapons: Learning from Labor History." *Labor Studies Journal* 37 (4): 337–344.

Carré, Françoise, and Chris Tilly. 2017. *Where Bad Jobs are Better: Retail Jobs across Countries and Companies.* New York: Russell Sage Foundation.

Chaison, Gary. 1980. "A Note on Union Merger Trends, 1900–1978." *Industrial & Labor Relations Review* 34: 114–120.

Chanin, Jesse. 2021. "Civil Rights, Labor Conflict, and Integration: New Orleans Educators' Struggle for Collective Bargaining 1965–1974." *Labor Studies Journal* 46: 286–317.

Chun, Jennifer Jihye. 2011. *Organizing at the Margins: The Symbolic Politics of Labor in South Korea and the United States.* Ithaca, NY: Cornell University Press.

Clawson, Dan. 2003. *The Next Upsurge.* Ithaca, NY: ILR Press.

Clawson, Dan, and Mary Ann Clawson. 1999. "What Has Happened to the US Labor Movement? Union Decline and Renewal." *Annual Review of Sociology* 25 (1): 95–119.

Cobble, Dorothy Sue. 2013. "Pure and Simple Radicalism: Putting the Progressive Era AFL in Its Time. *Labor: Studies in Working-Class History of the Americas* 10 (4): 61–87.

Cohn, Samuel. 1993. *When Strikes Make Sense—And Why: Lessons from Third Republic French Coals Miners.* New York: Plenum Press.

Cole, Peter. 2010. *Wobblies on the Waterfront: Interracial Unionism in Progressive-Era Philadelphia.* Chicago: University of Illinois Press.

Craft, Donna and Terrance Peck, eds.1998. *Profiles of American Unions.* Detroit: Gale Research.

Cregan, Christina. 2013. "Does Workplace Industrial Action Increase Trade Union Membership? An Exchange Relationship Approach to Union Joining and Leaving Behaviour." *The International Journal of Human Resource Management* 24 (17): 3363–3377.

De Leon, Cedric. 2015. *The Origins of Right to Work.* Ithaca, NY: Cornell University Press.

Devinatz, Victor G. 2005. "An Analysis of Strikes Led by the Trade Union Unity League After Passage of the National Industrial Recovery Act, 1933–1934." *Nature, Society, and Thought* 18 (2): 205–217.

Dixon, Marc. 2020. *Heartland Blues: Labor Rights in the Industrial Midwest.* New York: Oxford University Press.

Dixon, Marc, and Andrew W. Martin. 2012. "We Can't Win This on Our Own: Unions, Firms, and Mobilization of External Allies in Labor Disputes." *American Sociological Review* 77 (6): 946–969.

Dixon, Marc, Vincent J. Roscigno, and Randy Hodson. 2004. "Unions, Solidarity, and Striking." *Social Forces* 83 (1): 3–33.

Domhoff, G. William. 2015. *Myth of Liberal Ascendancy: Corporate Dominance from the Great Depression to the Great Recession.* New York: Routledge.

Domhoff, G. William. 2020. *The Corporate Rich and the Power Elite in the Twentieth Century.* London: Routledge.

Donner, Frank. 1990. "Protectors of Privilege: Red Squads and Police Repression." *Radical History Review* 1990 (48): 5–31.

Du Bois, William Edward Burghardt. 1935. *Black Reconstruction: An Essay toward a History of the Part Which Black Folk Played in the Attempt to Reconstruct Democracy in America, 1860-1880.* New York: Harcourt, Brace and Company.

Dube, Arindrajit, and Ethan Kaplan. 2010. "Does Outsourcing Reduce Wages in the Low-Wage Service Occupations? Evidence from Janitors and Guards." *ILR Review* 63 (2): 287–306.

Dubofsky, Melvyn. 1994. *The State and Labor in Modern America*. Chapel Hill: University of North Carolina Press.

Dubofsky, Melvyn, and Foster Rhea Dulles. 2004. *Labor in America: A History*. Wheeling, IL: Harlan Davidson.

Ebbinghaus, Bernhard, and Jelle Visser. 1999. "When Institutions Matter: Union Growth and Decline in Western Europe, 1950–1995." *European Sociological Review* 15 (2): 135–158.

Edwards, P. K. 1981. *Strikes in the United States 1881–1974*. Oxford: Basil Blackwell.

Edwards, Richard. 1979. *Contested Terrain: The Transformation of the Workplace in the Twentieth Century*. New York: Basic Books.

Eidlin, Barry. 2018. *Labor and the Class Idea in the United States and Canada*. New York: Cambridge University Press.

Fantasia, Rick. 1988. *Cultures of Solidarity: Consciousness, Action, and Contemporary American Workers*. Berkeley: University of California Press.

Fantasia, Rick, and Judith Stepan-Norris. 2004. "The Labor Movement in Motion." In *The Blackwell Companion to Social Movements*, edited by David Snow and Sarah Soule, 555–575. Malden, MA: Blackwell.

Faux, Jeff. 2013. "NAFTA's Impact on US Workers." *Economic Policy Institute Working Economics Blog*. https://www.epi.org/blog/naftas-impact-workers/.

Federal Mediation and Conciliation Service. 2000. *Fifty-Third Report of the Federal Mediation and Conciliation Service*. https://www.fmcs.gov/resources/documents-and-data/.

Fine, Janice. 2006. *Worker Centers: Organizing Communities at the Edge of the Dream*. Ithaca, NY: Cornell University Press.

Fink, Gary, ed. 1977. *Labor Unions*. Westport, CT: Greenwood Press.

Fisk, Donald. 2003. "American Labor in the 20th Century." *U.S. Bureau of Labor Statistics* https://www.bls.gov/opub/mlr/cwc/american-labor-in-the-20th-century.pdf.

Fletcher Jr., Bill, and José Alejandro La Luz. 2020. "Trump, Right-Wing Populism, and the Future of Organized Labor." In *Labor in the Time of Trump*, edited by Jasmine Kerrissey, Eve Weinbaum, Clare Hammonds, Tom Juravich, and Dan Clawson, 50–66. Ithaca, NY: Cornell University Press.

Fletcher, Bill, and Fernando Gapasin. 2008. *Solidarity Divided: The Crisis in Organized Labor and a New Path toward Social Justice*. University of California Press.

Flynn, Joan. 2000. "A Quiet Revolution at the Labor Board: The Transformation of the NLRB 1935–2000." *Ohio State Law Journal* 61: 1361.

Foley, James. 1947. "Union Unfair Labor Practices under the Taft-Hartley Act." *Virginia Law Review* 33 (6): 697–729.

Forbath, William E. 1989. "The Shaping of the American Labor Movement." *Harvard Law Review* 102 (1109): 1118–1256.

Form, William. 1987. "On the Degradation of Skills." *Annual Review of Sociology* 13: 29–47.

Form, William. 1995. *Segmented Labor, Fractured Politics: Labor Politic in American Life*. New York: Plenum Press.

Francis, Megan Ming. 2014. *Civil Rights and the Making of the Modern American State*. Cambridge: Cambridge University Press.

Friedman, Gerald. 1988. "Strike Success and Union Ideology: The United States and France, 1880–1914." *The Journal of Economic History* 48 (1): 1–25.

Frymer, Paul, and Jacob M. Grumbach. 2021. "Labor Unions and White Racial Politics." *American Journal of Political Science* 65 (1): 225–240.

Gallup Poll. 2022. "Approval of Labor Unions at Highest point Since 1965." *Gallup News.* https://news.gallup.com/poll/398303/approval-labor-unions-highest-point-1965.aspx.

Ganz, Marshall. 2000. "Resources and Resourcefulness: Strategic Capacity in the Unionization of California Agriculture, 1959–1966." *American Journal of Sociology* 105 (4): 1003–1062.

Garden, Charlotte. 2018. "Labor Organizing in the Age of Surveillance." *St Louis Law Journal* 63: 55.

Ghanbari, Lyda, and Michael McCall. 2016. "Current Employment Statistics Survey: 100 Years of Employment, Hours, and Earnings." *Monthly Labor Review.* U.S. Bureau of Labor Statistics. https://doi.org/10.21916/mlr. 2016.38.

Gifford, Courtney D. 1980–2016. *Directory of U.S. Labor Unions.* Washington, DC: The Bureau of National Affairs.

Glover, Robert W., and Cihan Bilginsoy. 2005. "Registered Apprenticeship Training in the US Construction Industry." *Education+ Training* 47 (4/5): 337–349.

Goldfield, Michael. 1987. *The Decline of Organized Labor in the United States.* Chicago: University of Chicago Press.

Goldfield, Michael. 1989a. "Public Sector Union Growth and Public Policy." *Policy Studies Journal* 18 (2): 404–420.

Goldfield, Michael. 1989b. "Worker Insurgency, Radical Organization, and New Deal Labor Legislation." *American Political Science Review* 83 (4): 1257–1282.

Goldfield, Michael. 2007. "The Impact of Globalization and Neoliberalism on the Decline of Organized Labour in the United States." In *Labor, Globalization and the State Workers, Women and Migrants Confront Neoliberalism,* edited by Debdas Banerjee and Michael Goldfield, 121–159. London: Routledge.

Greenstone, David. 1977. *Labor in American Politics.* Chicago: University of Chicago Press.

Griffin, Larry J., Michael E. Wallace, and Beth A. Rubin. 1986. "Capitalist Resistance to the Organization of Labor before the New Deal: Why? How? Success?" *American Sociological Review* 51 (2): 147–167.

Gross, James. 1974. *The Making of the National Labor Relations Board.* Albany: State University of New York Press.

Gross, James. 1981. *The Reshaping of the National Labor Relations Board.* Albany: State University of New York Press.

Hannan, Michael T. 1988. "Organizational Ecology of Labor Unions Project of Public-Release Data Set: American National Unions, 1826–1985." Catalog no. 448. Cornell Center for the Social Sciences. https://doi.org/10.6077/rfbj-y493.

Hatton, Erin. 2014. "Temporary Weapons: Employers' Use of Temps against Organized Labor." *Industrial and Labor Relations Review* 67 (1): 86–110.

Hegewisch, Ariane, and Julie Anderson. 2018. "Women-Only Pre-Apprenticeship Programs." National Center for Women's' Equity in Apprenticeship and Employment. https://iwpr.org/iwpr-issues/esme/women-only-pre-apprenticeship-programs-meeting-skills-needs-and-creating-pathways-to-good-jobs-for-women/.

Helwig, Ryan. 2004. "Worker Displacement in 1999–2000." *Monthly Labor Review* June: 54–68.

Henrickson, Kevin, and Wesley Wilson. 2008. "Competition, Unionization, and Deregulation in the Motor Carrier Industry." *The Journal of Law & Economics* 51 (1): 153–177.

Hill, Herbert. 1985. *Black Labor and the American Legal System: Race, Work, and the Law.* University of Wisconsin Press.

Hirsch, Barry, and David MacPherson. 2003. "Union Membership and Coverage Database from the Current Population Survey: Note. *ILR Review* 56 (2): 349–354.

Hodder, Andy, Mark Williams, John Kelly, and Nick McCarthy. 2017. "Does Strike Action Stimulate Trade Union Membership Growth?" *British Journal of Industrial Relations* 55 (1): 165–186.

Hoffman, Dennis E., and Vincent J. Webb. 1986. "Police Response to Labor Radicalism in Portland and Seattle, 1913–19." *Oregon Historical Quarterly* 87 (4): 341–366.

Honey, Michael. 1992. "Operation Dixie: Labor and Civil Rights in the Postwar South." *The Mississippi Quarterly* 45 (4): 439–452.

Honey, Michael. 1993. *Southern Labor and Black Civil Rights: Organizing Memphis Workers.* Champaign: University of Illinois Press.

Isaac, Larry, and Lars Christiansen. 2002. "How the Civil Rights Movement Revitalized Labor Militancy." *American Sociological Review* 67 (5): 722–746.

IWW History Project. University of Washington, Seattle. https://depts.washington.edu/iww/strikes.shtml.

Jacobs, David, and Marc Dixon. 2010. "Political Partisanship, Race, and Union Strength from 1970 to 2000: A Pooled Time-Series Analysis." *Social Science Research* 39 (6): 1059–1072.

Jacoby, Daniel. 1991. "The Transformation of Industrial Apprenticeship in the United States." *The Journal of Economic History* 51 (4): 887–910.

Johnston, Paul. 1994. *Success While Others Fail: Social Movement Unionism and the Public Workplace.* Ithaca, NY: Cornell University Press.

Jung, Moon-Kie. 2006. *Reworking Race: The Making of Hawaii's Interracial Labor Movement.* New York: Columbia University Press.

Juravich, Tom, and Kate Bronfenbrenner. 2000. *Ravenswood: The Steelworkers' Victory and the Revival of American labor.* Ithaca, NY: Cornell University Press.

Kalleberg, Arne. 2000. "Nonstandard Employment Relations: Part-Time, Temporary and Contract Work." *Annual Review of Sociology* 26: 341–365.

Kalleberg, Arne. 2009. "Precarious Work, Insecure Workers: Employment Relations in Transition." *American Sociological Review* 74 (1): 1–22.

Katz, Lawrence F., and Alan B. Krueger. 2019. "The Rise and Nature of Alternative Work Arrangements in the United States, 1995–2015." *ILR Review* 72 (2): 382–416.

Keefe, Jeffrey. 2015. *Laws Enabling Public-Sector Collective Bargaining Have Not Led to Excessive Public-Sector Pay.* Washington, DC: Economic Policy Institute. Briefing Paper # 409.

Kelley, Robin, D. G. 1990. *Hammer and Hoe: Alabama Communists during the Great Depression.* Chapel Hill: University of North Carolina Press.

Kerr, Clark, and Abraham Siegel. 1954. "The Interindustry Propensity to Strike: An International Comparison." In *Industrial Conflict*, edited by Arthur Kornhauser, Robert Dubin, and Arthur M. Ross, 105–147. New York: McGraw-Hill.

Kerrissey, Jasmine, and Nathan Meyers. 2022. "Public-Sector Unions as Equalizing Institutions: Race, Gender, and Earnings." *ILR Review* 75 (5): 1215–1239.

Kerrissey, Jasmine, and Evan Schofer. 2013. "Union Membership and Political Participation in the United States." *Social Forces* 91 (3): 895–928.

Kimeldorf, Howard. 2013. "Worker Replacement Costs and Unionization: Origins of the US Labor Movement." *American Sociological Review* 78 (6): 1033–1062.

Kitroeff, Natalie. February 2, 2019. "The Shutdown Made Sara Nelson into America's Most Powerful Flight Attendant." *New York Times*. https://www.nytimes.com/2019/02/22/business/sara-nelson-flight-attendant-union.html.

Klare, Karl. 1981. "Labor Law as Ideology: Toward a New Historiography of Collective Bargaining Law." *Industrial Relations Law Journal* 4: 450–482.

Klegon, Douglas. 1978. "The Sociology of Professions: An Emerging Perspective." *Sociology of Work and Occupations* 5 (3): 259–283.

Klein, Jennifer. 2020. "Between Home and State." In *Labor in the Time of Trump*, edited by Jasmine Kerrissey, Eve Weinbaum, Clare Hammonds, Tom Juravich, and Dan Clawson, 206–225. Ithaca, NY: Cornell University Press.

Krippner, Greta. 2005. "The Finalization of the American Economy." *Socio-Economic Review* 3: 173–208.

Kristal, Tali. 2013. "The Capitalist Machine: Computerization, Workers' Power, and the Decline in Labor's Share within US Industries." *American Sociological Review* 78 (3): 361–389.

La Follette Committee Report. 1941. *Subcommittee of the Committee on Education and Labor. U.S. Senate 77 the Congress 1st session pursuant to S. Res. 266.* Washington, DC: U.S. Government Printing Office.

Lafer, Gordon. 2017. *The One Percent Solution.* Ithaca, NY: Cornell University Press.

Lafer, Gordon, and Lola Loustaunau. 2020. *Fear at Work—An Inside Account of How Employers Threaten, Intimidate, and Harass Workers to Stop Them from Exercising Their Right to Collective Bargaining.* Washington, DC: Economic Policy Institute Report.

Laslett, John. 1984. "Socialism and American Trade Unionism." In *Failure of a Dream?*, edited by John Laslett and Seymour Martin Lipset, 118–150. Berkeley: University of California Press.

LeRoy, Michael. 1995a. "Employer Treatment of Permanently Replaced Strikers, 1935–1991." *Yale Law & Policy Review* 13 (1): 1–43.

LeRoy, Michael. 1995b. "Regulating Employer Use of Permanent Striker Replacements: Empirical Analysis of NLRA and RLA Strikes 1935–1991." *Berkeley Journal of Employment and Labor Law* 16 (1): 169–207.

Leonhardt, David. 2021, June 15. "The Amazon Customers Don't See." *New York Times.* https://www.nytimes.com/2021/06/15/briefing/amazon-warehouse-investigation.html.

Lewis, Penny, and Stephanie Luce. 2012. "Labor and Occupy Wall Street: An Appraisal of the First Six Months." *New Labor Forum* 21 (2): 43–49.

Lichtenstein, Nelson. 2002. *State of the Union.* Princeton, NJ: Princeton University Press.

Lin, Ken-Hou, and Donald Tomaskovic-Devey. 2013. "Financialization and U.S. Income Inequality, 1970–2008." *American Journal of Sociology* 118 (5): 1284–1329.

Lipold, Paul, and Larry Isaac. 2009. "Striking Deaths: Lethal Contestation and the 'Exceptional' Character of the American Labor Movement, 1870–1970." *International Review of Social History* 54 (2): 167–205.

Lipset, Seymour Martin, Martin Trow, and James Coleman. 1956. *Union Democracy.* Glencoe, IL: The Free Press.

Lissy, William. 1990. "Union-Free Statements in Employee Handbooks." *Supervision* 51: 22.

Logan, John. 1999. "Representatives of Their Own Choosing: Certification, Elections, and Employer Free Speech, 1935–1959." *Seattle University Law Review* 23 (3): 549–567.

Logan, John. 2006. "The Union Avoidance Industry in the United States." *British Journal of Industrial Relations* 44 (4): 651–675.

Loomis, Erik. 2018. *A History of America in Ten Strikes*. New York: The New Press.

Marsh, Ben. 1999. "Corporate Shell Games: Use of the Corporate Form to Evade Bargaining Obligations. *Journal of Labor and Employment Law* 2: 543–574.

Martin, Andrew. 2008. "The Institutional Logic of Union Organizing and the Effectiveness of Social Movement Repertoires." *American Journal of Sociology* 113 (4): 1067–1103.

Martin, Andrew W., and Marc Dixon. 2010. "Changing to Win? Threat, Resistance, and the Role of Unions in Strikes, 1984–2002." American Journal of Sociology 116 (1): 93–129.

Mason, Alpheus T. 1930. "Organized Labor as Party Plaintiff in Injunction Cases." *Columbia Law Review* 30 (4): 466–488.

McCammon, Holly J. 1990. "Legal Limits on Labor Militancy." *Social Problems* 37 (2): 206–229.

McCammon, Holly J. 1993. "From Repressive Intervention to Integrative Prevention: The US State's Legal Management of Labor Militancy, 1881–1978." *Social Forces* 71 (3): 569–601.

McCammon, Holly J. 1994. "Disorganizing and Reorganizing Conflict: Outcomes of the State's Legal Regulation of the Strike since the Wagner Act." *Social Forces* 72 (4): 1011–1049.

McCartin, Joseph A. 1997. *Labor's Great War: The Struggle for Industrial Democracy and the Origins of Modern American Labor Relations, 1912–1921*. Chapel Hill: University of North Carolina Press.

McCartin, Joseph A. 2006a. "PATCO, Permanent Replacement, and the Loss of Labor's Strike Weapon." *Perspectives on Work* 10 (1): 17–19.

McCartin, Joseph A. 2006b. "A Historian's Perspective on the PATCO Strike, Its Legacy, and Lessons." *Employee Responsibilities & Rights Journal* 18: 215–222.

MacLean, Nancy. 2017. *Democracy in Chains: The Deep History of the Radical Right's Stealth Plan for America*. New York: Viking.

McNicholas, Celine, Margaret Poydock, Julia Wolfe, Ben Zipperer, Gordon Lafer, and Lola Loustaunau. 2019. "Unlawful: U.S. Employers are Charged with Violating Federal Law in 41.5% of all Union Election Campaigns." Washington, DC: Economic Policy Institute.

Milkman, Ruth. 1987. *Gender at Work: The Dynamics of Job Segregation by Sex during World War II*. Chicago: University of Illinois Press.

Milkman, Ruth. 2006. *LA Story: Immigrant Workers and the Future of the US Labor Movement*. New York: Russell Sage Foundation.

Milkman, Ruth. 2016. *On Gender, Labor, and Inequality*. Chicago: University of Illinois Press.

Milkman, Ruth, and Ed Ott, eds. 2014. *New Labor in New York: Precarious Workers and the Future of the Labor Movement*. Ithaca, NY: Cornell University Press.

Millis, Harry, and Royal Montgomery. 1945. *Organized Labor*. New York: McGraw-Hill.

Mishel, Lawerence, and Jori Kandra. 2020. *CEO Compensation Surged 14% in 2019 to $21.3 Million*. Washington, DC: Economic Policy Institute.

Mishel, Lawrence, Lynn Rhinehart, and Lane Windham. 2020. *Explaining the Erosion of Private-Sector Unions: How Corporate Practices and Legal Changes Have Undercut the Ability of Workers to Organize and Bargain.* Washington, DC: Economic Policy Institute.

Moore, William J. 1998. "The Determinants and Effects of Right-To-Work Laws: A Review of the Recent Literature." *Journal of Labor Research* 19: 445–469.

Morris, Aldon, and Dan Clawson. 2005. "Lessons of the Civil Rights Movement for Building a Worker Rights Movement." *Working USA* 8 (6): 683–704.

Motley, James M. 1907. *Apprenticeship in American Trade Unions.* Baltimore, MD: Johns Hopkins Press.

Murolo, Priscilla, and A. B. Chitty. 2018. *From the Folks Who Brought You the Weekend: A Short, Illustrated History of Labor in the United States.* New York: The New Press.

Murphy, Marjorie. 1990. *Blackboard Unions: The AFT and the NEA, 1900–1980.* Ithaca, NY: Cornell University Press.

Nass, David. 1977. "American Federation of Teachers." In *Labor Unions*, edited by Gary Fink, 367–369. Westport, CT: Greenwood Press.

National Labor Relations Board, Annual Reports. Yearly, 1936–2010. https://www.nlrb.gov/reports/agency-performance-reports/historical-reports/annual-reports.

Neufeld, Maurice. 1956. "Structure and Government of the AFL-CIO." *ILR Review* 9 (3): 371–390.

North American Building Trades Unions. 2022 (access date). Advance Your Skills Advance Your Life. https://nabtu.org/wp-content/uploads/2021/09/NABTU_ApprenticeshipPrograms2021-Web.pdf.

Obenauer, Marie L. 1924. "Living Conditions among Coal Mine Workers of the United States." *The Annals of the American Academy of Political and Social Science* 111 (1): 12–23.

Parkin, Frank. 1983. *Marxism and Class Theory.* New York: Columbia University Press.

Perea, Juan F. 2011. "The Echoes of Slavery: Recognizing the Racist Origins of the Agricultural and Domestic Worker Exclusion from the National Labor Relations Act." *Ohio State Law Journal* 72 (1): 95–138.

Perrone, Luca. 1983. "Positional Power and Propensity to Strike." *Politics & Society* 12 (2): 231–261.

Peterson, Florence. 1937. *Strikes in the United States, 1880–1936.* Washington, DC: U.S. Government Printing Office BLS Bulletin No. 651.

Peterson, Florence. 1945. *American Labor Unions.* New York: Harper & Row.

Piazza, James A. 2005. "Globalizing Quiescence: Globalization, Union Density and Strikes in 15 Industrialized Countries." *Economic and Industrial Democracy* 26 (2): 289–314.

Pincus, Fred. 1980. "The False Promises of Community Colleges: Class Conflict and Vocational Education." *Harvard Educational Review* 50 (3): 332–361.

Polivka, Anne E. 1996. "A Profile of Contingent Workers." *Monthly Labor Review* 119: 10–21.

Prosten, Richard. 1979. "The Rise in NLRB Election Delays: Measuring Business' New Resistance." *Monthly Labor Review* 102 (2): 38–40.

Quadagno, Jill. 1992. "Social Movements and State Transformation: Labor Unions and Racial Conflicts in the War on Poverty." *American Sociological Review* 57 (5): 616–634.

Rabinowitz, Matilda. 2017. *Immigrant Girl, Radical Woman: A Memoir from the Early Twentieth Century.* Ithaca, NY: Cornell University Press.

Rajendra, Dania. 2022. "Organizing Megacorporations: Building a Movement for the 21st Century." *The Forge*. https://forgeorganizing.org/article/organizing-megacorporations-building-movement-21st-century.

Reed, Merl. 1977. "American Federation of Labor." In *Labor Unions*, edited by Gary Fink, 11–15. Westport, CT: Greenwood Press.

Reed, Stephen B. 2014. "One Hundred Years of Price Change: The Consumer Price Index and American Inflation Experience." *Monthly Labor Review* 137 (1).

Rhinehart, Lynn, and Celine McNicholas. 2020. *Collective Bargaining beyond the Worksite: How Workers and their Unions Build Power and Set Standards for their Industries*. Washington, DC: Economic Policy Institute Report.

Richardson, Damone. 2009. "Musician Strikes." In *The Encyclopedia of Strikes in American History*, edited by Aaron Brenner, Benjamin Day, Immanuel Ness, 675–684. London: M.E. Sharpe.

Rifkin, Bernard, and Susan Rifkin. 1979. *American Labor Sourcebook*. New York: McGraw-Hill.

Rolf, David. 2016. "The Labor Movement As We Know It Is Dying. Here's How It Can Survive." PBS News Hour, Economy. September 5. https://www.pbs.org/newshour/economy/whats-future-labor-movement.

Rosenfeld, Jake. 2006. "Desperate Measures: Strikes and Wages in Post-Accord America." *Social Forces* 85 (1): 235–266.

Rosenfeld, Jake. 2014. *What Unions no Longer Do*. Cambridge, MA: Harvard University Press.

Rosenfeld, Jake, and Meredith Kleykamp. 2012. "Organized Labor and Racial Wage Inequality in the United States." *American Journal of Sociology* 117 (5): 1460–1502.

Rosenzweig, Roy. 1983. "Organizing the Unemployed: The Early Years of the Great Depression, 1929–1933." In *Workers' Struggles, Past and Present: A "Radical America" Reader*, edited by James Green, 168–189. Philadelphia: Temple University Press.

Rothenbuhler, Eric W. 1988. "The Liminal Fight: Mass Strikes as Ritual and Interpretation." In *Durkheimian Sociology: Cultural Studies*, edited by J. C. Alexander, 66–89. Cambridge: Cambridge University Press.

Rubin, Beth A. 1986. "Class Struggle American Style: Unions, Strikes and Wages." *American Sociological Review* 51 (5): 618–633.

Ruiz, Vicki L. 1987. *Cannery Women, Cannery Lives: Mexican Women, Unionization, and the California Food Processing Industry, 1930–1950*. Albuquerque: University of New Mexico Press.

Sanes, Milla, and John Schmitt. 2014. *Regulation of Public Sector Collective Bargaining in the States*. Washington, DC: Center for Economic and Policy Research.

Schmalz, Stefan, Carmen Ludwig, and Edward Webster. 2018. "The Power Resources Approach: Developments and Challenges." *Global Labour Journal* 9 (2): 113–134.

Scopelliti, Demetrio. 2014. "Middle-Skill Jobs Decline as U.S. Labor Market Becomes More Polarized." *Monthly Labor Review*, October. https://www.bls.gov/opub/mlr/2014/beyond-bls/middle-skill-jobs-decline-as-us-labor-market-becomes-more-polarized.htm

Shaw, Randy. 2008. *Beyond the Fields: Cesar Chavez, the UFW, and the Struggle for Justice in the 21st Century*. Berkeley: University of California Press.

Silver, Beverly. 2003. *Forces of Labor*. New York: Cambridge University Press.

Slichter, Sumner. 1929. "The Current Labor Policies of American Industries." *The Quarterly Journal of Economics* 43 (3): 393–435.

Slichter, Sumner. 1947. *The Challenge of Industrial Relations*. Ithaca, NY: Cornell University Press.

Smith, Russell A. 1951. "Significant Developments in Labor Law during the Last Half-Century." *Michigan Law Review* 50 (8): 1265–1290.

Sobek, Matthew. 2001. "New Statistics on the US Labor Force, 1850–1990." *Historical Methods: A Journal of Quantitative and Interdisciplinary History* 34 (2): 71–87.

Southworth, Caleb and Judith Stepan-Norris. 2009. "American Trade Unions and Data Limitations: A New Agenda for Labor Studies." *Annual Review of Sociology* 35: 297–320.

Spedden, Ernest Radcliffe. 1910. *The Trade Union Label*. PhD diss., Johns Hopkins University.

Spero, Sterling D. 1972. *Government as Employer* (2nd ed.) Carbondale: Southern Illinois University Press.

Spomer, Cynthia, ed. 1992. *American Directory of Organized Labor*. Detroit: Gale Research.

Steinberg, Ronnie J. 1990. "Social Construction of Skill: Gender, Power, and Comparable Worth." *Work and Occupations* 17 (4): 449–482.

Stepan-Norris, Judith, and Caleb Southworth. 2010. "Rival Unionism and Membership Growth in the United States, 1900–2005." *American Sociological Review* 75 (2): 227–251.

Stepan-Norris, Judith, and Maurice Zeitlin. 1996. *Talking Union*. Chicago: University of Illinois Press.

Stepan-Norris, Judith, and Maurice Zeitlin. 2003. *Left Out: Reds and America's Industrial Unions*. New York: Cambridge University Press.

Stevens, George A. 1913. *New York Typographical Union No. 6: Study of a Modern Trade Union and its Predecessors*. Albany: J. B. Lyon Company, State Printers.

Stone, Katherine. 1981. "The Post-War Paradigm in American Labor Law." *Yale Law Journal* 90 (7): 1509–1580.

Stone, Katherine. 2004. "The Steelworkers Trilogy and the Evolution of Labor Arbitration." UCLA School of Law & Legal Theory Research Paper Series, No. 04–29.

Strom, Sharon H. 1989. "'Light Manufacturing': The Feminization of American Office Work, 1900–1930." *ILR Review* 43 (1): 53–71.

Summers, Clyde. 1946. "Admissions Policies of Labor Unions." *The Quarterly Journal of Economics* 61 (1): 66–107.

Sutch, Richard, and Susan B. Carter, eds. 2006. *Historical Statistics of the United States, Millennial Edition Online*. New York: Cambridge University Press.

Taft, Philip. 1976. "Expansion of Unionization in the Early 20th Century." *Monthly Labor Review* 99: 32–35.

Taft, Philip, and Philip Ross.1969. "American Labor Violence: Its Causes, Character, and Outcome." In *Violence in America: Historical and Comparative Perspectives*, edited by Hugh Davis Graham and Ted Robert Gurr, 221–301. A Staff Report to the National Commission on the Causes and Prevention of Violence. Washington, DC: U.S. Government Printing Office.

Taylor, Frederick W. 1911. *The Principles of Scientific Management*. New York: Harper Brothers.

Thelen, Kathleen. 2004. *How Institutions Evolve: The Political Economy of Skills in Germany, Britain, the United States, and Japan*. New York: Cambridge University Press.

Thornton, Robert, and Edward Timmins. 2015. "The De-licensing of Occupations in the United States." *Monthly Labor Review*, May. https://www.bls.gov/opub/mlr/2015/article/the-de-licensing-of-occupations-in-the-united-states.htm.

Tomlins, Christopher L. 1979. "AFL Unions in the 1930s: Their Performance in Historical Perspective." *The Journal of American History* 65 (4): 1021–1042.

Tomlins, Christopher L. 1985. *The State and the Unions*. New York: Cambridge University Press.

Troy, Leo. 1956. *Distribution of Union Membership among the States: 1939 and 1953*. New York: Columbia University Press.

Troy, Leo. 1965. *Trade Union Membership, 1897–1962*. New York: Columbia University Press.

Troy, Leo, and Neil Sheflin. 1985. *Union Sourcebook*. New Jersey: Industrial Relations Data and Information Services.

Ulman, Lloyd. 1955. *The Rise of the National Trade Union*. Cambridge, MA: Harvard University Press.

Ulman, Lloyd. 1961. "The Development of Trades and Labor Unions." *American Economic History*, edited by Seymour Harris, 366–482. New York: McGraw-Hill.

U.S. Government. Department of Labor. Bureau of Labor Statistics. 1926–2015, various years, various titles. *Directory of National and International Labor Unions in the United States*. U.S. Government Printing Office.

U.S. Government. Department of Labor. Bureau of Labor Statistics. 1934–1980, various years, various titles. *Analysis of Strikes and Lockouts*. U.S. Government Printing Office.

U.S. Government. Bureau of Labor Statistics. 1958. *A Guide to Labor-Management Relations in the United States*. Bulletin No. 1225. Washington, D.C: U.S. Government Printing Office.

U.S. Government. Bureau of Labor Statistics. 1993–2015. "Work Stoppages Involving 1,000 or More Workers, 1993–Present." https://www.bls.gov/web/wkstp/monthly-listing.htm.

U.S. Government. Bureau of Labor Statistics. 2015a. "Labor Force Statistics from the Current Population Survey." bls.gov/cps/cps_aa2015.htm.

U.S. Government. Bureau of Labor Statistics. 2015b. "News Releases." Union Membership (Annual).

U.S. Government. Bureau of Labor Statistics. BLS Reports. 2017a. "Labor Force Characteristics by Race and Ethnicity, 2016." April. Washington, DC: U.S. Government Printing Office.

U.S. Government. Bureau of Labor Statistics. BLS Reports. 2017b. "Women in the Labor Force: A Databook." April. Washington, DC: U.S. Government Printing Office.

U.S. Government. Equal Employment Opportunity Commission. https://www.eeoc.gov/sites/default/files/2020-06/OEDA_All%20Charges%20Infographic_052620.pdf.

U.S. Government. Federal Mediation and Conciliation Service. 1958. "Federal Mediation and Conciliation Since 1947." *Monthly Labor Review* 81: 388–392.

U.S. Government. National Labor Relations Board. 1947. *12th NLRB Report*. Washington, DC: U.S. Government Printing Office.

U.S. Government. National Labor Relations Board. 1952. *Decisions and Orders of the National Labor Relations Board*. Volume 96. Washington, DC: U.S. Government Printing Office.

U.S. Government. National Labor Relations Board. 1979 (also 1936–2009). *Annual Report of the National Labor Relations Board for the Fiscal Year*. Washington, DC: U.S. Government Printing Office.

U.S. Government. National Labor Relations Board. 2021. NLRB website. https://www.nlrb.gov/how-we-work/national-labor-relations-act.

Valletta, Robert, and Leila Bengali. 2013. "What's Behind the Increase in Part-Time Work?" *FRBSF Economic Letter*. 2013–24. August 26.

Valletta, Robert, and Richard B. Freeman. 1988. "The NBER Public Sector Collective Bargaining Law Data Set." In *When Public Sector Workers Unionize*, edited by Richard Freeman and Casey Ichniowski, 399–420. Chicago: University of Chicago Press.

Vaughn, Lea. 1990. "Article XX of the AFL-CIO Constitution: Managing and Resolving Inter Union Disputes." *The Wayne Law Review* 37: 4–88.

Viscelli, Steve. 2016. *The Big Rig: Trucking and the Decline of the American Dream*. Berkeley: University of California Press.

Voss, Kim, and Rachel Sherman. 2000. "Breaking the Iron Law of Oligarchy." *American Journal of Sociology* 106 (2): 303–349.

Wallace, Michael. 2007. "After Taft-Hartley: The Legal-Institutional Context of U.S. Strike Activity, 1948 to 1980." *The Sociological Quarterly* 48 (4): 769–799.

Wallace, Michael, Larry J. Griffin, and Beth A. Rubin. 1989. "The Positional Power of American Labor, 1963–1977." *American Sociological Review* 54 (2): 197–214.

Wallerstein, Michael, and Bruce Western.2000. "Unions in Decline? What Has Changed and Why." *Annual Review of Political Science* 3 (1): 355–377.

Weeden, Kim A. 2002. "Why Do Some Occupations Pay More Than Others? Social Closure and Earnings Inequality in the United States." *American Journal of Sociology* 108 (1): 55–101.

Weil, David. 2014. *The Fissured Workplace*. Cambridge, MA: Harvard University Press.

Western, Bruce. 1999. *Between Class and Market*. Princeton, NJ: Princeton University Press.

Western, Bruce, and Jake Rosenfeld. 2011. "Unions, Norms, and the Rise in US Wage Inequality." *American Sociological Review* 76 (4): 513–537.

Windham, Lane. 2017. *Knocking on Labor's Door: Union Organizing in the 1970s and the Roots of a New Economic Divide*. North Carolina: UNC Press Books.

Witte, Edwin E. 1930. "Labor's Resort to Injunctions." *The Yale Law Journal* 39 (3): 374–387.

Witte, Edwin E. 1932. *The Government in Labor Disputes*. New York: McGraw-Hill.

Wolman, Leo. 1936. *Ebb and Flow in Trade Unionism* (Publications of the National Bureau of Economic Research, Inc. Number 30). New York: National Bureau of Economic Research.

Wolman, Leo. 1924. *The Growth of American Trade Unions, 1880–1923*. New York: National Bureau of Economic Research.

Workman, Andrew. 1998. "Manufacturing Power: The Organizational Revival of the National Association of Manufacturers, 1941–1945." *The Business History Review* 72 (2): 279–317.

Woytinsky, Wladimir Savelievich, and Associates. 1953. *Employment and Wages in the United States*. New York: The Twentieth Century Fund.

Wright, Erik O. 2000. "Working-Class Power, Capitalist-Class Interests, and Class Compromise." *American Journal of Sociology* 105 (4): 957–1002.

Zeitlin, Maurice, and Frank Weyher. 2001. "'Black and White, Unite and Fight': Interracial Working-Class Solidarity and Racial Employment Equality." *American Journal of Sociology* 107 (2): 430–467.

Zieger, Robert. 2007. *For Job and Freedom: Race and Labor in America Since 1865*. Lexington: The University Press of Kentucky.

Zieger, Robert. 1969. *Republicans and Labor: 1919–1929*. Lexington: The University Press of Kentucky.

Zieger, Robert, and Gilbert Gall. 2002. *American Workers, American Unions: The Twentieth Century* (3rd ed.). Baltimore: The Johns Hopkins University Press.

Zinn, Howard, Dana Frank, and Robin D. G. Kelley. 2002. *Three Strikes: Miners, Musicians, Salesgirls, and the Fighting Spirit of Labor's Last Century*. Boston: Beacon Press.

Index

For the benefit of digital users, indexed terms that span two pages (e.g., 52–53) may, on occasion, appear on only one of those pages.